Comparing Constitutions

Comparing Constitutions

S. E. FINER
VERNON BOGDANOR
and
BERNARD RUDDEN

CLARENDON PRESS · OXFORD

SSCCA

Oxford University Press, Walton Street, Oxford OX2 6DP

Oxford New York
Athens Auckland Bangkok Bombay
Calcutta Cape Town Dar es Salaam Delhi
Florence Hong Kong Istanbul Karachi
Kuala Lumpur Madras Madrid Melbourne
Mexico City Nairobi Paris Singapore
Taipei Tokyo Toronto
and associated companies in
Berlin Ibadan

Oxford is a trade mark of Oxford University Press

Published in the United States
by Oxford University Press Inc., New York

British Library Cataloguing in Publication Data
Data available

Library of Congress Cataloging in Publication Data
Data available
ISBN 0-19-876345-X
ISBN 0-19-876344-1

Printed in Great Britain
on acid-free paper by
Biddles Ltd.
Guildford & King's Lynn

Contents

Preface

From 1974 to 1982 Samuel Edward Finer was Gladstone Professor of Government and Public Administration in the University of Oxford, and Fellow of All Souls College. In the course of a lifetime spent teaching comparative government he became increasingly dismayed at his pupils' ignorance of the actual words of the constitutions of the countries under examination. He concluded, however, that the students were rarely to blame for this: it was the texts themselves that were not readily accessible. There are, of course, two invaluable publications which give an English version of the text of every constitution in the world, but their very size and comprehensiveness make them available only in some libraries.[1]

As a partial remedy, Professor Finer brought out a paperback volume entitled *Five Constitutions* (Penguin, 1979), containing texts and commentary, together with a chapter on the constitution of Britain and two indexes. The edition was never reprinted and so the texts of major constitutions became once more hard to find. The present writers implored him to bring out a second edition, but his last months were devoted to his major work on the *History of Government*. He gave us his blessing, however, and, so fortified, we have prepared the present volume. Like the original it is designed to serve as a handbook for all those involved in the study of modern constitutions. Its core consists of the full texts of the present versions of the constitutions of the United States of America, the Federal Republic of Germany, the Fifth French Republic, and the Russian Federation. Of these, only the first—oldest and most durable—has seen few recent changes. The 1949 German text has been much amended, most fundamentally by the unification of that country in 1990. The French text of 1958 has also undergone a number of changes and,

---

[1] *Constitutions of Nations*, ed. Amos J. Peaslee (Nijhoff, 4 vols., 1970); *Constitutions of the Countries of the World*, ed. Albert P. Blaustein and Gisbert H. Flanz (Oceana Publications Inc., N.Y., 21 vols., looseleaf to date 1971–).

since it incorporates the 1789 Declaration and the Preamble to the 1946 Constitution, we also print translations of these documents. The most recent text is the constitution of the Russian Federation, adopted by referendum on 12 December 1993.

These documents are 'proper' constitutions in that they provide a textual source of the norms which aspire to govern the basic structure of power and of powers in a modern state. But we also include some other materials which a purist might decry, in the form of the basic institutional provisions of the Treaties establishing the European Community and the European Union. We willingly concede that these are not of the same nature as the constitutions properly so called. The Community is not a state, and the Union is not even a legal entity. Nonetheless, a comparison of the extracts with the provisions of real constitutions may enable us to study in embryo the formation of a United States of Europe. The Treaties have provoked basic changes in, and textual amendments of, the German and French constitutions, and the European Court of Justice has said more than once that 'the EEC Treaty, albeit concluded in the form of an international agreement, none the less constitutes the constitutional charter of a Community based on the rule of law'.[2]

Considered as such a charter, what the Treaty conspicuously lacks is a Bill of Rights. To remedy this the Community relies on, *inter alia*, the European Convention for the Protection of Human Rights and Fundamental Freedoms of 4 November 1950. There is something of a mismatch here, since this latter document is basically concerned to prevent the kind of official wickedness (torture, detention without trial, etc.) to which a Community dealing mainly with economic and monetary matters is unlikely to be tempted. But, since the Convention is also important for the protection of human rights within the United Kingdom, we thought it best to print extracts from this document also.

Our other addition deals with an entity which is certainly a sovereign state but has no constitution in the sense of a text. For this reason, among others, it is frequently an object of study, of fascination, and of bewilderment. The chapter on the constitution of the United Kingdom attempts to offer a précis of its main features, and has been guided by what the codified constitutions

---

[2] Opinion 1/91: [1992] 1 CMLR 245 at 269.

here printed single out as matters of such high importance as to qualify as the 'supreme' or 'basic' law of the land.

To assist further comparison we have built on a feature of Professor Finer's earlier edition and have compiled two indexes. The first is analytical: that is to say the components of governance are broken down into the major categories commonly employed by political scientists, and the contents of the various texts are cross-indexed accordingly. The second index is traditional: topics are listed in alphabetical order—but here again in such a way as to facilitate cross-comparison between the various provisions.

The order in which to present the material has caused us some difficulty. In the end we decided to give the four main texts in the order of historical appearance so that the USA comes first and the Russian Federation last. We then add the European texts—the Human Rights Convention and extracts from the EC and EU Treaties. The United Kingdom of Great Britain and Northern Ireland, awkward as always, appears as Chapter Three.

For the Federal Republic of Germany we have used the official translation of 1991 and are grateful for having been given permission to do so. The English versions of more recent German amendments are our own, as are the entire texts of the French and the Russian constitutions. As usual with the exercise of translation, we have been frequently forced to choose among a number of imperfect renderings. The first problem is that of mood. The American constitution uses 'shall' for both the imperative and—to denote conditions or circumstances—for the future and future perfect indicative: 'No person shall be a senator who shall not have attained to the age of thirty'. The official German translation renders the German present indicative by 'shall' where its meaning is imperative: 'Die Todesstrafe ist abgeschafft' becomes 'Capital punishment shall be abolished'. Following these examples, we have used 'shall' where the French or Russian indicative mood seems to denote obligation. We have not used it in the American way to describe conditions or circumstances— for those we use the simple present. We have normally rendered *Gesetz* and *zakon* by 'law', although occasionally, where precision is needed, we use 'statute'. The French constitution, however, opposes *loi* (enacted by the legislature) to *règlement* (adopted by the executive) and so, where this distinction needs to be brought out, we translate *loi* not by 'law' but by 'legislation' for the general sense, and 'statute' or 'enactment' for the particular.

The initial work on Chapter Three was done by Vernon Bogdanor, and Bernard Rudden drafted the rest of the book. We then collaborated on the final version, and would like to express our gratitude for the help given by Mr Michael Beloff QC and Anthony Teasdale. As regards all errors of fact and judgement we respectfully absolve the spirit of Sammy Finer, and freely admit that they are jointly and severally our very own.

V.B.
B.R.

Brasenose College
Oxford
June 1994

Abbreviations

art.	article
CMLR	Common Market Law Reports
EC	European Community
ECB	European Central Bank
ECHR	European Convention on Human Rights and Fundamental Freedoms
ECJ	Court of Justice of the European Communities
ECR	European Court Reports
EEC	European Economic Community
EU	European Union
FRG	Federal Republic of Germany
HL	House of Lords
para.	paragraph
RF	Russian Federation
RSFSR	Russian Soviet Federated Socialist Republic
TEU	Treaty on European Union
UK	United Kingdom of Great Britain and Northern Ireland
US	United States
USA	United States of America
USSR	Union of Soviet Socialist Republics

1

On Whether Constitutions Matter

Constitutions are codes of norms which aspire to regulate the allocation of powers, functions, and duties among the various agencies and officers of government, and to define the relationships between these and the public.

Nowadays many political scientists play down the study of constitutional texts, or accord it a low priority and, perhaps surprisingly, some academic lawyers seem to share this view. They give many good reasons for this. First, they argue—and in this they are perfectly right—that these documents are highly incomplete, if not misleading, guides to actual practice, that is to what is often called the 'working constitution' or the 'governance' of a country. It would be a serious error, for instance, to contrast art. II 1(2) of the US constitution with art. 6 of the French, and then conclude without more ado that the American president is not elected by the people.

Second, it is demonstrably the case that rules included in one constitution may be omitted from others, so that each may be *pro tanto* incomplete—the treatment of political parties is an obvious example. Third, in countries where the law is respected, the constitutional text frequently becomes permeated with the interpretation given it by the courts. This process is demonstrated in the statement of a standard introductory work that 'the study of constitutional law, as that term is used in the United States, is chiefly the study of those decisions of the Supreme Court of the United States that have interpreted the federal constitution'.[1] And even in a country such as France, long hostile to 'government by judges', it is certainly the case that the 1958 Constitution must now be read in the light of the decisions of that body which it calls a mere council but which has become in effect a constitutional court. Fourth, the texts themselves say little of the

[1] E. Allan Farnsworth, *An Introduction to the Legal System of the United States* (2nd edn., Oceana, 1983), 131.

extra-constitutional organizations which generate and conduct the political process: the churches, the pressure groups, the bureaucracy, the great business corporations, ethnic and other minorities, the media, the armed forces, and so on.

But although constitutions are not textbooks on the governance of a particular country, it does not follow that such textbooks should, or even can—without peril—ignore the constitution of that country. A constitution resembles a sharp pencil of light which brightly illuminates a limited area of a country's political life before fading into a penumbra where the features are obscured—even if that surrounding darkness may conceal what are the most potent and significant elements of the political process.

To the arguments about incompleteness, others have added one concerning the ineffectiveness of constitutions. Almost every state in the world today possesses a codified constitution. Yet the vast majority of them are either suspended, or brazenly dishonoured, or—if neither of these—are constantly and continually torn up to make new ones. Moreover—so this line of argument goes—Britain, New Zealand, and Israel have no codified constitutions but nevertheless follow with remarkable consistency and continuity what constitutional rules they do possess. Hence—it is concluded—constitutions are otiose: if the powerholders exercise self-restraint, the written constitution is unnecessary, and if they do not then it is useless. This last contention is quite correct: the majority of states today are either in the throes of revolution or of civil war, or have rulers entirely indifferent to legal norms. But this is not a sound reason for rejecting the study of constitutions, rather for pursuing it with sensitivity and common sense, otherwise one might just as well deny the usefulness of door locks. These are clearly unnecessary to honest people who pass the door, and equally are useless against the determined burglar. But they can and do deter the casual strollers who might otherwise come in and help themselves.

In any case, it is perfectly clear from the most superficial comparative survey that not all constitutions are dishonoured all the time and that certain parts of certain constitutions are obeyed most of the time. Just as no one constitution is an entirely complete and realistic description of what actually happens, so very few are entire fictions, bearing no relationship whatsoever to what goes on. Most constitutions fall between the two extremes, in that they contain fictive or decorative passages as well as omitting many of the powers and processes met with in real life. But the constitutions of the USA, France, and Germany are largely non-fictive. Those of the USSR and the RSFSR were largely fictive but, with the collapse of the Communist Party and its single ideology, it is possible that the new constitution of the Russian Federation may come to have some genuine impact on, and even control of, the political life of that country.

One reason for studying these texts is that, in so far as they are 'realistic', they channel and to that extent constrain the scope and direction of the power of government in general and the various organs of government in particular. At its crudest, there are certain laws infringing human rights which the legislatures of the USA, France, or Germany would be legally unable to enact and therefore are politically unlikely to attempt. Another reason is that such constitutions provide an exact knowledge of what happens, or who does what where and when, on highly important occasions. We know from the US Constitution, for instance, that every four years the electors will vote for a President and Vice-President. And suppose the French President dissolves the National Assembly and dislikes the result of the new elections—can the new body be dissolved? To this, the answer is plain—not until one year has elapsed.

Similar safeguards are now written into the Russian text for the case where the new House passes a motion of no confidence in the existing government. Even if the reader doubts the reality or durability of the Russian constitution printed here, the text was put to a popular vote, is hard to amend, and does, at the very lowest level of political understanding, identify the main legal authorities within the Federation and lay down the framework within which they are supposed to operate.

When we look at those elements of a written text which are wholly or partly fictive, the first and most stimulating question to ask is *why* political life has departed from them. Examples include the US provisions on the election of the President, or the requirement of the EC Treaty that the Parliament be directly elected by a uniform procedure in all Member States. Sometimes the artlessness of the text highlights the complexity of the political process and reveals the reality of political power: a striking example is the EC provision that the seat of the institutions shall be settled 'by common accord of the governments of Member States'—so that, at the time of writing, the European Parliament holds its plenary sessions in Strasbourg, its committee meetings in Brussels, and its documents in Luxembourg.

It would be improper to conclude this recital of the rewards to be gained from the study of the actual texts of constitutions (instead of the study of what scholars or judges have made of these texts) without referring to what is arguably the most important single factor that has made for the neglect of constitutional texts. We refer to American 'behavioralism', a movement both timely and wholesome in so far as it reacted against the formalism and literalism of much earlier political science and stressed that the constitutional law of the lawbooks might conceal more political reality than it revealed. It is perfectly right to distinguish legalism and legitimacy. But these share a common ground with law; and the observance of laws and the sanctity that attaches to law as such are sociological and behavioural facts of profound, and indeed central, political importance. Respect, or at any rate an equal respect, for law is not found in all societies, and it is precisely this fact that explains the difference between the realistic constitutions and the fictive ones.

Some societies—notably those of the West—are profoundly law-bound. It is no accident that the rapid recent changes in the former Soviet Union were so often justified by appeals to the Russian calque of the word *Rechtsstaat*, or that the European Community Court insists that the EC Treaty creates 'a community based on the rule of law'.[2] In Western societies on the whole the laws are felt *in foro interno*, and not just by reason of their sanctions. In societies such as these, the provisions of a constitution do effectively constrain the organs of government and empower large sections of the public; a stark testimony to that fact is the number of guns in the hands of American citizens.

This simple example can take us further. There may well be dispute about the precise meaning of any particular constitutional provision and, for centuries, there have been different schools of interpretation. Some aver that one can say what 'the text means'. Some cleave to what 'the drafters meant', some to

---

[2] Case 294/83, *Parti Ecologiste, Les Verts* v. *Parliament* [1986] ECR 1365.

what 'the reader understands', while there is a long common law reverence for what 'the judges say it means'. The uncommitted observer at such debates may occasionally suspect that the method of interpretation selected is to some extent determined by the outcome sought to be achieved, and may want to know whether or not a particular commentator on the Second Amendment owns a hand-gun. But the main point is that, for whatever motive, every contestant argues that their view of a particular text is correct and that their opponents are mistaken about the *very same text*.

In brief: in neither the USA, Germany, France, nor the Russian Federation does a knowledge of the constitutional text alone equate, even nearly, to an understanding of political reality; but it is a necessary condition of that understanding. Whence it follows that there is no substitute for reading the texts themselves.

2

On the Variety among Constitutions

All the classical commentators on constitutions have drawn attention to the wide differences between them. Indeed, among modern states roughly comparable in economic position and political attitudes, the private law is likely to be essentially similar (in substance if not appearance), while the public law will be very different.

There are of course obvious reasons for many of the major varieties. Some have to provide for a federal or confederal structure; others are unitary; and some (like the British) include quite different legal systems within the one state. Some have to handle serious internal ethnic, linguistic, and religious differences, while others are written for a homogeneous population. Some are largely restricted to a set of justifiable rules of law, while others contain manifesto-like proclamations and show a tendency to the picturesque by, for instance, the adoption of a national animal (always attractive, but rarely edible). A few are contained in no given text or texts. Some are never meant to be taken seriously.

These distinctions are both evident and indispensable, but it will be seen that the motivations which underlie them fall into distinct categories. That a federal document should contain material absent from a unitary one reflects a mechanical consideration, whereas whether the constitution should include manifesto-like pronouncements or a Bill of Rights reflects value preferences. And as soon as we begin to ask what has influenced these preferences we stumble on an additional reason for the wide variety among constitutions. It is a very easy and obvious reason, but that does not make it any the less significant. It is, quite simply, that the constitution-makers in different countries, or for that matter at different moments in the history of any one country, have quite different preoccupations. The reason they are drafting a new instrument of government at all can only be that they are reacting to what is perceived to be a new set of circumstances. Were this not so, the old constitution would go on serving perfectly well.

So all constitutions contain elements that are autobiographical and correspondingly idiosyncratic. Such features are sometimes made explicit in preambles and often in transitional provisions. They are less apparent in the main text unless and until we adopt the comparative method. Then they begin to stand out. Different historical contexts have generated different preoccupations and priorities, and these in turn have led to quite different constitutional structures. Even among those drafters who admired the oldest enduring text which lies to hand—that of the USA—it is striking that, while its first three words and first ten amendments may often be imitated, no one ever copies the Constitution itself.

The following pages will frequently refer to these autobiographical features in offering a brief comparison of the main issues dealt with by the various constitutions—the UK version is given rather fuller treatment in the next Chapter. Use of the analytical index ought to provide a more detailed overview, while for the beginnings of deeper understanding there is no substitute for the constitutional texts themselves.

ADOPTION AND AMENDMENT

Adoption

The Constitution of the USA, which is the oldest text in this collection, reflects two urgent preoccupations. The first was to replace the integrative functions (and organs) especially in matters of commerce and defence, which had previously been supplied by the British Crown, by something more forceful than the arrangements under the Articles of Confederation. The second was to guarantee to citizens the limitations on government power and the common law freedoms for which the colonists had rebelled. As far as the first is concerned, the problem was seen as grafting a federal government on to thirteen flourishing and well-established states, each with its own constitution, legal system, and political institutions. This is why the new Constitution devotes itself almost exclusively to the new, federal machinery and says almost nothing about the form of state governments except that this shall be 'republican', and nothing about their revenue-raising powers or local government. Compare this with the German Constitution which minutely records a long list of 'concurrent powers' and devotes an entire chapter to the division of finance between the federal government and the Länder, or with that of the Russian Federation which (whether wisely or not, we do not yet know) glosses over the problems of a multi-national state. The latest version of the European Community Treaty shows (art. 3) a considerable extension in the concurrent competences of the Community and an attempt to balance this by the express introduction of the 'principle of subsidiarity' (art. 3b).

It is a curious feature of these texts that there are some doubts about the method by which most of them were constituted. First, there may be uncertainties over the earlier normative context by virtue of which the new instrument was enacted, and here the question is whether the authority to make the new constitution, and the method adopted in so doing, are derived both legiti-mately and legally from the procedures prescribed by the previ-ous constitution. Secondly, some of the present texts say that they were made into a constitution by 'the people', but this is not so. Thirdly, the EC and EU structures were, of course, put into place by juridical acts not of national but of international law, where they were negotiated by national executives and ratified by the Heads of State. But lastly, it seems as if all (save perhaps one) can now derive political legitimacy from the popular sup-port which, in very general terms, they currently enjoy.

France

Our technical doubts over the constituent power and methods are rather hard to explain, and it may be easier to begin with the exception. The present constitution of France was drafted under threat of force occasioned by the Algerian conflict; yet technically it was adopted by a careful application of the procedures laid down by its predecessor and was then approved by a large majority of the electorate. After World War II the—basically parliamentary—constitution of the Fourth French Republic was adopted by a small majority in a referendum. The following years saw economic difficulties, colonial problems, parliamentary logjams, deadlocks, and futile coalitions leading to twenty-three governments in twelve years. By June 1958, the failure of the Fourth Republic's government to resolve the Algerian problem led to the threat of an army coup against parliamentary institutions. To avoid this, leading parliamentarians called upon Charles de Gaulle to form a government. De Gaulle agreed to do so only if he was allowed to draw up a new constitution giving much greater power to the executive. The 1946 Constitution provided (art. 90) that amendments could be introduced only by an absolute majority of the National Assembly and could proceed to enactment if so resolved by a similar majority of the Upper House. In 1955 the requisite majorities resolved to alter art. 90 itself, and on 3 June 1958 the ensuing amendment was enacted by a two-thirds majority of the National Assembly as required under the original art. 90. The new constitution was then drafted, debated, and adopted under the procedures set out by the Amendment Act. A leader was needed who could command widespread popular support and in June 1958 the National Assembly recalled Charles de Gaulle with very wide powers for a period of six months, and then fashioned the constitutional changes on which he insisted. The text which ensued was approved by referendum in which, in metropolitan France, almost 80 per cent of the voters (over 66 per cent of the electorate) voted in favour. Indeed, neither parliament nor people had very much choice if they wished to avoid a breakdown of public order and the possibilities of military rule. Transitional provisions of the text enabled the new institutions to be set up by government, rather than parliamentary, law-making.[1]

Three other texts in this collection aver that they were made by the people. That of the USA begins with words well-known throughout the world 'We, the people . . . do ordain and establish this Constitution'. That of the FRG states that 'the German People have adopted, by virtue of their constituent power, this Basic Law'. The 1993 RF text begins 'We, the multi-national people of the Russian Federation . . . adopt the Constitution'.

---

[1] See, for the circumstances in which the Fifth Republic came into existence, P. M. Williams, 'The Fourth Republic: murder or suicide?', Chap. 7 of P. M. Williams, *Wars, Plots and Scandals in Post-War France* (Cambridge, 1970)—a highly detailed account; and P. M. Williams and Martin Harrison: *De Gaulle's Republic* (London, 1960).

USA

Of course, the American people themselves never drafted, nor voted to accept, their constitution. The delegates to the 1787 Philadelphia convention met in the context of the Articles of Confederation which could be amended only by all thirteen states (art. XIII), and whose opening paragraph named all the states in order from north to south. Yet the new text which emerged stated that it was to become a constitution for those who ratified it when nine states did so (art. VII). Since, at the time of agreeing the draft, it was not known which states would ratify, it would have looked strange to begin the text with a list of all thirteen names. The solution was a stroke of political genius: 'We, the people'.

FRG

Needless to say, the constitution of the Third Reich did not serve as the basis for the adoption of the present structure. Although the Basic Law did owe a great deal to earlier German constitutional tradition, yet for all practical purposes 1945 constitutes the beginning.[2] On the defeat of Germany in that year the USA, Britain, France, and the USSR divided the conquered Reich into four zones of military occupation, plus a separate command structure for Berlin. This was to pave the way for the eventual reconstruction of German political life on a democratic basis. In the event, the Soviet Union on the one hand, and France, Britain, and the USA on the other, proceeded to build up separate German governments in their respective spheres. Step by step the three Western powers united their zones for economic purposes, licensed political parties, inaugurated municipal elections, and re-carved the country into provinces (Länder), in which were established local legislatures and governments. For its part, the Soviet Union set about building the Eastern Zone into a 'German Democratic Republic', and in early 1948 denounced the common Western policy, walked out of the four-power Control Council, and began a blockade of Berlin. The three Allies responded by issuing (on 1 July 1948) an authorization for the heads of the eleven Land governments to convene a constituent

[2] See Nevil Johnson, *Government in the Federal Republic of Germany*, Chap. 1 (Oxford, 1973).

assembly (a 'Parliamentary Council') of Land representatives which was required to draft a constitution both democratic and federal. The Land legislatures elected delegates who unanimously chose Konrad Adenauer to head the Parliamentary Council.

In formal juridical terms there is some doubt as to who made the Basic Law. Both the original and the current versions of its Preamble aver that it was adopted by the German people 'by virtue of their constituent power'. Yet it was never submitted for approval by popular vote or referendum as were the French and Russian constitutions. Indeed in the conditions of the Cold War this would have been impossible. Instead the text as finally approved by the Parliamentary Council entered into force (rather like that of the US constitution) when notice of its ratification by representative assemblies in over two-thirds of the Länder was published: on 23 May 1949. It seems, then, that the term 'constituent power' should be understood as an allusion to the constitution's basis of legitimation rather than to the mode of its enactment. The Basic Law's last words foretell its own ending. Art. 146 provides that it shall one day be superseded by a constitution adopted by a free decision of the German people. So the future should see a new text, adopted by referendum.

The constitution's promulgation was followed by federal elections, when Theodor Heuss became Head of State (President) and Konrad Adenauer Head of Government (Chancellor). This did not of itself entirely abrogate the jurisdiction of the Occupying Powers, but (by a convention of 26 May 1952) the three Western Allies terminated their regime and thus restored to the FRG sovereignty over its internal and external affairs. In 1968 the Allies relinquished their last-resort emergency powers, but the status of Berlin itself remained quite distinct until the wall which split the city came down in 1989.

Russia

The Russian regime's attitude to law and the constitution displays a striking contrast between its words and its deeds. The USSR leader, Mikhail Gorbachev, successfully upgraded the electoral process and the role of the legislature at the expense of the Party, and the years of *perestroika* (1987–91) resounded with sermons extolling and slogans proclaiming the Rule of Law. But laws soon became weapons, first in the doomed struggle to save the Union, and then in the battle between the Russian Parliament and the President. Whether the USSR was ever legally dissolved is a matter of doubt. The heads of state of three of its members (Russia, Ukraine, Belorussia) announced its end at the Minsk Agreement of 8 December 1991, and four days later the Russian Supreme Soviet ratified the Agreement and denounced the 1922 Union Treaty. On 25 December 1991 Mikhail Gorbachev resigned as USSR President and on the following day an inquorate Union parliament wound up the legislative, executive, and judicial branches. Perhaps the legal niceties do not matter, save as a testimony to the official disdain for constitutional propriety.

During the next two years the same disdain, or rather contempt, was displayed by both the Russian Congress and the President. Constitutional amendments, requiring a two-thirds majority of the Congress, were constantly being introduced and immediately adopted. At the same time President Boris Yeltsin was issuing a stream of presidential edicts of all kinds. Throughout the next eighteen months competing drafts of a new constitution were produced and debated. On 22 September 1993, on the ground that 'the security of Russia is a higher value than formal conformity to contradictory norms created by the legislative branch of government', the President dissolved the legislature. He had no legal power to do so, as the Constitutional Court promptly pointed out, so on 7 October he suspended that body. The physical challenge of removing the members of parliament was overcome by arms: the House of Parliament (the 'White House') was fired on, killing scores of occupants; it was then taken by force, and the Speaker and others were detained and imprisoned. Afterwards the Russian media described these events as being, on the part of the members of parliament, a 'failed *coup d'état*' or an 'armed revolt'. The BBC calls it 'an uprising'.

The opportunity for political challenge occurred on 12 December 1993. On that day the new constitution, a translation of which is printed here, was submitted to the electorate by presidential edict and was approved by referendum. According to the official returns, 54.8 per cent of the electorate voted, of whom 58.4 per cent were in favour. In place of the Congress and Supreme Soviet it provides for a bi-cameral legislature, elections for which were held on the same day. The Lower House of 450 deputies is given the same name—Duma—as that of the first pre-revolutionary representative assemblies (1905–17). The Upper House is a council of representatives of the component entities of the Federation. An electoral edict provided that half of the Lower House candidates were to be elected from federal party lists based on proportional representation, and the other 225 seats were to be filled by majority vote in single-member constituencies. According to official returns, the first method resulted in the representation of eight parties. One had fourteen seats, four had about twenty seats each, the Communist Party had thirty-two, the broadly government party, Russia's Choice, had forty and the so-called Liberal Democratic party of Russia led by Vladimir Zhirinovsky had fifty-nine. The other 225 deputies include members of many differing parties and movements, and a number who stood as independents.

Amendment

The provisions on the means by which a constitution may be amended are of both juridical and political importance: they are themselves an exercise of the constituent power in spelling out how its own creation may be changed; they divide the amending power among people, legislature, and executive, or between a federation and its components; and they may express basic values. The last are revealed in those features stated to be unamendable: the republican form of government in France, and in Germany the basic human rights and the federal structure.

In the USA, amendments require a special majority in Congress followed by ratification by three-quarters of the states. The last amendment dealt with members' salaries and was adopted in 1992; the 'equal rights amendment' has not yet succeeded. The French provisions give the President a certain leeway. The amendment bill must be passed by both Houses, but he or she may then either put it to the people or resubmit it to both Houses of Parliament convened together in one body (called Congress), in which case it requires three-fifths of the votes cast. The constitution's own provision on amendment envisages no method which does not involve the legislature. Yet it seems that the constitution can be amended by the art. 11 procedure allowing the President to submit directly to the people, and without the intervention of the legislature, any government bill dealing with (*inter alia*) the organization of the public authorities. Art. 3 of the constitution declares indeed that 'sovereignty belongs to the people which they exercise through their representatives *or* by referendum'. In 1962, after an attempt on his life, De Gaulle put to the people directly, under art. 11, an amending Act providing for the direct election of the President. After its passage by a convincing majority, and before its promulgation, the Constitutional Council (by an unpublished majority of 6:4) declined jurisdiction to review the validity of the amendment Act. Since no other French court will ever entertain an argument that a statute is unconstitutional, the constitution was effectively amended. The decision of the Constitutional Council was much criticized by jurists but, with hindsight, was politically very shrewd.

In fact, the Fifth Republic Constitution has never so far been amended by a referendum under the provisions of art. 89. Indeed, no such referendum has ever been held, although the Constitution has on a number of occasions been amended through the Congress method. The main reason for this is the difficulty of securing the assent of the legislature to a text to be submitted to approval by referendum under art. 89. Admittedly, the Assembly is normally under the control of the government, but the Senate is not. In 1962 it would certainly have vetoed a referendum, since it was strongly opposed to the direct election of the President. Use of the art. 11 procedure for amending the constitution seems now to have become broadly acceptable. Indeed, this is very much in the spirit of the Fifth Republic Constitution, since its main purpose was to insulate the executive from the legislature so that government was no longer dependent upon shifting coalitions or localist interests.

By contrast to this process, and mindful of the Weimar provisions for referendum and initiative (which were alleged to have assisted the rise of Hitler), the German Constitution does not involve the people at all in the amendment procedure, but requires a special majority of each House. A similar method used to be employed to amend the previous Soviet and Russian constitutions. But this proved very easy for a body which, under Party rule, had long been accustomed to enthusiastic unanimity, and the years of *perestroika* saw the enactment of hundreds of amendments in the Union and the Republic constitutions. The new text makes the process much more difficult. Nothing is utterly immune from change, but amendments to the basic state structure, the Bill of Rights, and the amendment provisions themselves can be achieved only through the adoption of an entirely new constitution by a constitutional convention or referendum (art. 135). The rest of the constitutional machinery can be changed only with the consent of at least two-thirds of the component members of the Federation (art. 136).

That the basic treaties establishing the EC and EU are far from being a full constitution is illustrated by the fact that, in their own terms, they, and any amendments to them, take effect only after a ratification in accordance with the national constitutions of all the Member States.

The American constitution is very brief. The founders' determination to limit government, both in range and procedure, explains the design of its first three articles, each devoted to a separate branch of federal power, and all interlocking with a system of checks and balances designed to ensure that neither legislature nor executive acquires undue might. None of the other constitutions printed here attempts anything quite as terse or as intricate. The brevity of the American text is largely offset by its age, by the accretions of customary procedures in the legislative and executive branches, and of course by the enormous achievements and awesome responsibility of the judicial branch of government.

The German Constitution is quite lengthy. As a matter of practical politics, the Land representatives who hammered out the text had a number of major concerns. The first was to do nothing that would perpetuate, let alone legitimate, the *de facto* division of Germany. The second was to steer a course between the loose federalism pressed on them by the French and Americans and favoured by some of the Christian Democrats, and the tight centralization on which the German Social Democrats insisted, even to the point of quitting the discussion at one stage. The third, and perhaps overriding, concern was to prevent a replay of the immediate past in its perversions of both the organs of government and all human values.

The drafters' response to the division of their country found expression in the name of their text (Basic Law, not Constitution), in its preamble's reference to a transitional period, in its announcement that 'for the time being' it applied in certain Länder (old art. 23), and in the final article's statement that 'This Basic Law . . . shall cease to be in force on the day on which a constitution adopted by a free decision of the German people comes into force'.

The Basic Law was so written as to facilitate the admission of the provinces to the East, for the old art. 23 stated that it was to come into force for them on their accession. In the summer of 1990 the German Democratic People's parliament (Volkskammer) restored the five easterly Länder (which had been demoted to districts in 1952) and voted to merge itself with the Bundestag. Both legislatures approved a lengthy unification treaty, the Volkskammer dissolved itself, and 3 October 1990 became the official Day of Unity. Next day the 663 members of the Federal Diet for the whole of Germany met in the renovated Reichstag in Berlin, and in December were held the first all-German elections in fifty-seven years.

The federal nature of the German Constitution is underlined by the fact that the legal instrument for its extension to the East was the accession of the Länder under art. 23. That provision was then repealed under the Unification Treaty, art. 4(2) (the number 23 was allotted in 1992 to constitutional amendments dealing with European Union). The second paragraph of the preamble now lists the sixteen Länder and states that the unity of Germany has been achieved. This statement (along with the repeal of the old art. 23) precludes the accession of any further eastern regions of the old Reich and, together with the 1992 ratification of the Treaty between Germany and Poland reconfirming the Oder–Neisse border, seems to have solved a potentially grave problem of territory.

The other fundamental concerns of the Basic Law are federalism and democracy, both victims of the unitary centralized state which Germany became after 1933. Consequently the text spells out and guarantees two main sets of rights: those of the Federation *vis-à-vis* the Länder and vice versa, and those of the people *vis-à-vis* the state. The essentials of both are, as it were, engraved for ever in provisions whose substance is immutable: according to art. 79(3) (the 'perpetuity clause') the principles of art. 1 (basic human rights) and art. 20 (a democratic and social *federal* state) may not be amended. This is, at least in formal terms, quite different from the position elsewhere: in the UK a parliamentary majority (of votes cast) is sovereign; in the USA and Russia no part of the constitution is declared to be unamendable (although there are procedural safeguards of varying strength); while in France only the republican form of government is immune from alteration (art. 89, final paragraph).

For a modern constitution, the French text is unusually short. This is explained by a number of factors. First, of course, it has no federal problems to resolve. Second, it does not expressly set out its own Bill of Rights; instead it operates by incorporating those proclaimed by the 1789 Declaration with the additions laid down in the 1946 preamble. This last document in turn incorporates expressly the 'fundamental principles recognised by the laws of the Republic'. The third reason for the brevity is the technique of the *loi organique*. A number of matters which are too fundamental to be left to ordinary legislation, but too detailed for inclusion in the constitution, are confided to the special procedure of the organic statute (art. 41). These deal with such matters as the electoral system, the judiciary, and the like. The Russian Federation's provision for 'federal constitutional laws' perhaps borrows something from this method. Their subject-matter is important (e.g. martial law, state of emergency) and they can be enacted only by special majorities of both Houses (art. 108).

The Russian Constitution was born amid the ruins of the Soviet Union as a political entity, and of communism as a political creed. Just as Western economic institutions have been adapted to a post-socialist context, so the constitution shows traces of Western texts. It begins, of course, with 'We the . . . people', and art. 1(1) describes the state as 'democratic, federative, law-governed and republican'—all epithets which echo the German art. 20. Art. 3 locates sovereignty in the people and— like art. 3 of the French text—alludes to its direct expression via referendum, while the statement that the constitution is directly effective (art. 15(1)) seems to owe something to EC law. The text is longer than the French but slightly shorter than the German version, and somewhat different in structure. The first chapter's sixteen articles spell out the principles of human rights, federalism, the social state, and the separation of powers, enshrine private property of land and other natural resources, and recognize ideological diversity. They end by making the rest of the constitution subject to the principles enunciated in that first chapter.

FEDERALISM

Of the countries treated in this book, the USA, Germany, and Russia are explicitly federal states. The UK is not, but it embraces four different legal systems: of England and Wales, of Scotland, of Northern Ireland, and of the UK. In addition, the British government is responsible for the defence and international relations of the Channel Islands and Isle of Man, which are not part of the UK. Their citizens are not represented in (and therefore not taxed by) the UK Parliament but, with their consent, laws are made for them by the Queen in Council (i.e. the British executive). The European Community is not a federation, still less is the European Union. Nonetheless it has many features of incipient federalism, not least the fact that, according to Community law, Community law takes precedence over even the constitutions of the Member States.

USA

The American constitution created a federal Union. Secession was neither permitted nor forbidden, but South Carolina's attempt to leave triggered the Civil War of 1861–5. The Congress of the United States was given a list of matters on which it might legislate. The states were told that there were certain things they could not do. Everything else was, according to the Xth Amendment, 'reserved to the States respectively or to the people'. But Congress was given the important powers 'to regulate commerce with foreign nations and among the several states' and to make all laws 'necessary and proper' to carry out its tasks. In this way, the federal competence has grown enormously, although it is worth remembering that a constitutional amendment (the XVIth) was needed in order to permit a federal income tax. The Constitution is declared to be the supreme law of the land and so, in case of conflict, overrides any other federal or state provision. Nonetheless, it should be emphasized that, where the states have jurisdiction, this extends to all branches of government, legislative, executive, and judicial. One result of this is the fifty different versions of the basic areas of criminal and civil law (property, succession, contract, and the like).

FRG

By contrast with the US text, the provisions dealing with the German federal structure are both lengthy and complex. The Länder have general legislative competence, but there is a list of exclusive federal powers, and a longer list of powers in art. 74 which are described as 'concurrent' (a better rendering would be 'alternative'). This has its counterpart in the new Russian constitution's art. 72, but the elaborate financial provisions of the Basic Law's Chapter X are unique in their caution. The provisions for the Land exercise of governmental powers and execution of federal laws (arts. 30, 83) mean that—unlike the situation in the USA—there are few federal agencies, and no first or second-instance federal courts within the Länder. Although in theory the Länder have the general residual legislative power, federal law is supreme, and the erosion of local competence has provoked much discussion: the attempt in art. 72(2) to specify the conditions under which the Federation may exercise legislative powers in fields of concurrent competence seems to have inspired the European Community's new notion of subsidiarity (EC Treaty, art. 3b paragraph 2).

Russian Federation

When the RSFSR was part of the Soviet Union, the constitutions of both the Union and the Republic contained a secession clause. There is no such provision in the 1993 Constitution of the Russian Federation. Of the many problems facing the country, the most intractable is surely the fact that it resembles the Roman Empire in the number and complexity of its ethnic components and in their cultural, linguistic, and social diversity. At the same time a 'Russian problem' stems from the Tsarist legacy, the decades of 'democratic centralism', the Russians' numerical supremacy, and the fact that Russia is the *de facto* heir to the USSR's capital city and much of its capital resources.

The present provisions on the federal question are neither innovative in substance nor clear in formulation. Broadly speaking the component entities retain the relative status accorded to them on paper when they were parts of the RSFSR which was itself within the Union: and the roots of the divisions are more a matter of geography and history than of politics. Art. 5 defines and art. 65 lists the different component entities. There are twenty-one republics, each with its own constitution and legislature. Broadly speaking, this title is accorded to nations which are fairly numerous in population (such as the six million Tatars in the East of European Russia) and which usually make up a majority of the inhabitants of their traditional territory. The lower status of region is accorded to six areas ranging from Krasnodar in the Caucasus to Khabarovsk in the Far East; then come the numerous provinces, the cities of Moscow and St. Petersburg, and the autonomous districts—a status allocated to smaller nations living within a larger, often non-Russian, group. Each of these components is entitled to send two representatives to the Upper House of the legislature, the Federation Council.

As in the German Basic Law, the RF constitution goes on to list a large number of matters within the exclusive federal jurisdiction, and a number of matters within the joint jurisdiction of the RF and its components (arts. 71–2). Everything else is for the latter, but within areas of exclusive or joint jurisdiction, federal law is supreme (art. 77) and, under the transitional provisions, the RF constitution itself prevails over any conflicting provisions of the various internal federative treaties signed during 1992. The main thrust of this system seems to be towards greater decentralization, together with concessions to ethnic ambition, but the text itself contains several crucial overlaps and ambiguities; see, for instance, the power to tax (arts. 71(h), 72(i), 75(3)), the double cover of human rights (arts. 71(c), 72(d)), the generalities of the provisions on local government (arts. 130–3), and the laconism on border disputes (arts. 67(3), 102(1)(a)).

EC/EU

The American 'inter-state commerce clause' is perhaps a pointer to the federalizing tendency of the European Community. Some entity over and above the Member States is needed to secure the free movement of goods, persons, services, and capital within the

EC, and the common commercial treatment of the outside world. That entity is supplied by the institutions of the Community—Commission, Council, and Parliament—and the laws they make prevail. The supremacy of Community law is almost an automatic consequence, for if the relationship between it and any given national law were determined by the constitution of the Member State involved there could be a dozen different results and the law in question would cease to be common to the Community as a whole. On the accession of new states, the Commission's formal opinion is careful to spell this out, and of course the European Court of Justice has frequently held that, in case of conflict, Community law takes precedence over national law. This factor reaches out into the domestic legal systems, for the national judge is then bound by Community law to give precedence to Community law, even over the provisions of his or her own constitution.

GOVERNANCE

The 1789 French Declaration proclaimed that a society which lacked the separation of powers had no constitution at all. All the states dealt with in this book have, to a greater or lesser extent, adopted the principle; the latest convert—after seven decades of denial—is the Russian Federation (art. 10). In the United Kingdom, however, the principle refers mainly to the independence of the judiciary. Executive and legislative powers are at least as closely fused today as they were when Bagehot published *The English Constitution* in 1867.[3]

Political parties find no formal mention in the US Constitution. Given the Nazi law of 1933 which permitted only one party in the Third Reich, it is not surprising that they are specifically mentioned in art. 21 of the FRG Constitution (and can be ruled unconstitutional). They appear also in the French and Russian texts. Further, the 1993 Maastricht amendments introduced political parties into the EC Treaty, where they are 'important as a factor for integration within the Union' and are said to 'contribute to forming a European awareness' (art. 138a).

[3] See, for the separation of powers, M. J. C. Vile, *Constitutionalism and the Separation of Powers* (Oxford, 1967).

USA

The American Constitution devotes each of its first three articles to a separate branch of government. Legislative powers are vested in a bicameral Congress whose members are elected. The House of Representatives is composed of members apportioned among the states and elected for two years. Each state is represented by two senators, elected for a term of six years, and cannot be deprived of this right without its consent. The Lower House exemplifies the principle of the representation of individuals, the Upper House that of the representation of the geographical units comprising the Federation. The equality of representation in the Senate is, of course, out of all proportion to the size or population of the different states, and this is one of the reasons for the present movement to divide California. The Houses are equal in that both must concur to pass any law unlike, for instance, the position in Germany, France, Russia, and the UK where the Upper House may, in certain circumstances be overruled by the Lower.

The executive power is vested in a President, elected (in formal terms by an electoral college) for four years, who may not serve more than two terms. The Vice-President is elected in the same manner but separately. The American (and French and Russian) President can be removed only by impeachment, a process in which the legislature becomes the court. The President selects his or her own cabinet, but presidential appointments require confirmation by the Senate. He or she may veto bills, but can be overruled by special majority of the legislator. Conversely, he or she has to persuade Congress to enact his or her own agenda into legislation.

In short, the main features of the presidential form of government as developed in the USA are the following. The President combines ceremonial status and political power. Legislature and executive are elected separately and for different terms, which means that the President may be of one political party and the majority of the legislature of another. The USA is well accustomed to this while, in the 1980s and 1990s, the French Constitution proved able to withstand the strain of *cohabitation* between a socialist President and a legislative majority of the right. A presidential system gives the chief executive length of tenure and wide control over subordinates. Furthermore, since the US executive is no part of Congress, there is little temptation for the latter to federalize the whole system and to overlook states' rights. The legislature cannot remove the President save by impeachment, in which the Lower House lays the charge and the Upper House tries the case.

RF

The new Russian structure embodies several of these features, but expands the presidency in a number of ways. First, the office does not seem to exercise merely the executive power. Although art. 10 recites the traditional triad of separate powers, the following article suggests there are four, for it says that state power is exercised by the President, the Federal Assembly (clearly the legislature), the government (executive), and the courts (judiciary). And art. 110 states that executive power is exercised by the government, consisting of its chair, vice-chairs, and ministers. Second, following a tradition going back to the Tsars, the office of the President is given wide power to rule by edict (*ukaz*). Apart from the need to comply with the constitution and with federal legislation, this power seems virtually unlimited (art. 90). Third, the President appoints the prime minister (with the consent of the Lower House). Fourth, the President seems to be able to dismiss the government, although the Russian is ambiguous, meaning both resignation and dismissal (arts. 83(c), 117(2)). As in the USA, the Russian President may veto legislation, but can then be overridden by special majority (art. 107(3)). Finally, the President can dissolve the lower House and call new elections if it thrice rejects his or her candidate for premier (art. 111), or if it passes a motion of no confidence in the government (art. 117(3)(4)).

FRG

The German Constitution, embodying as we have seen a strong reaction against the past, represents a determined attempt to revert to the law-governed state: the German for this is *Rechtsstaat*, a word whose Russian calque is also prominent in the first article of the 1993 RF Constitution. The German safeguards are designed to eliminate the possibility of Nazi-style absolutism, and to correct any possible faults in the Weimar Constitution which might have contributed to its rise. The institutional arrangements derive from awareness of the alleged loopholes which the Nazis had exploited.

Thus, art. 73 of the Weimar Constitution permitted the President to submit a law passed by the Reichstag to popular vote. The present constitution (unlike that of France) contains no such power. Yet an important feature of the constitution is that it seeks to create a representative democracy marked by general elections at regular intervals.

Because of its federal structure, Germany has always had a bicameral system. The Bundestag, the Lower House, is elected by popular vote for a four-year term. In contrast to the provisions under both the Empire and Weimar, it can be dissolved only under the very exceptional circumstances of arts. 63 and 68. The Upper House (Bundesrat) is selected by neither direct nor indirect elections. It is made up of sixty-eight members nominated by the sixteen Land governments, who are in effect delegates of the government rather than of the people or of the Land legislature. Unlike the US Senate, the number—and voting power—of the members (three, four, or five) depend on the population of the Land they represent.

Legislation is by joint action of both Houses, although—as elsewhere—most bills are introduced by the government. The Bundesrat has an absolute veto in certain cases and can otherwise, in the last resort, merely suspend the passage of legislation. Bills duly passed go to the President for formal signature and counter-signature of the Chancellor.

The office of President, allegedly abused by Hindenburg after 1930, is shorn of authority and preserved only as that of a largely ceremonial Head of State. The President is no longer directly elected by the people, but indirectly by a Federal Convention of members of the Federal and Land legislatures. He or she is not in charge of the armed forces, and has no emergency powers; appoints the federal judges and ministers, but does not select them and ratifies international Treaties, but usually only with the consent of the legislature. Like other Heads of State, the President's duties include the formal assent to federal statutes: but this is valid only on countersignature by the Chancellor.

It is this latter office which carries the real power of Head of Government, and the Chancellor is—in legal terms—rather better protected than the British Prime Minister. The President must appoint to the office the person who obtains a majority of the votes of the members of the Bundestag. Only if no one has such a majority may the President choose whether to appoint the person with a majority of the votes cast or to dissolve the Bundestag. Once installed, the Chancellor nominates and demotes Ministers (whose formal appointment and dismissal are for the President) and is well-protected against a 'no confidence' defeat in the legislature. It is not enough for the Bundestag to outvote him; a majority of the members must agree on the alternative Chancellor. Thus 'unnatural' combinations of left and right may defeat a Chancellor but they will not force a resignation as they could in the Weimar Republic. In fact this process has worked only once when in September 1982 Helmut Kohl was elected to the office following the constructive dismissal of Chancellor Schmidt.

There is no unlimited power in the executive to dissolve the Bundestag and call an election. On the other hand, the Chancellor may use the 'no confidence' procedure in order to demonstrate ability to govern with authority. If his or her motion for a vote of confidence fails, the President may be asked to dissolve the Lower House; and the only way the Bundestag can stop this is by promptly electing another Chancellor by a majority of its members. This device was used by Willy Brandt after an unsuccessful attempt to oust him in 1972. He put a motion of confidence to the Bundestag, planning to lose it, asked the President to dissolve Parliament, and won the next election. Chancellor Kohl did much the same in 1983, and his tactics and the dissolution decision of President Carstens survived challenge in the Constitutional Court which, after a lengthy examination, concluded that the only constraint was on the use of this procedure as a sham: that is, where a Chancellor, sure of a majority, contrives a negative vote in order to get the President to call an election. The particular political drama ended when the new elections gave support to the Kohl coalition. It may now be a convention of the FRG that a change of government in mid-term should be endorsed by the electorate.

France

The French system has features of both the presidential and the parliamentary models. The 1958 constitution devoted half of its ninety-two articles to the executive, the legislature, and the relations between them. This was an attempt to avoid the problems which had bedevilled the Fourth Republic. In the event, however, the governments of the Fifth Republic have usually been able to command a majority in the Assembly. The importance of the executive is emphasized by the fact that, after the first articles devoted to the people, the next section deals with the President (a similar pattern is found in the new Russian text). The President is far from being merely a titular Head of State. Since 1962 he or she is directly elected by the people, has arbitral powers under art. 5, and emergency powers under art. 16, and signs the regulations emanating from the executive's very extensive lawmaking powers (arts. 37, 13). In association with the government he or she can present bills to the people to enact by referendum, thereby bypassing the parliament, and can dissolve the National Assembly and call new elections. By contrast, the legislature is trammelled. Its power to enact laws is laid down in terms not merely of form but of subject-matter, and (under art. 41) the government may block any bill which does not fall within the areas listed in art. 34. Much of its internal procedure is now defined in the constitution and this gives the Prime Minister and his or her Cabinet great procedural advantages over the Opposition (cf. for example the 'block vote' provision of art. 44).

EC/EU

In the institutional structure of the European Community the legislative powers are dispersed, in a highly complex pattern, among three institutions: Commission, Council, and the body called the European Parliament, directly elected for a term of five years. But this last entity can, of its own motion, neither make laws nor impose taxes, and the strength of its powers varies enormously depending on the subject-matter of the proposed legislation. In fact until 1993 its functions were described in the Treaty of Rome as merely 'advisory and supervisory' (art. 137). These epithets were removed by the Treaty on European Union, but were not replaced by the word 'legislative', although both the Single European Act and the Maastricht Treaty gave the Parliament important new powers. In most cases only the Commission has the power of legislative initiative, and drafts the regulations and directives which make up the EC's general norms. Its members have always been selected by the Member States' governments, although from 1995 the Parliament's approval will be required. The instruments they draft are, in the end, adopted or rejected by the Council, made up of representatives of each Member State at ministerial level. Between drafting and adoption, however, the Parliament is brought into the process. Its powers vary according to the subject-matter (art. 189a–c) but at their strongest amount to a veto. The fact that the exact balance of power among Commission, Council, and Parliament differs according to the issue involved has the rather strange consequence of bringing the institutions into court against each other. In particular, the Parliament—unlike national legislatures—has more than once descended into the courtroom and sued the Council to assert its rights in the lawmaking process. The checks and balances of the Community structure are often to be found in the different voting requirements laid down for the various sectors of competence, and what the Parliament seeks is a judicial decision favouring that particular Treaty procedure whose voting rules give it most power.

Voting generally

Perhaps a general word should be said on this matter. The machinery of democracy often functions by way of voting, and the majority carries the day. But a majority of what—of those who could vote, or of those who do vote; and what kind of majority? One widespread model seems to be a simple majority of those who in fact choose to vote. This appears to be taken for granted in the US Constitution for ordinary matters, in the UK Parliament for all legislation, and is expressed as a general residual principle both in Germany (art. 42(2)) and for the European Parliament (EC art. 141). By striking contrast (and following the unbroken Soviet tradition), the Russian constitution provides (arts. 102(3), 103(3), 105) that normally the Houses of the legislature act by a majority of their members—so absence or abstention counts against the proposal.

Many other patterns are possible. A majority of the votes in the Bundesrat can be rejected by a majority of the members of the Bundestag (under art. 77(4)). Thirteen States participated in the drafting of the US Constitution but it took effect (for those which did) when nine ratified; by contrast the TEU took effect (on 1 November 1993) only after all twelve Member States had ratified. To approve the ratification of Treaties or to impeach the American President requires the consent of two-thirds of the

Senators present, whereas amendments to the constitution must be proposed by two-thirds of the members of both Houses and ratified by three-quarters of the States. The French constitution can be amended by a three-fifths majority of the votes cast when both Houses are sitting together. In order to adopt the 1993 Russian constitution votes by a majority of the electorate and approval by a majority of the votes were required. A two-thirds majority of members of both Houses is needed to override the Russian President's refusal to sign a statute and, by the same majority, the Lower House may overrule the Upper.

The EC Commission acts by a majority of its members. So in principle does the Council but, as this would mean that small states could outvote much larger ones, the Treaty occasionally insists on unanimity, and generally requires what it calls a 'qualified' (i.e. special) majority of weighted votes (art. 148). Finally, the relative powers of the Parliament and the Council in the European legislative and budgetary processes are articulated in an extremely complex set of requirements for voting in each body (arts. 189a–c, 203).

THE JUDICIAL BRANCH

When it comes to the judiciary, separation of powers is taken quite seriously, although in England this is obscured by the fact that the Upper House of the legislature has the same name as the highest court, and its Speaker (the Lord Chancellor) is the senior judge. In all the systems here dealt with, judges are independent and irremovable. In Russia this is expressly stated, but is a frail novelty. In the USA and UK it is not stated but is the case.

The only topic which merits brief discussion here is the relation between the constitution, the courts, and the legislature. For almost 200 years the USA has led the way in discussion and practice in this area, although—or perhaps because—the actual text of the US Constitution is not pellucid on the point. Art. VI provides that the Constitution and federal laws made under it and treaties 'shall be the supreme law of the land' and shall bind state judges: thus the supremacy of federal over state law is clearly stated. But nothing expressly subordinates federal legislation to the federal constitution and art. III on the judicial power does not in so many words confer jurisdiction to do this. Nonetheless the Supreme Court assumed such a jurisdiction and in 1803 held that 'an Act of the Legislature repugnant to the Constitution is void' (*Marbury* v. *Madison*[4]). As a result, any court of general jurisdiction seems to have power to declare any statute unconstitutional. In practice this power is wielded ultimately by the Supreme Court. But that body does not deal with only constitutional questions. It has some primary and more appellate jurisdiction over a whole host of other issues of public and private law. In short, its function is that of an ordinary court: to decide disputes. In consequence, it will rule on questions of constitutionality only if they arise in an actual case, and it will not give abstract or advisory opinions.

The general continental European pattern is much more recent (dating from the 1920s) and tends to differ from the American model in a number of respects. First, the whole topic is expressly dealt with in the constitutional text. Second, the tribunal given a power of constitutional review is quite separate from the ordinary courts of general jurisdiction. Third, and a consequence of this, its jurisdiction is exclusive: other courts cannot decide issues of constitutionality but must, where such questions need to be settled to dispose of the case in hand, refer them to the Constitutional Court. Fourth, process may be instituted in a number of different ways: by ordinary courts in the manner just described; by ordinary citizens complaining that their individual constitutional rights are being infringed by some legislation; by certain high officials (President, Speaker etc.) seeking, in the absence of any particular dispute, to obtain a general and 'abstract' ruling on the constitutionality of a statute; and occasionally the constitutional tribunal is even given the power to review legislation on its own initiative. Finally, the Court's decision that a particular legislative provision is unconstitutional is itself given the force of law so as to bind all courts and officials. The texts printed in this volume adopt varying versions of these features, and add their own particular extensions or limitations.

The German Constitution sets up a Constitutional Court, the name emphasizing its main function.[5] It is divided into two

---

[4] 1 Cranch 137.
[5] See Donald P. Kommers, *Judicial Politics in West Germany: A Study of the Federal Constitutional Court* (Sage, Beverley Hills, 1976), and *The Constitutional*

senates of eight judges each, the first handling basic rights cases
(with a screening committee of three judges) and the second the
inter-institutional and political disputes (thus it was this senate
which ruled on the constitutionality of accession to the TEU). It
is the only court in Germany where dissenting opinions are permissible. Its decisions bind all legislative, executive, and judicial
bodies.

The Court's powers are listed in ten different articles of the
Basic Law (and of course completed in a fuller statute on the
Court itself). They cover some sixteen areas, although it has
never been called upon to decide on the impeachment of the
President or dismissal of a judge. One most interesting function is
that of ruling on the constitutionality of political parties (art.
21(2)), though it can be seised only by legislature or government,
and has in fact heard only two such cases: in 1952 the neo-Nazi
Socialist Reich Party and in 1956 the Communist Party were held
to be unconstitutional. It also handles disputes as to jurisdiction
between Federal organs (art. 93(1)(1)) and between Federal and
State organs (arts. 93(1)(3), 84(4)). At the request of the government or one-third of the Bundestag members, it may rule on the
compatibility of legislation with the constitution—and thus does
so in the abstract, in the absence of any litigated case. During
ordinary lawsuits, however, a German court which thinks that
legislation might be unconstitutional, and needs to know in order
to decide the dispute before it, must refer the question to the
Constitutional Court (art. 100)—the notion is not unlike that of
EC art. 177(b) empowering any national court to refer a question
of the validity of Community legislation to the ECJ. A German
court may also ask the Federal Constitutional Court whether a
rule of international law directly creates rights for the litigants
before it (arts. 100(2), 25).

In all these types of proceeding, access to the German
Constitutional Court is open only to governmental and parliamentary entities and the courts. But a 1969 amendment incorporated in the Constitution an avenue previously opened by statute
(art. 93.1(4a) and (4b)) whereby anyone who considers that his
constitutional rights have been violated by the state may, after

Jurisprudence of the Federal Republic of Germany (Duke U. P., Durham, N.C.,
1989); and Nigel Foster, *German Law and Legal System* (Blackstone, London,
1993).

exhausting all other legal remedies, file a complaint directly with the Constitutional Court.

In terms of textual appearance, the basic powers of the Russian Constitutional Court are not dissimilar to those of its German counterpart. In terms of political reality, however, it is difficult to see how, after its humiliation by Mikhail Gorbachev's refusal to obey an injunction to appear, and its unconstitutional but effective suspension by Boris Yeltsin, it can readily gain respect.

Just as the French institutional structure is unique, so is its forum for constitutional review.[6] The body in question is, quite deliberately, not established as, or given the name of, a court: it is the Constitutional Council. Its members sit for only nine years, save for ex-Presidents who are *ex officio* members for life. Three of the appointed members are selected by the President of the Republic, and three each by the Speakers of each House. They are not necessarily trained lawyers, but tend to have held high ministerial or academic office.

This forum is an innovation of the Fifth Republic, and its primary functions may be summed up by saying that the Constitutional Council judges only the Parliament; and the Parliament is judged only by the Constitutional Council. It was devised by de Gaulle's advisers mainly to provide a means of stopping legislation. The parliament's law-making power is confined to a list of (admittedly important) matters in art. 34. Everything else is for the government. Consequently it was necessary to provide some method whereby a private member's bill on some topic outside the range permitted to parliament could, if the government so wished, be halted. Art. 41 allows the government to object to such a bill and, in case the parliament is determined to proceed, to refer it to the Constitutional Council for a ruling on whether it falls within the competence of the legislature or the executive. Until 1971 this was perceived as the Council's main function.

But the Constitution also allows any bill—before promulgation—to be referred to the Council for an assessment of the bill's conformity with the Constitution (art. 61 para. 2), and goes on to enact that a provision declared unconstitutional can be neither promulgated nor implemented. In 1971 a Council decision began

---

[6] See John Bell, *French Constitutional Law* (OUP, 1992).

with the formulaic words 'Having seen the Constitution and particularly its Preamble'. This latter text incorporates the Bill of Rights contained in the 1789 Declaration and the 1946 preamble and, via the latter, 'general principles recognized by the laws of the Republic'. Since then, the Constitutional Council has held a number of bills to be unconstitutional for contravention of human rights and has become, *de facto* if not *de jure*, a constitutional court.

However, the following points need to be stressed. First, statutes which have been promulgated are, as in the UK, entirely immune from constitutional challenge in any jurisdiction whatever. Second, and following from this, ordinary citizens and ordinary courts may not refer matters to the Council. That power is reserved to the President, the prime minister, the two Speakers, and (since a 1974 amendment) any sixty Deputies or Senators. But this last group is, of course, usually the Opposition which frequently refers Government bills in the hope that it will achieve by a lawsuit what it could not attain by a vote. By this process the Council was called on to play a delicate role during the 1980s when a socialist parliamentary majority proceeded to large-scale nationalization, only to be succeeded by the rapid privatization programme of the next government. On the whole the Council performed its difficult functions with great tact.

It may finally be worth pointing out that the American-inspired method of permitting an *ex post facto* declaration of unconstitutionality means that statutes can, many years after their enactment and implementation, be held to be null and void. This is costly. By contrast, the French system operates rather like a check on motor-cars before they leave the factory. It is not perfect, since the occasional defective statute may be promulgated without having been referred to the Council. But it is cheap.

EMERGENCY POWERS

The greater the constitutional commitment to a Bill of Rights, the more difficult it is to frame emergency powers. The following issues have to be resolved: the events or circumstances which count as an emergency; the body which can decide whether these circumstances obtain; the body which can exercise emergency powers; the extent to which these powers can contravene normal rights and liberties; and the procedure for and the supervision of their exercise.

By comparison with later documents, these matters receive little attention in the US constitution. The United States is bidden to protect every state against invasion and, if asked by the state legislature or executive 'when the legislature cannot convene', against domestic violence. Congress declares war and can use the militia (whose commander will be the President) to suppress insurrection and repel invasion; and art. I on the legislative power provides that 'the writ of habeas corpus' may be suspended when, in cases of rebellion or invasion, the public safety may require it (art. I 9(2)).

Events in the twentieth century lead modern constitution-framers to devote much more anxious attention to the problem. On the one hand the executive must be permitted to take emergency action; on the other the emergency power should not be capable of being used to subvert both the legislature and the Bill of Rights.

The position in Germany has been particularly complicated. Under the Occupation Statute and its modification by the 1955 Convention the Allies retained certain powers to safeguard their own forces serving in West Germany and to cope with internal and external subversion. The late 1960s and 1970s saw West Germany under violent attack from terrorists of left and right with numerous attacks on public persons. In the mid-1960s the Federal Government, under the control of the CDU, wanted to insert emergency provisions into the constitution and drafted several alternative bills. The SPD opposed them until, as part of the Grand Coalition Government formed in late 1966, it was able to insist on substantial modifications. Amendments to a number of separate articles of the constitution were enacted by the law of 24 June 1968, despite violent opposition outside parliament and vigorous protests by the FDP in the Federation Council. With the passage of this Act the Allies declared that their residual powers had lapsed.

The changes themselves fall into several categories, including those which amend the basic rights clauses (for instance, to permit telephone tapping—a prerogative previously reserved to the Occupying Powers). The bulk of the legislation deals with three separate situations: the 'state of defence' (*Verteidigungsfall*) which, elsewhere, would be called a 'state of war'; the 'state of tension' (*Spannungsfall*), and the 'internal state of emergency' (*innerer Notstand*). The first two require a two-thirds majority in parliament, but in the first case, if parliament cannot function, most of its powers are taken over by a Joint Committee of members of the Bundestag and of the Federation Council (arts. 2, 8, 53a). Care is also taken to ensure that the Constitutional Court shall continue to function.

Art. 16 of the French Constitution defines the circumstances which will enable the President to take 'such measures as are required'. He or she must consult the prime minister, both Speakers, and the Constitutional Council; parliament convenes as of right; and the National Assembly cannot be dissolved. This provision has been invoked only once, in 1961 to resist a military coup in Algeria.

Since the Russian President's unilateral exercise of strength was the foundation for the abolition of the old and adoption of the new constitution, it is not surprising that that document is fairly terse on emergency powers (arts. 56, 87, 88, 102(1)(b), (c)). The President may introduce martial law or a state of emergency (which must be confirmed by the Upper House) and may then restrict most individual rights. Circumstances and procedures are left to be spelled out in a federal constitutional law.

INTERNATIONAL AFFAIRS

On the whole, most constitutions deal with international affairs in generalities, and in some cases it is not entirely clear who has what powers. Outside the UK, only the legislature can declare war, but (except in Germany) the President is Commander-in-Chief of the armed forces. The extent to which this latter office allows the executive to order military intervention without a declaration of war is a matter of doubt. The USA fought a long defeat in Vietnam without benefit of a Congressional declaration, and the Supreme Court regularly avoided review of challenges to this involvement. Congress and the President remain in disagreement about the war powers.

But in all the constitutions, the general conduct of international affairs in peacetime is, for obvious practical reasons, confined to the executive. The Head of State appoints and receives ambassadors and ratifies treaties negotiated by the executive, although the constitution may require the President to obtain the consent to ratification of the legislature or some branch thereof. The US President needs the consent of a special majority of the Senate while, for a wide category of important Treaties, the French President may ratify only under the authority of a law. This would normally, of course, be passed by the parliament but the law authorizing the ratification of the TEU was enacted by referendum. The EC general pattern requires the Commission to negotiate, the Parliament to consent to, and the Council to conclude international agreements (art. 228). The UK is the odd one out: there seems to be no general rule that the executive needs parliamentary authority to ratify treaties, though in practice Parliament is informed before ratification. Of course Parliament can change this if it wishes to, and section 6(1) of the European Parliament Elections Act 1978 enacts that 'no treaty which provides for any increase in the powers of the European Parliament shall be ratified unless it has been approved by an Act of Parliament'.

There seems to be a relation between the bodies involved in the ratification process and the effect in the internal legal order of any treaty once ratified. The UK is quite logical here: while (as in Germany) the general rules of international law are part of the national system, each particular treaty is ratified by the executive, and so has no internal effect on the legal position of citizens—for that, legislation is required. The USA, where treaties are ratified with the consent of part of the legislature, gives them internal effect similar to that of Acts of Congress. France, which requires full parliamentary approval for the ratification of treaties which will change French law, then accords them an authority superior to that of national legislation. The Russian provisions seem imperfect. The President negotiates and signs treaties and executes instruments of ratification. It is not clear to what extent he or she needs the consent or authority of the legislature to ratify treaties. As in France (art. 54) and the EC (art. 228(6)), treaties before ratification may be submitted to the Constitutional Court for a ruling on whether they conform to the constitution. If they do not, they cannot be ratified without renegotiation or amendment of the constitution. Once ratified, international treaties (as in France) prevail over inconsistent national legislation. Short of involving the Constitutional Court, however, the powers of the Russian legislature to control executive negotiation and presidential ratification are obscure. One would expect the Lower House to be empowered to authorize the ratification of important treaties, but there is no express provision to this effect. Yet some such power seems to be presumed, for the Upper House is enjoined to examine the Lower House's action on 'the ratification and denunciation of international treaties' (art. 106(d)).

The relation of France, Germany, and the UK to the EC and EU treaties is (according to Community law) determined not by the national constitutions (under which its effect could vary from state to state), but by Community law as laid down by the European Court of Justice.

Perhaps a more fundamental question, however, is whether, with the appropriate consent of the legislature, the executive may make treaties of any kind whatever, including those which transfer to other inter-state entities some part of national sovereignty. Such a power is expressly granted by the German and Russian constitutions, while the 1946 French text permits it in order to safeguard peace. France may cede territory, however, only with the consent of the populations concerned (compare the UK's Northern Ireland Constitution Act 1973). But the ratification of the TEU required constitutional amendment in both France (arts. 88(1) to 88(4)) and Germany (particularly arts. 23, 24, 28) in order to provide for voting rights of Community citizens and the transfer of the power to issue money.

HUMAN RIGHTS

The first ten amendments to the US Constitution commit the Union to a respect for certain basic rights, and the XIVth Amendment subjects the states to the same discipline. The rights in question are usually expressed by a negative: Congress shall make no law abridging the freedom of the press; the right to keep and bear arms shall not be infringed; the right to be secure shall not be violated; no person shall be deprived of life, liberty, or property without due process of law; no fact tried by a jury shall be otherwise re-examined than according to the rules of the common law.

The 1789 French Declaration, although somewhat more rhetorical, covers much the same ground and, as we have seen, operates via the 1958 preamble and the powers of the Constitutional Council to restrict the powers of the legislature. The Bill of Rights is deliberately placed at the very beginning of the German constitution (arts. 1–19). The rights are acknowledged to be inviolable and inalienable, directly enforceable, and binding on legislature, executive, and judiciary. Furthermore the provisions which describe them are, as we have seen, entrenched against any amendment of their essentials. They are not all, however, expressed in absolute terms. On the contrary, the text seeks to balance the rights of any given individual against those of others, for instance to prevent their being used 'to offend against the constitutional order or against morality' (art. 2(1)). But 'the essential content of a basic right may never be encroached upon' (art. 19(2)). The society in which these rights are to be enjoyed is that of a representative democracy with separation of powers, described in art. 20 as a democratic, social, and federal state in which all state authority emanates from the people, who exercise it by elections and voting and by specific legislative, executive, and judicial organs. Furthermore, the legislator is bound by the constitution, and the executive and judiciary by the law *stricto sensu*—and by justice.

As to content, the substantive values enshrined in the Basic Law are rooted in the three main currents of opinion which made up the 1949 drafting Council: the liberal tenets espoused by the Free Democratic Party, the socialist values of the Social Democratic Party, and the Christian 'natural-law' tradition found in the Christian Democratic Union and its Bavarian counterpart, the Christian Social Union. From the first come the standard commitments to freedom of personality, belief, expression, assembly, movement, occupation, and property, and the assertion of a right of privacy, of immunity from unauthorized search and seizure, and of a right to judicial protection against the state. The second tradition inspired the maxim that 'property imposes duties', the guarantee of trade union rights, the provision that the means of production may be nationalized, and the inclusion of the word 'social' in the constitutional description of the state. The Christian heritage ensured that the preamble mentions God, that freedom may not be used to offend against morality, and that the issue of private, including religious, education is fully covered.

The above division into three main sources is of course too simple. In particular, it should not be thought that each current of opinion was necessarily hostile to all the tenets espoused by the others. Quite to the contrary, the resulting text contrives to combine the main values of each into a workable ensemble. But the Bill of Rights is not, and is not intended to be, a set of merely procedural safeguards of the individual. The German constitution is imbued with a ranked set of values of which the most basic is the principle of human dignity, and comes equipped with a unique mechanism for its own and for their protection. Anyone who abuses his or her constitutional freedoms 'in order to combat the free democratic basic order shall forfeit these basic rights' (art. 18), and 'all Germans have the right to resist anyone seeking to abolish the constitutional order' (art. 20(4)).

The Russian treatment places the Bill of Rights in its second chapter and declares the rights to be directly effective. The core of the list is similar to that found in the 1936 Stalin and 1977 Brezhnev constitutions, and includes numerous claims on the state—to housing, health care, legal aid, and the like. However, the new era is indicated by several provisions such as those ensuring freedom of entrepreneurial activity, private ownership of land, and the right to one's lawful judge.

The fact that the European Community Treaty contains no Bill of Rights posed an initial threat to the supremacy of Community law. Several agricultural regulations were felt by those affected—especially in Germany—to contravene the national Bill of Rights. The European Court of Justice needed to persuade the judges of the Member States that they should not hear challenges to the legality of such regulations but should instead refer the problem to the ECJ. To do so it declared that the protection of human rights formed a part of the Community legal system. Its textual justification was found in art. 164 which enjoins the Court to ensure that 'the law' is observed, and in art. 173 which provides for the annulment of Community legal acts which contravene 'any rule of law'. The details of this protection were to be deduced from the 'constitutional traditions of the

Member States' and the European Convention on Human Rights (invoked three times by the TEU). In this way, the Court has considered such matters as double jeopardy, the right to a hearing, and the principle of proportionality. Amendments introduced by the TEU include the right to petition the parliament (as in the US First Amendment and the German art. 17) and the setting up of an Ombudsman to handle complaints of Community maladministration (arts. 138d, 138e).

LAST THOUGHTS

This survey has stressed those autobiographical elements in the history of the various countries which have led to the particular features of their constitutional order and to the variety among them. Yet at a more general level it can be seen that the systems selected here have much in common. Each is democratic in the sense that it makes the legislature and the executive ultimately dependent on popular vote, and each gives the final say to a majority of those entitled to vote (though there are important differences in the kinds of majority needed to carry the day). Each provides an avenue of individual access to political power, with the right to vote and to be elected, and confers protection against abuse of state power. Political rights are, of course, conferred only on citizens, but there are very few provisions aimed against foreigners (though the American President must have been born in the USA). None contains any strident territorial claims or devices to protect state possessions. Each constitution (expressly or impliedly) accords a special role to political parties set up by individuals in order to run or to oppose the government. In each there is some version of separation of powers and some system of checks and balances between them, although constitutions later than that of the USA contain some residual device to prevent an endless deadlock. Finally, of course, in none of them does the constitution itself give a full or accurate depiction of the polity: each text operates within a matrix of custom, convention, case law, and cautious compromise.

3

On the Constitution of the United Kingdom

1 We have seen that the codified constitutions contain, among programmatic matters and the like, a self-consistent set of laws which control the conduct of government. We have also seen that these laws are merely a selection: for instance, while the German Constitution now contains clauses relating to political parties, the American Constitution does not. A second characteristic of these constitutions is that these laws have a special, indeed a superior, status *vis-à-vis* all other laws. Indeed the very words for the document as found in Germany or the USA underline this point. The German Constitution is called the *Grundgesetz*, or Basic Law; that of the USA contains the phrase 'This Constitution . . . shall be the supreme Law of the Land (art. VI, cl. 2).

2 Each of these constitutions contains three elements to secure this higher or special status to the constitution relative to any other laws. They are: (a) an arrangement for signalling repugnancy of the ordinary law to the constitution—in the USA and Germany this is a court of law, in France it is the Constitutional Council; (b) nullification of the said law in the case of repugnancy to the constitution; and (c) where it is desired to change the constitution rather than the law which is repugnant to it, a more arduous procedure for the abrogation or alteration of a constitutional provision than that established for ordinary laws. So, the French Constitution requires either a referendum or a three-fifths vote of the two Houses of Parliament convened as a Congress (art. 89). Moreover, in two of these constitutions there exist clauses which cannot be changed at all: arts. 1 and 20 of the Bonn Constitution, and art. 89(5) of the French Constitution.

3 None of these characteristics applies to the United Kingdom. On the contrary, its constitution is marked by three striking features: it is indeterminate, indistinct, and unentrenched.

4 *Indeterminate content*   Her Majesty's Stationery Office publishes the Official Revised Edition of the statutes in force. The two volumes devoted to 'Constitutional Law' give the text of 138 Acts of Parliament (from the Tallage Act 1297 to the Welsh Language Act 1993), while a quite separate volume on 'Rights of the Subject' gives another thirty-two (including what is left of Magna Carta). From these hundreds of pages, what is or is not 'the Constitution' is a matter for scholars' individual judgements. Furthermore, many matters regulated with great precision in codified constitutions—such as the procedure on a finance bill, or that covering a vote of no confidence in the government—are in the UK governed entirely by custom, convention, or Standing Orders of the House. There is no authoritative selection of statutes, conventions, common law rules, and the like which together comprise 'the Constitution'; every author is free to make a personal selection and to affirm that this is the one, even the only one, that embraces all the most important rules and excludes all the unimportant ones—though nobody has ever been so foolish as to assert this. As Dicey put it, a writer on the Constitution 'has good reason to envy professors who belong to countries such as France ... or the United States, endowed with Constitutions on which the terms are to be found in printed documents, known to all citizens and accessible to every man who is able to read'.[1]

5 Despite this indeterminacy at the edges, since we are concerned with the constitution of a 'United Kingdom', all scholars must agree on the importance of the specific legal acts which constituted that entity. Great Britain was brought into being by a Treaty followed by two distinct Acts of two different legislators. The 'Acts of Union' of 1707 are complex but fundamental. From 1603 the crowns of England and Scotland had been united in the same person, but the two countries remained distinct sovereign states each with its own parliament, laws, courts, and (customary) constitution. In 1706, commissioners for England and separate commissioners for Scotland agreed Articles of Union—also called a Treaty. As Queen of Scotland, Anne 'with advice and consent of the estates of (the Scottish) Parliament' enacted a statute which established the Presbyterian Church in Scotland,

---

[1] A. V. Dicey, *Introduction to the study of the Law of the Constitution* (10th edn., E. C. S. Wade (ed.), Macmillan, 1958), 4.

declaring that it was to be inserted in any (Scottish) Act ratifying the Treaty of Union and was to be a fundamental and essential condition thereof. The Scottish Parliament then passed an 'Act for the Union with England'. The English Parliament with Anne as Queen of England then passed a lengthy Act for the Union with Scotland which recited and approved the Treaty of Union and the Scottish statutes. This process gave birth to an entity described in the Acts as 'the United Kingdom of Great Britain'. The Scottish Act for the Union with England (in a provision repeated in the English Act for a Union with Scotland) stated that henceforth Scots law was alterable by the Parliament of Great Britain but that no alteration could be made in private law 'except for evident utility of the subjects within Scotland'. It is therefore argued by some jurists that, by the very act of its creation, the UK Parliament is not empowered to alter Scots private law to the prejudice of the people there, and so is not absolutely supreme.[2] The issue has never been finally tested by litigation, although it is conceivable that English courts might take one view of the outcome and Scottish courts another.

6 In 1800 the kingdoms of Great Britain and Ireland were united by similar legal procedures—Articles of Union followed by an Act of each parliament. In 1922 a UK Act recognized the 'Irish Free State' comprising the island of Ireland minus six counties in the north-east, and gave force of law to an agreement between the UK government and an Irish delegation. The Ireland Act 1949 finally declared that Ireland had ceased to be part of His Majesty's dominions, though the statute also enacts that Ireland is not a foreign country (so its citizens are not aliens or foreigners for the purposes of UK law). Since 1922 legislation of the UK Parliament has in effect limited the United Kingdom to Great Britain and Northern Ireland (the latter is dealt with later).

7 *Indistinct structure* The second striking feature of the UK position is that there is no special device to signal the repugnancy of 'ordinary' laws to those we choose to regard as laws forming part of the constitution. The constitution is a rag-bag of statutes

[2] There are other provisions of the Scots Act of Union which may limit the powers of Parliament. See generally, Neil MacCormick, 'Does the United Kingdom have a Constitution?' (1978) 29 *Northern Ireland Legal Quarterly* 1; Denis J. Edwards, 'The Treaty of Union: more hints of constitutionalism' (1992) 12 *Legal Studies* 34; and *Pringle, Petitioner*, 1991 SLT 330.

and judicial interpretations thereof, of conventions, of the Law and Custom of Parliament, of common law principle, and jurisprudence. Inside this miscellany all that we can assert with certainty is that statutes override non-statutory provisions, and that among statutes the latter overrides the earlier one. So if it be a statute relating to political practices that is being broken, this will be cognizable and dealt with by the ordinary courts and not by any specially constituted tribunal. And an infraction will be handled just like an infraction of, let us say, the Highways Act. If on the other hand the law being broken is not a law but a convention, the only way in which this is signalled is by private persons like the authors writing or making speeches on the subject, supported by some and opposed by others.

8 *Unentrenched* One of the main reasons for the UK constitution's indistinct structure and indeterminate content is the absence of any special *formal* requirements for enacting or amending constitutional norms. Codified constitutions are adopted and can be altered only in certain ways—by special voting requirements, by referendum, and the like. But in the UK, statutes relating to political practices, that is 'constitutional law', are changed or repealed in exactly the same way as any other statute.

9 Now statutes are made, and made exclusively, by one organ. This is the Queen-in-Parliament. Often in this particular context this is simply called Parliament. The Queen-in-Parliament therefore becomes the starting-point for the exposition of the Constitution of Britain.

THE SUPREMACY (OR SOVEREIGNTY) OF PARLIAMENT

10 For present purposes Parliament is the Queen, the House of Lords, and the House of Commons combined. Except as when otherwise laid down by statute, a statute is made by the Queen assenting to a Bill which has been passed by each of the two Houses. The Parliament Acts of 1911 and 1949 lay down the circumstances in and the procedures by which a Bill can become law without the consent of the House of Lords, that is by being passed only by the Commons and thereafter receiving the Royal Assent.

11 Until recently, the law assumed that Parliament was omni-

competent and paramount. It could make or unmake law on any matter whatsoever and, indeed, it could do so with retrospective effect. No court in the kingdom was competent to question the legal validity of any Act of Parliament, that is of a statute. Every lawmaking body in the country was subordinate to it, since even if it did not derive its original authority from Parliament, it exerted this authority only as long as Parliament cared to suffer it.

12 This attribute is sometimes called the sovereignty, sometimes the supremacy, of Parliament. There are many difficult questions arising from this concept and both lawyers and politicians have debated them widely.[3] But on the basic proposition stated in the preceding paragraph there was no doubt at all, at least until the European Communities Act of 1972 (see below), and if we were codifying the constitution of Britain, we should be safe in leaving it at that, allowing lawyers and other commentators to argue the niceties, just as they do about the clauses of the constitutions in Bonn, Washington, and Paris. In Blackstone's famous lines:

The power and jurisdiction of parliament, says Sir Edward Coke, is so transcendent and absolute, that it cannot be confined, either for causes or persons, within any bounds. And of this high court he adds, it may be truly said *'si antiquitatem spectes, est vetustissima; si dignitatem, est honoratissima; si jurisdictionem, est capacissima.'* It hath sovereign and uncontrollable authority in making, confirming, enlarging, restraining, abrogating, repealing, reviving, and expounding of laws, concerning matters of all possible denominations, ecclesiastical, or temporal, civil, military, maritime or criminal: this being the place where that absolute despotic power, which must in all governments reside somewhere, is entrusted by the constitution of these kingdoms. All mischiefs and grievances, operations and remedies, that transcend the ordinary course of the laws, are within the reach of this extraordinary tribunal. It can regulate or new model the succession to the crown; as was done in the reign of Henry VIII and William III. It can alter the established religion of the land; as was done in a variety of instances, in the reigns of King Henry VIII and his three children. It can change and create afresh even

---

[3] See e.g. Dicey, n. 1 above, Chaps. I, II, III, and the introduction (by E. C. S. Wade), pp. xxiv–xcvi, cxciv–v; W. I. Jennings, *The Law and the Constitution* (5th edn., University of London Press, 1959) Ch. IV; Geoffrey Marshall, *Parliamentary Sovereignty and the Commonwealth* (Oxford University Press, 1957); Geoffrey Marshall, *Constitutional Theory* (Oxford University Press, 1971) Ch. III.

the constitution of the kingdom and of parliaments themselves; as was done by the act of union, and the several statutes of triennial and septennial elections. It can, in short do everything that is not naturally impossible; and therefore some have not scrupled to call its power, by a figure rather too bold, the omnipotence of parliament.[4]

13 When, however, the United Kingdom entered the European Community in 1973, it was committing itself to the 'new legal order' created by the Community Treaty,[5] a legal order which took precedence over rules of domestic law. There was, therefore, the possibility of a conflict between the doctrine of the supremacy of Community law and that of the sovereignty of Parliament. In order to see the effect of EC law on the UK constitution it is important to bear in mind that we have to deal with two distinct legal orders: that of the Community and that of the national constitution of any given Member State. This will be so whenever a particular matter falls within the scope of application of the EC and EU Treaties, and a convenient comparison is to recall that in the USA 'inter-state commerce' falls within the federal jurisdiction. So where we are concerned with, for instance, the free movement of goods, persons, services, or capital the subject-matter may be dealt with by two legal orders. The Community law is interpreted by the European Court of Justice and has to operate throughout the territories of the Member States. It must follow, therefore, that *as a matter of Community law*, Community law does not depend on a national constitution: for if it did there could be as many different versions of its application as there are Member States with their own constitutions. But it might be the case that, *according to the national constitution*, Community law is subject to that constitution; and where, as in the UK, the national constitution affirms the absolute legal supremacy of 'the Queen-in-Parliament' it might be thought that EC law could be overridden by parliamentary legislation: such an action might be a breach of Community (and public international) law, but not of UK law.

14 It seems, however, that the UK constitution now recognizes the supremacy of Community law (within the latter's jurisdiction)

---

[4] Sir William Blackstone, *Commentaries on the Laws of England*, 1765–9, I, Ch. 2, 156.

[5] Case 26/62, *Van Gend en Loos* v. *Nederlandse Administratie der Belastingen* [1963] ECR 1.

together with the power of Community law to determine what matters do fall within its own jurisdiction—what the Germans call *die Kompetenz-kompetenz*. There are three sources of this rule of recognition: the UK Parliament, government statements, and court decisions.

15 By section 2(4) of the European Communities Act 1972 (and in a complex piece of drafting) 'any enactment . . . to be passed . . . shall . . . have effect' subject to any relevant Community law: and it is a rule of UK law (embedded in section 2(1)) that the question of relevance is to be decided by Community, not by UK, law.

16 In one of the *Factortame* fisheries cases before the ECJ, the British Government acknowledged that where UK legislation was inconsistent with Community law the latter should prevail; it is reported as saying:

With regard to legislation, the courts did not have the right, under the British constitution, to nullify an Act of Parliament or to treat it as void or unconstitutional. It was otherwise in the case of legislation which was contrary to Community law since section 2(1) and (4) of the European Communities Act 1972 empowered the courts to uphold the primacy of rights arising from Community law.[6]

17 Furthermore, the courts have now accepted that, as a matter of national law, Parliament has no power to infringe Community law. If possible, of course, that legislation will be construed so as to be compatible with Community law; but an Act of Parliament that cannot be so interpreted will not be applied. In such a situation, the court does not of course repeal the statute. Nor need it hold the conflicting national law to be absolutely ineffective, for the provision may well operate perfectly validly in a case with no Community element. What the court does is to refuse to apply the provision to the extent to which it conflicts with Community law. In one of the Sunday trading cases, Hoffman J stated that:

The Treaty of Rome is the supreme law in this country, taking precedence over Acts of Parliament. Our entry into the Community meant that (subject to our undoubted but probably theoretical right to withdraw from the Community altogether) Parliament surrendered its sover-

---

[6] *R.* v. *Secretary of State for Transport, ex parte Factortame Ltd and Others (No. 2)* [1990] 3 WLR 818 at 826.

eign right to legislate contrary to the provisions of the Treaty on matters of social and economic policy which it regulated.[7]

18 A simple example of the judicial recognition of the supremacy of Community law is to be found in its treatment of the Sex Discrimination Act 1975 which provided—in perfectly lucid English—that a compensation order must not exceed a specified limit (£6,250 at the material time). The discrimination in question was also a breach of Community law, and Community law requires adequate financial recompense so British courts, where necessary, disregard the upper limit which Parliament imposed on their powers.[8]

19 The possibility of conflict remains in the perhaps unlikely circumstance of Parliament deliberately legislating in breach of the European Community or Union Treaty by passing a statute which cannot be made compatible with Community law. It is not clear whether, in such circumstances, the courts would uphold the doctrine of the sovereignty of Parliament; or alternatively, whether, by refusing to apply the statute in question, they would uphold the doctrine of the supremacy of Community law. Short of this extreme possibility, however, it seems difficult to deny that, by passing the European Communities Act 1972, a sovereign Parliament has voluntarily yielded its sovereignty.[9]

---

[7] *Stoke-on-Trent City Council* v. *B. & Q. plc* [1991] 4 All ER 221 at 223–4.

[8] Case C–271/91 *Marshall* v. *Southampton and South West Hampshire Area Health Authority (No. 2)* [1993] 4 All ER 586 (ECJ) and [1994] 1 All ER 736 (HL); and *R.* v. *Secretary of State for Employment, ex p. Equal Opportunities Commission* [1994] 1 All ER 910 (HL).

[9] See, on the difficult questions raised by the potential conflict of doctrines, *inter alia*, E. C. S. Wade and A. W. Bradley, *Constitutional and Administrative Law* (11th edn., Longman, 1993), Chap. 8B, L. Collins, *European Community Law in the United Kingdom* (4th edn., Butterworths, 1990), N. Gravells, 'Disapplying an Act of Parliament Pending a Preliminary Ruling: Constitutional Enormity or Community Law Right' [1989] *Public Law* 568; H. W. R. Wade, 'What Has Happened to the Sovereignty of Parliament' (1991) 107 *LQR* 1; Dawn Oliver, 'Fishing on the Incoming Tide' (1991) 54 *MLR* 442; P. P. Craig, 'Sovereignty of the UK Parliament after *Factortame*' [1991] *Yearbook of European Law* 221; A. W. Bradley, 'The Courts, Community Law and Equal Pay: a Constitutional Case?' [1988] *Public Law* 485; and Neil MacCormick, 'Beyond the Sovereign State' (1993) 56 *MLR* 1.

STATE AND RELIGION

20 In England and in Scotland there are established churches, the Church of Scotland being a Presbyterian church. An established church is one recognized by law as an official church by contrast with, for example, the United States where church and state are separated and Congress is prohibited from establishing a state religion (First Amendment).

21 The Sovereign is described in the Preface to the thirty-nine articles of the Church of England as 'Being by God's Ordinance, according to our just Title, Defender of the Faith and Supreme Governor of the Church'. The Sovereign must be in communion with the Church of England, and in her coronation oath she promises to preserve it. Officials of the Church of England are also officials of the state; thus archbishops and bishops of the Church of England are appointed by the Queen on the advice of the Prime Minister, taking an oath of allegiance to the Sovereign on their appointment and paying homage to the Queen after their consecration. The Lords Spiritual—twenty-six archbishops and bishops of the Church of England—sit in the House of Lords for as long as they retain episcopal office.

22 The supremacy of Parliament is reconciled with the freedom of the Church of England, like that of other churches, to regulate its own worship and doctrine, through a process of devolution of authority. Under the Church of England Assembly (Powers) Act 1919, the General Synod, the supreme authority of the Church of England, has the power provided for in the Synodical Government Measure, 1969—delegated to it by Parliament—to approve Measures (statute laws) on any matter concerning the Church of England. These Measures, once approved, are laid before both Houses of Parliament, which must approve, or reject, but cannot amend, them. The Synod can also make ecclesiastical regulations known as Canons, which must be submitted to the Crown before coming into effect, and which are binding on the clergy, though not on the laity without an Act of Parliament. Under the Worship and Doctrine Measure 1974, the Church of England was given devolved power to determine its own doctrine and forms of worship, except that use of the 1662 Book of Common Prayer cannot be discontinued without the agreement of Parliament.

23 In Scotland, by contrast with England, the Queen is a member of the established church but not its Supreme Governor. She is required by the 1707 Treaty of Union to preserve the Church of Scotland and to 'inviolably maintain and preserve the foresaid settlement of the true Protestant religion with the government, worship, discipline, rights and privileges of this Church as above established by the laws of this Kingdom'. She takes an oath to preserve the Church of Scotland not, as with the Church of England, at her coronation, but at the meeting of the Privy Council immediately following the accession. The supreme authority of the Church of Scotland is its General Assembly which has the power to pass resolutions having effect without Royal Assent, provided only that they are within the law of the land. Thus, while in England, the freedom of the church is secured through devolution, in Scotland it is secured through a division of powers between church and state. Thus the concept of an established church is reconciled with ecclesiastical self-government; and the existence of established churches has proved perfectly compatible with full toleration for those of other creeds and for those who hold no religious beliefs at all.

24 In Northern Ireland, there has been a separation of church and state since the Irish Church Act, 1869; and in Wales, a separation since the Welsh Church Act of 1914, which came into effect in 1920.[10]

TREATIES

25 Constitutions generally identify the source of the treaty-making power. In the United States, for example, this power is vested in the President 'by and with the Advice and Consent of the Senate', provided that two-thirds of Senators present concur (art. II, section 2). In Britain, by contrast, there is no parliamentary involvement in the ratifying of treaties, such ratification being an executive act. By the so-called Ponsonby rule of 1924,

[10] See Moore's *Introduction to English Canon Law* 2nd edn., E. Garth Moore and Timothy Briden (eds.) (Oxford, 1985), especially Chap. II; St. John A. Robilliard, *Religion and the Law: Religious Liberty in Modern English Law* (Manchester University Press, 1984), especially Chap. 5, and T. M. Taylor, *Juridical Review*, 1957.

however, the government is required to notify Parliament of a treaty and not to ratify it until twenty-one parliamentary days have elapsed.[11]

26 Where a treaty, in altering rights and obligations, requires national law to be altered, this must be done through implementing legislation so as to incorporate the treaty into national law. Where such implementing legislation has not been passed, as in the case of the UK with the European Convention of Human Rights, a treaty cannot be a source of domestic rights and obligations.[12]

27 The treaties creating and amending the European Community—the Treaty of Rome, the single European Act, and the Treaty of Maastricht—are ratified in a similar way to other treaties, save that by section 6(1) of the European Parliament Elections Act 1978, any treaty increasing the powers of the European Parliament must be approved by Parliament before it can be ratified by the government of the United Kingdom.

TERRITORIAL PROVISIONS

28 The United Kingdom is, like France, a unitary state, unlike the USA and Germany which are federal. In the United Kingdom there exist many territorial bodies with rule-making powers: none of these, whether they be the local councils or the former parliament of Northern Ireland at Stormont, are co-ordinate with the British Parliament at Westminster. All are subordinate.

29 But although the United Kingdom is a unitary state whose seat of government is at Westminster and whose unique sovereign organ is the Queen-in-Parliament, this does not signify that the form of administration and the provisions of law are identical throughout the United Kingdom. For special provisions apply in Northern Ireland, in Scotland, and, to a lesser extent, in Wales.

30 It is important from the very beginning to be clear about nomenclature. The United Kingdom signifies, in constitutional law, Great Britain and Northern Ireland, exclusive of the Channel Islands and the Isle of Man. Great Britain means

---

[11] HC Debs., 1 Apr. 1924, cols. 2001–4.
[12] See *R.* v. *Home Secretary, ex p. Brind* [1991] 1 AC 696.

England, Wales, and Scotland. Northern Ireland is part of the Crown's Dominions, and an integral part of the United Kingdom.

31 The Channel Islands and the Isle of Man are known as the British Islands. Their defence and international relations are undertaken by the government of the United Kingdom: but these islands all have their own legislatures, local government arrangements, and fiscal and legal systems as well as their own law courts. For the most part, their legislation becomes valid only on the passage of an Order in Council, made by the Privy Council (to wit, the Crown). In practice, the Order is made by the Home Secretary acting on behalf of the Crown. Appeal lies from the islands' courts to the Judicial Committee of the Privy Council.[13]

32 Northern Ireland, which comprises six counties (Antrim, Armagh, Down, Fermanagh, Londonderry, and Tyrone), possessed its own parliament from 1921 (the Government of Ireland Act 1920) to 1972. The authority of this parliament was, however, restricted; first, by the 'excepted matters', which included matters relating to the Crown, to defence and international relations, naturalization and control of aliens, foreign trade, currency, radio communication, patents, and copyrights; and also by 'reserved matters', which were to be dealt with by the United Kingdom Parliament and which include the postal services and such taxation as the United Kingdom Parliament continued to levy, for example income tax. In the United Kingdom Parliament, Northern Ireland was represented by twelve Members of Parliament (MPs). Northern Ireland thus represented a devolution of power by the United Kingdom Parliament, which remained sovereign. The subordinate nature of the Northern Ireland Parliament was clearly demonstrated by the Northern Ireland (Temporary Provisions) Act 1972, which transferred all legislative and executive powers concerning Northern Ireland to the United Kingdom Parliament and to the Secretary of State for Northern Ireland.

33 Since 1972, Northern Ireland has been governed directly from Westminster through the Secretary of State for Northern Ireland. Northern Ireland has, since 1983, returned seventeen

---

[13] See below. The status of these islands is considered as one category, and the detail concerning individual islands is immensely more complicated than this summary suggests.

MPs to Westminster, and in 1994 the government established a Select Committee on Northern Ireland. During the period of direct rule, British governments, whether Conservative or Labour, have sought to reintroduce devolution into Northern Ireland but, by contrast to the period between 1921 and 1972 when government was monopolized by the Unionists, they have also sought to ensure that any new arrangements for devolved government allow for the participation of both the Unionist and the Nationalist communities. So far, it has proved impossible to reach agreement on such new arrangements.

34 Northern Ireland is unique in the United Kingdom and indeed in Western Europe, in that the constitution of another country, the Irish Republic, lays claim to it (arts. 2 and 3 of the Irish Constitution, 1937: 'the national territory consists of the whole island of Ireland'). The position of Northern Ireland within the United Kingdom is therefore given special protection. Until 1972, this was achieved by means of section 1(2) of the Ireland Act 1949, which provided that Northern Ireland would not cease to remain part of the United Kingdom without the consent of the parliament of Northern Ireland. In 1973, section 1 of the Northern Ireland Constitution Act provided that Northern Ireland would not cease to remain part of the United Kingdom without the consent of the majority of the people of Northern Ireland voting in a poll. So far, only one poll has been held, in 1973, and it resulted in 57.5 per cent of the electorate of Northern Ireland voting to retain Northern Ireland's position in the United Kingdom. The parties representing the Nationalist minority advised their supporters to abstain, so that only 0.6 per cent of votes were cast by those seeking to join Northern Ireland with the Irish Republic.

35 In 1985, the Anglo-Irish Agreement[14] gave the government of the Irish Republic wide consultative powers over issues affecting Northern Ireland and provided a forum, based on a standing intergovernmental conference, within which such issues could be discussed, while in the Declaration of Principles signed by the British and Irish governments in 1993, the British government reaffirmed that it had no 'selfish strategic or economic interest in Northern Ireland'.[15]

[14] Cmnd. 9690.
[15] See P. Arthur, *The Government and Politics of Northern Ireland* (2nd edn.,

36 Following the Acts of Union, 1707, the formerly distinct parliaments of Scotland on the one hand and of England and Wales on the other, were extinguished and replaced by a new common parliament of Great Britain in which Scotland is currently represented by seventy-two MPs. In agreeing to the Treaty of Union, the Scots also accepted the English Act of Settlement (1701) and, in this way, it was ensured that the union of the two Crowns which had come about in 1603 would be preserved. Thus the independent Kingdom of Scotland came to form a part of the new political entity entitled Great Britain.

37 The Treaty of Union reserved to Scotland a number of existent rights and privileges. Consequently, to this day, it has its own legal system, its own established church, and its own local government and educational systems. Since 1885, there has been a Scottish Secretary, who became a Secretary of State in 1892. Since 1926 the Secretary of State has been a member of the Cabinet, except in wartime. The Secretary of State heads a Scottish Office, whose staff are almost entirely located in Edinburgh, the capital city of Scotland. To this office very substantial areas of administration have been transferred. In addition, the main central government departments have regional offices for Scotland, most of them with Scottish directors. There exist also a number of boards and commissions catering to various aspects of Scottish life such as, for instance, the Highlands and Islands Development Board and the Crofters Commission. Most Scottish legislation is dealt with by committees on which Scottish MPs predominate. The Scottish Grand Committee takes the Second Reading of almost all Scottish bills, and there are Scottish standing committees for the committee stage. There is also a Select Committee on Scottish Affairs to supervise the administration of the Scottish Office.

38 The Principality of Wales, by contrast, was fully incorporated into the English political and administrative system by statutes of 1536 and 1542, while the judicial systems of the two countries were fully amalgamated in 1830. Wales, like Scotland, has no parliamentary assembly of its own but many of the personnel of the Welsh Office are located in Cardiff, the capital

Longman, 1984); Padraig O'Malley, *The Uncivil Wars* (Blackstaff, Belfast, 1984); and David Watt (ed.), *The Constitution of Northern Ireland: Problems and Prospects* (Heinemann, 1981).

of Wales. Since 1964, the Welsh Office has been headed by the Secretary of State for Wales who is a member of the Cabinet. There is a considerable degree of administrative decentralization, but less than in Scotland. Wales returns thirty-eight MPs to the House of Commons. There is a Welsh Grand Committee and a Select Committee on Welsh Affairs.[16]

39 During the 1970s, following the rise of nationalism in Scotland, there was considerable debate on devolution to Scotland and Wales. The Scotland Act and the Wales Act, which provided for the establishment of assemblies in Scotland and Wales, were passed by Parliament in 1978, but failed to secure sufficient support in referendums held in 1979 and were, in consequence, repealed in that year. More recently, following the publication of *A Claim of Right for Scotland* (1988), the debate on devolution has been renewed.[17]

LOCAL GOVERNMENT

40 Whatever the structure of the state, whether unitary or federal, every democracy has, in addition to the institutions of central government, one or more layers of local government. For it is neither necessary nor desirable for all public services to be provided from the centre. In Britain, the modern system of elected local government began with the Municipal Corporations Act of 1835, and today local councillors constitute the only elected representatives of the people apart from Members of Parliament. Local authorities are either empowered or required to provide services for their areas under specific powers conferred by Parliament. They are subject to the *ultra vires* rule, their powers being derived strictly from statute.

41 The structure of local government differs significantly in the different parts of the United Kingdom. England, outside Greater London, and Wales were divided by the Local Government Act of 1972 into counties and each county was divided into districts.

---

[16] See J. G. Kellas, *The Scottish Political System* (4th edn., Cambridge University Press, 1989); M. J. Keating and A. Midwinter, *The Government of Scotland* (Humanities Press, 1983); and J. A. Andrews (ed.), *Studies in Welsh Public Law* (Cardiff, 1970).

[17] See the reports of the Scottish Constitutional Convention, 1989–92.

In six metropolitan counties, covering the main conurbations outside Greater London—Tyne and Wear, West Midlands, Merseyside, Greater Manchester, West Yorkshire, and South Yorkshire—there is now, following the 1985 Local Government Act, a single tier of local government, based upon thirty-six metropolitan districts. In the other thirty-nine counties of England, there is a two-tier system of local government, based upon the counties and 296 non-metropolitan districts. In Greater London, the London Government Act of 1963 was modified by the Local Government Act of 1985, which abolished the Greater London Council and provided for local government functions to be undertaken by thirty-six London boroughs and by the Corporation of the City of London as well as by various *ad hoc* bodies. In Wales, local government functions are until 1996 divided between eight counties and thirty-seven district councils but, from 1996, the Local Government (Wales) Act of 1994 provides for a new unitary structure of local government comprising twenty-two councils. In addition, there are parish councils in many rural areas of England, and in small towns, and in Wales community councils which cover the whole of the country.

42 In Scotland, the structure of local authorities is, until 1996, governed by the Local Government (Scotland) Act 1973, which established a two-tier system on the mainland, comprising nine regions and fifty-three districts, and three all-purpose island authorities—Orkney, Shetland, and the Western Isles. There is also statutory provision for the establishment of community councils. From 1996, the Local Government (Scotland) Act of 1994 provides for a new unitary structure of local government comprising thirty-two councils.

43 In Northern Ireland, local government was reorganized under the Local Government (Northern Ireland) Act of 1972 which provided for a single-tier structure of twenty-six local authorities. These authorities have comparatively minor functions—local public health, entertainment and recreation, cleansing and sanitation, and various regulatory services. Administration of other services formerly undertaken by local authorities is now carried out by the offices of central departments or by nominated area boards. These functions may be transferred back to the provincial level if and when a devolved assembly for Northern Ireland is established.

44 In England, Wales, and Scotland, local authorities remain responsible for a broad range of services including education, social services, housing, planning, highways and traffic, fire, and the police. Except in Northern Ireland, local authorities now raise between 15 per cent and 30 per cent of their revenue from local taxation, the council tax, as provided for in the Local Government Finance Act of 1992, but this is subject to capping if the Secretary of State for the Environment believes that a particular local authority has spent excessively. The rest of local revenue is derived primarily from non-domestic rates and from government grants. In Northern Ireland, rates remain the main form of local taxation as they were in England and Wales before 1990.

45 At the time of writing, much of local government is in a state of flux. The Local Government Act of 1992 provided for a Local Government Commission for England to review the structure of local authorities with a view to creating unitary authorities in the non-metropolitan counties, while in Scotland and Wales, current legislation provides for a new structure of government on a unitary basis.[18] Since 1979, a number of education and housing functions have been transferred from local authorities either to central government or to individual institutions, such as grant-maintained schools or housing associations. The Police and Magistrates Court Act 1994 reduces local authority representation on police authorities. Nevertheless, democratically elected local government, subordinate to Parliament, is likely to remain as a significant element of the British Constitution.[19]

THE SOVEREIGN AUTHORITY

46 The supreme legal authority in the United Kingdom, then, is the Queen-in-Parliament. In law, the Queen is the executive branch of government, so that the very expression, Queen-in-Parliament, suggests the fusion in one organ of the two tradi-

---

[18] See para. 41 above.
[19] See C. A. Cross and S. Bailey, *Cross on Local Government Law* (8th edn., Sweet & Maxwell, 1991); T. Byrne, *Local Government in Britain* (Penguin, 1990); and M. Loughlin, *Local Government in the Modern State* (Sweet & Maxwell, 1986).

tional branches of government, namely the executive and the legislature. But the Queen-in-Parliament is also regarded, in law, as
the High Court of Parliament; a court of record, whose record,
the Parliament Roll, must be accepted as valid by all other courts
in the kingdom which, *ex hypothesi*, are inferior to it. 'Parliament' therefore is the supreme executive, legislative, and judicial
authority all rolled into one, and this state of affairs, sometimes
called the fusion of powers, stands in contrast to the USA, where
there is a system of separated powers.

47 However, the concept of the 'separation of powers' has been
shown to be imprecise, confused, and confusing when closely
examined. For our present purpose, it is more useful to use the
related concept of 'checks and balances', since this can be defined
and evaluated by asking whether, how far, and in what respect
any one of the three branches of government can either impose its
will on the others or, alternatively, prevent them from taking
action. The American Constitution goes furthest in this respect. A
statute requires the concurrence of President and Congress and, if
challenged in proceedings involving its constitutionality, may be
declared invalid by the Supreme Court. The Congress and the
President are each independently elected, and for different terms,
the latter being unable to dissolve the former, while the former is
able to remove the President only by the difficult and highly circumscribed process of impeachment. The Supreme Court is admittedly appointed by the President and the Senate, but once the
judges are appointed they can be removed only by impeachment.
In practice it is very hard or even impossible for the incumbents of
one branch to remove the incumbents of the others or to pressure
them by threat of removal; yet each branch can seriously obstruct,
even where it is not permitted to veto, the plans of the others. To
speak very broadly, these three branches have co-ordinate status
and in certain circumstances each can veto the others. In Britain,
however, these three branches do not have co-ordinate status,
since the Crown, whose origin is certainly independent of
Parliament, must by law exercise most of its functions via ministers whose authority depends on Parliament. As to the judges, the
effects of their judgments can be (and have been) altered retrospec-
tively by Act of Parliament. The authority to veto a parliamentary
Bill is still vested in the Queen, it is true, but it has not been used
since 1707.

48 Thus authority ultimately rests in the legislature, on whose confidence the Ministers of the Crown depend, and although a prime minister may ask the Queen to dissolve Parliament and call a general election in the hope of securing such confidence, his Cabinet could not continue to govern if the election returned a hostile majority. A new prime minister and Cabinet would have to be installed, such as can command the confidence of the new parliamentary majority.

49 These remarks are intended to do no more than point to the contrast between, on the one hand, a system of effective checks and balances among the three branches of government, as in the USA, and, on the other, one where this hardly exists, as in Britain. However, all the constitutions printed in this volume do acknowledge the existence of the 'branches' of government—executive, legislative, and judicial—and much (in some constitutions the greater part) of their text is devoted to detailed explanation of the precise relationships between them. This detail is the 'fine print' and it is precisely because it qualifies in so many ways the simplistic generalizations of the kind that have just been made that this collection of the constitutions is desirable and an elaborate cross-index to them necessary, for the student of government. As Figgis once observed: 'Liberty will be found secreted in the interstices of constitutional procedure.' Hence the foregoing remarks should be read as a general orientation in whose light we can proceed to examine the details of the respective powers and duties of the executive, legislative, and judicial branches.

THE LEGISLATIVE BRANCH

50 In each of the constitutional texts the legislature is described as consisting of two assemblies: an Upper and Lower House or Chamber. Nowhere does a text give a rationale for this arrangement and, indeed, this varies from one country to another. In federal states—the USA, Germany, Russia—the obvious rationale is that the component units of the federation shall be represented as such, in contradistinction to the population at large.

51 No such justification can be urged for the Upper Chambers

of France or of the UK. It is arguable that the widespread adoption of an Upper House throughout most of Europe and, then, through the wider world springs from the historical accident that Britain had a bicameral legislature in 1815, when her institutions were regarded as a model for western Europe. However, the arrangement was subsequently justified on supposedly rational grounds: a century and a half ago, one of the supposed advantages of having an Upper House was to check the pretensions of the democracy that was expressing itself in the popularly elected Lower House. It is unfashionable nowadays to see this as anything but a drawback, so that quite other advantages of a second Chamber are the ones that are stressed today: notably its value as a body for revising the texts produced in the Lower House, together with the assumed advantages of more, and slower, deliberations.

52 Apart from this similarity, the British Parliament may be contrasted notably with the legislatures of the USA and of France in two different ways. It is unlike the former in that the executive authority resides in and is dependent upon the confidence of this legislature, instead of being independently elected, all but irremovable, and constitutionally endowed with a great number of powers in its own right. It is unlike the French Parliament in a different way: the British Parliament is omnicompetent, whereas the powers of its French equivalent are restricted to what the constitution stipulates, with the unspecified remainder of governmental authority inhering as of right in an autonomous executive power, that is to say, in the presidency, the prime ministership, and the ministers themselves. Thus, the domain of legislation is exceptional, while that of regulations constitutes, juridically, the common rule.

THE HOUSE OF LORDS: COMPOSITION AND PROCEDURE

53 The House of Lords is perpetual and it is non-elective. Its members, who are styled 'Lords of Parliament', sit there by virtue of one of three possible characteristics. First, they may be hereditary peers. Such peers are created by the Crown under its prerogative powers (though, effectively, via the nomination of the prime minister). A hereditary peer is by law entitled to receive a

writ of summons to sit and vote in the House of Lords: but he must be 21 years of age and is disqualified if he is an alien (the Act of Settlement 1701) or a bankrupt, or has been convicted of treason or felony, or sentenced to a term of imprisonment, such disqualification lasting until he has discharged his term of punishment or has been pardoned, or (where relevant) has discharged his bankruptcy.

54 Since 1963, peeresses in their own right may take their seats, but the great majority of hereditary peerages are restricted to male heirs. In December 1992, there were only seventeen peeresses out of 758 peers by succession. Any person who can prove his or her right to a peerage to the Lord Chancellor is entitled to a writ of summons. Since 1963, a peer who has inherited a title may disclaim it for life; but by December 1992, only eleven had done so. The vast bulk of the membership of the House still sits by virtue of hereditary descent, although no new hereditary peerages were created between 1965 and 1983. In December 1992, there were 776 hereditary peers of whom eighty-six were, for various reasons, without a writ of summons and, accordingly, not members of the House while another ninety-three were on leave of absence.

55 The second category of membership consists of life peers, created under the Life Peerages Act 1958 by the Crown on the recommendation of the prime minister and in December 1992 numbered 391, of whom fifty-four were peeresses. Third, and finally, a number of persons are peers *ex officio*: the two archbishops and the twenty-four diocesan bishops of the Church of England, and the Lords of Appeal (active and retired), who are known as the Law Lords. Altogether, in 1992 the total membership of the House was 1,213.

The presiding officer is the Lord Chancellor. The House is the sole judge of its own procedure, as laid down in its standing orders or as sanctioned by custom. Unless it otherwise resolves, its meetings are public. Its sessions tend to coincide with those of the Commons but the Lords can adjourn at discretion and resume its sittings at a different time from the Commons. Proceedings on pending legislation lapse immediately the Queen prorogues Parliament. The Lords then ceases to sit and reconvenes on receipt of a writ of summons to the next Parliament at the date therein stated.

56 Like the Commons, the Lords is the guardian of its own privileges and the sole judge of anything that appears to it to infringe them. Again, like the Commons, it has the right to punish breaches of such privileges. Some are similar to those of the Commons, notably freedom from arrest except on a criminal charge or bankruptcy; exemption from jury service; and the famous freedoms of 'speech, debate and proceedings in Parliament'.

THE HOUSE OF COMMONS

57 The House of Commons is elected for a period not exceeding five calendar years (Parliament Act 1911). The Bill of Rights (1689) stipulates that parliaments ought to be held 'frequently'. By convention Parliament must meet at least once a year because certain legislation, like the Finance Acts, requires the assent of the House and is introduced on an annual basis.

58 For electoral purposes the country is divided into a number of single-member constituencies (currently 651). In each of these the candidate who secures the highest number of votes is elected. The electorate (see below) comprises all citizens of the United Kingdom and (anomalously) of the Irish Republic above the age of 18 who have satisfied the residence requirements in a constituency—with the exception of peers, convicts, and the mentally ill. The distribution of seats by constituencies is kept under review by four boundary commissions for England, Wales, Scotland, and Northern Ireland respectively. These commissions are politically neutral. They have the right, and in certain circumstances the duty, to report to the relevant ministers. Their reports are laid before Parliament. If the commissions have recommended a boundary change the relevant ministers lay a draft Order before Parliament to give effect—with or without modifications—to the recommendations.

59 To be validly elected, candidates must be at least 21 years old. Certain categories of citizens are precluded from sitting in the House. They are: clergymen of the Church of England, the Church of Scotland, and the Roman Catholic Church; those undergoing prison sentences of over a year; mental patients; bankrupts; those found guilty of corrupt electoral practice; civil

servants; the police; members of the regular armed forces; and most judicial officers. Although Irish peers may sit, English and Scottish peers are debarred unless they have disclaimed their titles under the Peerage Act 1963.

60 MPs receive an annual stipend plus a tax-free secretarial allowance. Although the maximum legal term of a parliament is, under the Parliament Act 1911, five years, Parliament may—and in this case uniquely the assent of both Houses is necessary—prolong its life by passing an appropriate Act. Correspondingly, the prime minister may, and normally does, ask the Queen to dissolve the Parliament before its five-year term is complete.

61 The chief officer of the House is its Speaker, elected by the MPs at the beginning of each session and, by custom, re-elected annually until retirement or death. The first of the Speaker's two principal functions is to regulate debate and enforce the rules of the House. The second is to guard the privileges of the House *vis-à-vis* all external bodies—Crown, courts, or the public. In presiding over debates and interpreting the standing orders the Speaker is bound to the strictest impartiality. He or she votes only when members' votes are tied, and in such cases must by convention support the *status quo*, not the innovation that has been proposed.

62 The House is complete master of its own procedure. The chief of its privileges are freedom from arrest save for certain criminal and bankruptcy charges, exemption from jury service, and above all the freedom of speech, debate, and proceedings in the House. This body of privileges is subsumed in the Law and Custom of Parliament, which is a body of true law independent of the common law, so that on certain occasions collisions have occurred between the House and the courts of law. For contempt of the House or a breach of its privileges, the House can punish and imprison. Its own members as well as the public are subject to these enforcement powers. The House can also expel one or more of its own members, as it is the sole judge of its own composition.

63 Immunities for the elected members of legislatures, somewhat similar to the ones just related, are to be found in all of the constitutions printed here. Such immunities are essential to the authority of an elected assembly. But two are sufficiently idiosyncratic to Britain to warrant special attention. If ever the British

constitution were to be codified in a single document, then certainly these two immunities would have to be specified.

64 They are on the one hand the protection of the dignity and freedom of the Commons as a corporate body, and on the other the freedom and dignity of the individual MP. Disrespects to the House as such are styled 'contempts'; for instance, libels on the House, the Speaker, or the Select Committees. Statements that MPs are, generally speaking, drunkards or parasites, would come under this heading of 'contempts'. At the same time, threats and intimidation of individual MPs are 'breaches of privilege', and come under the general heading of 'molestation'. A former Clerk to the House (Lord Campion) advising the Select Committee on Privileges in 1947 stated the matter thus: 'Any punitive or discriminatory action by an outside body or persons against a Member for speeches or votes in Parliament, or the threat of such action, is a breach of the privilege of freedom of speech'.[20] This threat has become very salient in the last half-century, since large numbers of MPs have begun to receive financial assistance, and/or have entered into certain contractual arrangements with outside bodies, notably with trade unions.

65 When these or other outside bodies are disappointed at the way such MPs speak or vote in the House the possibility arises that they may withdraw or threaten to withdraw the assistance they are affording. There have been a number of such threats: in each case the warning that the House might consider this a breach of its privileges has been enough to cause the threat to be withdrawn. Now, in France and Germany this kind of threat is not countered by the law and custom of the legislatures, as it is in England, but by specific clauses in the Constitution. The French text says (art. 27(1)): 'Tout mandat impératif est nul'. The German Constitution states (art. 38(1)) that the Deputies to the Bundestag 'shall be representatives of the whole people, not bound by orders and instructions, and shall be subject only to their conscience'.

66 *The Powers of the Upper House.* In the USA, neither of the two Houses of the legislature can overrule the other, which means that the Upper House has a full veto over the bills passed in the Lower House. In Germany the same is true for a range of

---

[20] *Select Committee on Privileges: Case of A. J. Brown*, 1947, 83 ff.

items duly specified in the text as requiring the consent of the Upper House, which in that country is the Bundesrat, the Council of States, that is the House specifically charged with the protection of the interests of the Länder into which this federal republic is divided. On all other matters, however, the Lower House can override the Upper House provided it does so by a majority vote which is not less than that by which the Upper House made its decision.

67 The French Constitution, however, contains a rare if not unique provision relating to this matter (art. 45). When the Senate (the Upper House) rejects the text of the National Assembly (the Lower House), the outcome depends on the government of the day, that is on the executive. It may decide to do nothing, which is tantamount to upholding the veto of the Upper House, since the Constitution requires that both Houses pass an identical text. Alternatively, however, it can override the veto of the Senate by asking 'the National Assembly to make a final decision'.

68 It should be noted in conclusion that in every one of these constitutions a Bill may originate in either of the two Houses, with the exception of money Bills which must originate in the Lower House.

69 The relationship between the two Houses in Britain is regulated by the Parliament Acts 1911 and 1949. Money Bills, duly certified as such by the Speaker of the House of Commons, can become law without the assent of the Lords provided they are sent to this House for consideration at least one month before the end of the parliamentary session. With one important exception—a Bill to prolong the life of a parliament beyond the statutory five years—all other public Bills (see below) do not require the assent of the Lords provided that: (1) the Bill has been passed by the Commons in two successive sessions, whether of the same Parliament or not; and (2) one year has elapsed between the date of second reading of the Bill in the first of these two sessions and the final passing of the Bill in the second of these two sessions. This procedure has been used to pass only one bill, the War Crimes Bill 1991.[21]

70 *Legislation.*   The sole constitution among the texts here

---

[21] See Gabrielle Ganz, 'The War Crimes Act 1991—Why No Constitutional Crisis?' (1992) 55 *MLR* 87.

that devotes considerable attention to parliamentary procedure is the French. The main object of the constitution of the Fifth Republic was, indeed, to exalt the executive and to constrain the legislature. So it includes much material prescribing procedure, and makes any alteration of this subject to the decision of the Constitutional Council. Because this is exceptional—other constitutions devote little attention to the matter—what follows will be the most summary outline of the British Parliament's legislative procedure.

71 *Private Bills.* Private Bills confer special powers or advantages on any persons or body of persons (e.g. corporations, local authorities), as distinguished from public Bills, which apply to the community or categories of the community generally. The procedure for deliberating on private Bills is, apart from the requirements that such Bills must be read three times in each House, substantially different from that for public Bills; it resembles a judicial hearing more than an act of legislation.

72 *Public Bills.* When these are introduced (in either House) by individual members, as they may be, they are known as Private Members' Bills as distinct from government Bills, although the procedure is identical for both categories. Since the Cabinet controls the parliamentary timetable the passage of Private Members' Bills is highly dependent on its benevolence.

73 The first reading is a formality. Debate on the text begins with the second reading. In the Commons, after receiving its second reading, the Bill goes to a committee: either a standing committee, which is a microcosm of the entire House, or to the entire House itself, operating under more relaxed rules and known as a Committee of the Whole House. The text as amended is then brought back to the House for a report stage, and then proceeds to the third-reading debate. After this it goes to the Lords, where the procedure is similar, though not identical. In particular, the Lords have no standing committees, and the committee stage of all legislation is taken on the floor of the House.

74 *Voting procedure.* The quorum for the House of Commons is forty members but, as the Standing Orders now provide that the House shall never be counted, absence of a quorum does not end a sitting. It does, however, mean that if fewer than forty members (including Chair and Tellers) take part in a vote, the matter under consideration is postponed to the next

sitting (in the House of Lords the figure is thirty). Apart from this, a simple majority of votes cast carries the day. Indeed the first vote is always by voice, it being for the Speaker in the Commons (or the Lord Speaker in the Upper House) to decide from the loudness of the response which side has the majority. Only if the Speaker's decision on the vocal outcome is challenged will a division be ordered so that the numbers on each side can be counted.

75 *Subordinate Legislation.* Ministers may make subordinate legislation by virtue of statutory authority. This is an untidy field, but most of it is regulated by the Statutory Instruments Act 1946. This Act stipulates that a Statutory Instrument is an instrument made under this Act or under a subsequent Act which is exercisable either by Order in Council or by another Statutory Instrument. The Act does not require that all Statutory Instruments shall be laid before Parliament. Whether this is required or not is decided by the parent Act in question. Where a Statutory Instrument is to be laid it is usually provided that it is laid before both Houses. In financial matters, however, it is laid only before the Commons. Nor is there uniformity in the other requirements. Some Statutory Instruments take immediate effect when laid, subject to subsequent annulment by a resolution of both Houses. This is the commonest form. A rarer form is for the instrument or its draft to take no effect unless it is expressly approved by resolutions of both Houses.

76 *Financial Legislation.* The basic principles of financial legislation, as opposed to the details of the procedure itself, are these. First, only the Crown, that is ministers, may propose additional expenditure or a new charge on the public revenue. Characteristically, this is not stipulated in a statute but by a standing order, to wit SO 46, which is the very oldest, dating back to 1713. Next, proposals to raise or spend money must originate in the Commons, not the Lords. Third, by the Bill of Rights 1689, taxation requires the consent of Parliament. Similarly, money can be expended only under the authority of an Act of Parliament. Most expenditure is authorized by annual Acts, or grants incorporated annually into an Act, and this device ensures that Parliament must meet at least once every year. Some expenditure, however, is authorized under permanent Acts; the purpose here is to insulate the recipients from parliamentary control. Not surprisingly, the Queen's Civil List (annual

allowance) and the salaries of judges of the higher courts, of the Speaker, and of the Comptroller and Auditor-General are all paid out in this way. Fourth, the House not only votes the totals of expenditure requested by Ministers in the 'Estimates', but specifies how the money is to be spent. The 'Estimate' is broken down into 'Votes' and these into heads and subheads, and it is in this form that the money is granted in an Appropriation Act, passed annually. The Comptroller and Auditor-General, by means of his post-audit, together with the subsequent help of the Public Accounts Committee of the Commons, ensures that the various departments spend the money exactly as appropriated and in no other wise, unless following the express permission of either the Treasury or the House itself. Fifth, the arrangements for taxation are introduced by way of another annual Act, the Finance Act. Lastly, taxation may be imposed by simple resolution of the House until 5 May of any year where the resolution was passed in the previous November or December. If the resolution should be passed at some other time, it has taxable effect for four further months, provided that the Bill which will incorporate this resolution has received its second reading within thirty days of the passing of the resolution.

77 The administration of each government department is scrutinized by a Select Committee comprising back-bench MPs and broadly reflecting the party composition of the whole House. Most of these departmentally related Select Committees were established in 1979. In addition, there are nine other Select Committees of the Commons, the oldest of which, the Public Accounts Committee, was established in 1861. The other Select Committees include a Statutory Instruments Committee, a Committee on the Parliamentary Commissioner for Administration (the Ombudsman), and a Select Committee on European Legislation. The Lords has also established Select Committees including a highly influential Select Committee on the European Communities and a Select Committee on Science and Technology. Select Committees generally work, by contrast with standing committees, in a non-partisan fashion, and indeed some chairmen are opposition members.[22]

[22] See G. Drewry (ed.), *The New Select Committees* (2nd edn., Oxford, 1989); and the House of Commons Procedure Committee's review of the departmentally related Select Committees, HC 19, 1989–90.

78 The day-to-day conduct of administration is challengeable on the floor of the House in Question Time, when ministers appear according to a roster to answer oral questions on their departments. Question Time occurs every day of the parliamentary week except Friday. Further opportunities for challenge are provided by debates on the adjournment of the House; by the set debates, whose topics are nominated by the Opposition; and, finally, by the rare motions of censure put down by the Opposition and, traditionally, always accepted by the government for debate.

79 *The Cabinet's Responsibility to the Commons.* The meaning of the convention of collective responsibility will be considered below. Here we have to ask whether there exists in the constitution a definition of the circumstances in which a government, having suffered a defeat on the floor of the House, must resign. It seems fairly clear that if a government says in advance that it is treating a particular vote as a 'matter of confidence', this is tantamount to its stating that, if defeated, it intends to resign. Accordingly, if defeated in these circumstances, we might confidently expect it to do so. If the Opposition puts down a motion of censure and carries it, then, too, we might expect the government to resign: but one cannot be absolutely sure that it will do so since it might argue that the vote was a 'snap' vote, or freakish and unrepresentative of the government's majority in one or other of a number of ways. However, the probability that a government would resign after defeat on a censure motion is certainly very high indeed.

80 However, apart from these two highly formal occasions, certain traditions concerning when a government ought and ought not constitutionally to resign used to exist in the past. A defeat in committee is not a confidence matter, since in principle this could always be reversed by the House as a whole. But defeats on the second reading of a Bill used to be regarded as a matter of confidence entailing the government's resignation. It is traditional also that snap votes and defeats by 'ambush' might be disregarded by a government since, *ex hypothesi*, such defeats do not express the normal balance of votes in the House. These traditions worked well enough in the heyday of majority one-party governments but became more and more elastic under the minority governments of Wilson and Callaghan, between 1974 and

1979. Mr Callaghan's government lost a Bill (the Redundancy Rebate Bill, on 7 February 1977) at its second reading, but ignored the defeat and simply carried on. It is increasingly clear that the usages governing the occasions on which it is requisite for a government to resign are much more flexible in the case of a minority government than where the government has an absolute majority in the House; and that such a minority government is allowed a good deal of latitude to disregard occasional defeats on the way. In such circumstances only a motion relating to 'confidence', whether formulated by the Opposition or by the government itself, seems to be the appropriate mechanism for bringing such a minority government down.

THE EXECUTIVE BRANCH

81 Nowadays the executive branch of a government is organized into various strata of authority, from high to low. The relationship between these strata may be as important as the relationship of the branch as a whole to the legislature and the judiciary.

82 A comparison of the constitutions printed in this book shows that the branch is headed by a single individual who in some sense personifies the state, and who may be styled generically, therefore, the head of state. In every case this individual is styled the President. In Britain, however, the head of state is the Queen.

83 Further comparison reveals also that we may have to distinguish between constitutions where the head of state is the effective chief executive officer—and this is the case in the USA—and those constitutions where the role of the head of state is part of what Bagehot called the 'dignified' rather than the 'efficient' element of the constitution, the effective headship of the executive branch being vested in an officer who is nominally inferior. Such is the situation in Germany, where this officer is the Chancellor, and so also in Britain where he is styled the prime minister.

84 The French constitution, with its seemingly bicephalous executive, at first appears to stand midway between these two types of constitution. But, in general, it is the President who normally

enjoys effective power, except in periods of *cohabitation*, such as the years 1986 to 1988 and 1993 to 1995, when the majority in the National Assembly is opposed to that of the President. Under such circumstances, it is the prime minister rather than the President who becomes the effective executive. Thus, the Fifth Republic constitution can sustain two quite different systems of government depending upon political and electoral vicissitudes.

85 In those constitutions which vest effective headship of the executive in a prime minister or Chancellor, however, it is necessary to inquire further and ask in what sense is such an officer a chief executive? For in all these constitutions, and this applies equally to Britain, the executive branch is divided laterally as well as vertically between a number of individuals who head government departments, that is between ministers. And questions about three distinctions immediately suggest themselves here. First, does the constitution prescribe that these ministers shall act collegiately, that is as a body? Second, what is the relationship between this body and the chief executive where such an office exists? And third, in what relationships do these ministers stand towards the chief executive in their individual—as opposed to their collective—capacities? With the exception of the American Constitution, all of them envisage colleges of ministers styled the Council of Ministers (France), and the government (*Regierung*) in Germany. In Britain this body is the Cabinet. Certain duties have to be performed by such bodies collectively. Next: the relationship between these bodies and the chief executive may vary from being the keystone of the arch in Britain to primacy, as in Germany where the Chancellor is responsible for general policy. Finally, as in the French Constitution, it may be laid down that individual ministers have certain rights and duties in respect of the departments they lead, and that likewise they may stand in a relationship of equality with the chief executive in certain matters and subordination in respect of others. In this connection, it may be noted, whether the chief executive has the authority to dismiss a minister is of major importance.

86 But even this catalogue does not exhaust the constitutional concept of the executive branch. Heads of state, chief executives, and ministers who are usually both temporary and politically partisan are the directing heads of the very numerous body of subordinate officials known as the 'civil service' or 'the bureau-

cracy' or 'Whitehall' who are, on the whole, permanent, paid, full-time professional career officers. A constitution like the German one may devote a fair amount of space to the nature, rights, and responsibilities of such officers, or say relatively little except in connection with the highest posts, as in the French and American constitutions. Or, indeed, it may say nothing at all, as was the case with the old Soviet Constitution of 1977. Using these distinctions as signposts it is possible to outline the main features of the British constitution dealing with this area.

87 *The Head of State: the Queen.* Unlike the American Constitution (and to a lesser extent the French) the convention of the British constitution (totally contrary to its strict law) distinguishes sharply between the head of state and the chief executive. Again, unlike other constitutions, the head of state in Britain is neither appointed nor elected for a fixed term but is the holder for life of a hereditary office, namely the Crown. A third distinction is this: whereas all these other constitutions have created an office (the presidency) and invested it with certain powers, in Britain the converse obtains. The office is primeval, and the historical role of the constitution has been to whittle away its powers and transfer them to other offices. The head of state, then, is a hereditary queen (or king) and the form of government is not a republic but a monarchy. However, it is a constitutional monarchy, in the following sense: virtually all the executive powers which legally inhere in the monarch must—by virtue either of statute or of convention—be exercised by her officers. Yet, for all that, the monarch is still invested with a range of powers some of which have been and others of which conceivably might be exercised in circumstances in which the existing laws or conventions or precedents give no clear guidance. These personal prerogatives, as they are generally called, include the powers to appoint a prime minister and to dissolve Parliament. Normally their use is uncontroversial but they could be of importance in the not inconceivable case of a hung parliament, that is a parliament in which no single party enjoyed an overall majority. They could also be of importance in grave crises, but even in these circumstances they would be exercised only with the utmost circumspection—such is the political tradition. In so far as this tradition persists, its rationale has best been expressed by Benjamin Constant, who wrote, in 1815:·

The royal authority (by which I mean that of a head of state irrespective of the precise title he may bear) is a neutral authority. The authority of Ministers is an active one ... Constitutional monarchy established the neutral authority in the person of the head of state. The true interest of this head is no way that one or other of the (three) branches of government should impede the other, but that all of them should sustain and understand one another and act in concert.[23]

88 A trace of this view of the function of the head of state is to be found in art. 5 of the French Constitution, which states that the President of the Republic is the 'guardian of the constitution. By the exercise of his judgement (*arbitrament*) he shall ensure the regular functioning of the public authorities, and the continuity of the state'. (However, this notion of an arbiter or umpire was soon interpreted by the first president of the Fifth Republic, Charles de Gaulle, to be that of the *Guide de la Nation*, and far from being used neutrally, was utilized to permit the presidency to dominate the other organs of the government.)

89 *Succession to the Throne.* The descent of the Crown is principally regulated by the Bill of Rights (1689) and the Act of Settlement (1701). The Crown is vested in the heirs of the Princess Sophia of Hanover subject to these conditions: (a) an heir who is a Catholic or is married to a Catholic is excluded from the succession, and the Crown then descends to such an heir, being Protestant, as would have inherited in the case of the excluded heir's being dead; (b) any person coming into possession of the Crown must join in communion with the Church of England; and (c) such a person must, under the Acts of Union 1707, take oaths to preserve the Church of England and the Presbyterian Church of Scotland.

90 The King never dies. There is no interregnum. On the death of the reigning monarch the Crown vests immediately in the person entitled to succeed and such a person, being King or Queen, is entitled to exercise his or her full regalia without further ado. If the sovereign is a minor, however, provision is made for a Regency under the Regency Acts 1937–53. Provision is also made for a Regency if the sovereign becomes permanently incapable.

91 *The powers of the Crown.* The Queen (or King) is the supreme executive officer in the state. She is Supreme Governor

[23] Henri Benjamin Constant de Rebecque, 'Principes du Politique' in *Œuvres* (Pléiade (ed.), Paris, 1937), 1079.

of the Established Church in England, the head of the army, navy, and air force; she is the source of justice and all courts in the country are her courts. It is in her name that foreign affairs are conducted, treaties made or dissolved, and laws administered. She appoints and dismisses ministers, dissolves, prorogues, or convenes Parliament, creates peers, and distributes titles and dignities. She assents to legislation. But by convention she must—subject to certain exceptions explained below—act only on the advice of her ministers and through the recognized departments and officers. In particular she, by convention, appoints as her prime minister a person who can acquire or has the confidence of the House of Commons; she must also appoint as minister and to the Cabinet (see below) those persons her prime minister recommends to her; she normally accedes to her prime minister's request to dissolve Parliament; and she must normally assent to every Bill that has been passed by the two Houses or, if the Parliament Acts of 1911 and 1949 are being applied, that has been passed by the House of Commons in due form.

In certain exceptional circumstances, however, the Queen may or must act without the advice of ministers. The most obvious case is the appointment of a prime minister. In circumstances where no single party with a duly recognized leader commands a majority in the House of Commons, a so-called 'hung parliament', the Queen may have a genuine discretion. She retains the right to refuse her prime minister's request for a dissolution of Parliament. This power has not been used in modern times in Britain, but there are Commonwealth examples where the Governor-General, acting as the Queen's representative, has refused a dissolution. The Queen has the theoretical right to dismiss a prime minister. It was last exercised in 1834, to be sure, but it is possible to imagine circumstances in which she might legitimately still use it. The very passion with which the contrary has been argued in the two cases above suggests that the view that these prerogative powers of the Crown are in desuetude (a concept which is unknown in English law, in any case) is, to put it at its lowest, contestable. The Queen retains the right to refuse to create new peers in order to secure a majority in the House of Lords favourable to the government of the day. Circumstances might arise to make such an action on her part useful or desirable. At present, the Parliament Act of 1949 permits the House of

Lords to delay non-money bills of the Commons for a period of just over one year. A prime minister might desire that a particular measure pass immediately, only to find a majority of peers refusing to pass his Bill. It is in a circumstance of this kind that he might request the Queen to create new peers in sufficient numbers to create a majority for the measure. Perhaps the best judgement one can make in a case like this is that the Crown's power to refuse is extant, but, depending on the precise circumstances which generated the prime minister's request for its exercise, it might be very impolitic for the Crown to refuse.

The Crown possesses the right to refuse assent to bills passed by the two Houses of its Parliament. But this power, last exercised in 1707, by convention is never used, although George V contemplated using it in 1914 with regard to the Government of Ireland Bill, providing for Home Rule for Ireland. Some powers of the Crown must be exercised by the sovereign in person or, in her absence or indisposition, by Counsellors of State under the Regency Acts 1937–53. Among such actions are assent to such subordinate legal instruments, known as Orders, as have to be made in her Privy Council (hence their full title, Orders in Council). Other such actions include the appointments or actions that are required by law to be made under the sign manual, for instance, a Royal Pardon. This distinction between actions that must be performed personally and those that need not is clearly not of major constitutional importance. What matters is that, except for the instances noted above, the Queen is only the head of the executive. In modern terminology she is the head of state but not the chief executive. In Britain this position is occupied by the prime minister and his Cabinet. For purposes of comparative analysis it is desirable to discuss these separately.

92 *The Chief Executive: the Prime Minister.* In the United States the head of state is also the chief executive; only France and Germany have an office even comparable to that in Britain. Yet in Germany the Chancellor (who is the chief executive) and in France the prime minister, are both clearly recognized and their roles defined in the respective constitutional texts. In contrast, even the existence of a British prime minister is but marginally recognized by statute, while his powers and duties are not laid down by law at all. A future historian who had nothing but the statute book to consult could certainly infer that there had

once been an office of prime minister: he would do so by consulting the Chequers Estate Act 1917, which accepted the gift of a country house called Chequers as an official residence for somebody called the prime minister, and a similar gift under the Chevening Estate Act 1959. He would learn of the existence of the office, too, by way of the Ministers of the Crown Act 1937, for example, and the Ministerial and Other Pensions and Salaries Act 1991, which lay down how much the prime minister is to be paid, and a few other statutes. But the office, its powers and duties, are determined wholly by convention and usage.

93 *Appointment.* A Prime Minister is appointed by the Queen who must choose someone capable of commanding the support of the House of Commons. Where, as is normally the case, one political party has an absolute majority and where it has a recognized leader or has procedures for acquiring one (and this is true of all three major national parties in Britain today), the Queen is obliged to appoint the leader of the majority party in the Commons. She enjoys discretion only when no single party commands an absolute majority in the Commons, or when normal party ties break down, as occurred in both world wars. In such circumstances, the Sovereign may still appoint the leader of the largest party in the Commons, but this is by no means necessary. In 1924, King George V sent for the leader of the second largest party, the Labour Party, to form a government. In 1931, George V used his discretion to reappoint Ramsay MacDonald as prime minister, even though MacDonald was becoming the leader of a small rump of the Labour Party. This was because MacDonald was best placed to lead a coalition government able to resolve the financial crisis. In some circumstances, the Sovereign may appoint someone who is not a party leader. In 1916, George V appointed Lloyd George prime minister although he was not then the leader of any party; and George VI similarly appointed Winston Churchill in 1940.

94 *Dismissal.* The German President has no personal discretion to dismiss a Chancellor whatsoever; he or she can do so only at the request of the Bundestag (art. 67). The French Constitution states that the President shall dismiss the prime minister on the latter tendering the resignation of his government, but is silent as to the motives for such a resignation. Clearly this motive might well be the prime minister's defeat in the legislature

on a confidence vote, but the practice of the French Constitution shows that it is more likely to have been the request, or even the demand, of the President that the prime minister resign, since each one of the Fifth Republic's four Presidents has in fact dismissed his prime minister(s) at will. Such a discretionary power continues to reside in the British Crown but, as already explained, would be exercisable—if at all—only in bizarre, one might almost say revolutionary, circumstances. For everyday purposes the dismissal comes about either because the prime minister has already tendered his resignation for personal reasons, like Sir Harold Wilson in 1976, or because her position as party leader has become untenable as with Margaret Thatcher in 1990, or because he or she has been defeated in the House of Commons or at a general election.

95 The German Chancellor, however, is better protected than a British prime minister against a 'no confidence' defeat in the legislature. It is not enough for the Bundestag to outvote him or her: the majority must also agree on the name of the alternative Chancellor. Thus 'unnatural' combinations of right and left can defeat a Chancellor but not force a resignation. In Britain, the conventions of the constitution make no such requirement.

96 *Eligibility.* The French Constitution makes only one condition respecting the eligibility or otherwise of a candidate for the prime ministership, namely, that he or she must not be a Deputy. The German constitution merely debars a candidate from following a number of secondary occupations. In Britain there is apparently no restriction at all on the class of person the Crown may invite to become prime minister. In law, a prime minister could be of half-Persian half-Mongolian descent, of indeterminate nationality, perhaps born in an aircraft as it passed over the International Date Line: but provided that he (or she) could command the support of the Commons, it would appear that such an exotic individual would be eligible.

97 In practice, however, questions of eligibility reduce themselves to two. Must the person selected by the Queen be a member of one of the Houses of Parliament, and if the answer is 'yes', must he or she be a Member of the House of Commons? The practical imperatives of commanding the confidence of a majority of the Commons suggest that the answer to both questions is 'yes'; in 1963, Lord Home was appointed by the Queen, but he

immediately renounced his peerage and entered the Commons in a by-election.

98 *Powers.* The British prime minister is always, by convention, the First Lord of the Treasury (the Second Lord is always the Chancellor of the Exchequer), draws the salary and pension by virtue of holding that post, and, as First Lord, is also generally responsible for civil service matters, his approval being required in the appointment of Permanent Heads of the departments.

99 For the rest, the powers depend wholly on convention and usage and derive from his position as leader of the government and, normally, party leader, not from any statutory powers. The prime minister recommends to the Queen, who must give her assent, the persons he or she wishes her to appoint as principal ministers, and from those he or she selects his Cabinet (see below, paras. 101 ff.). He or she can require a minister to resign at any time and for any reason, and if the minister chooses not to do so, he or she can advise the Queen to dismiss him, as occurred with a junior minister, Eric Heffer, in 1975, the only example of a dismissal in modern times. It is he or she who presides over the Cabinet, draws up its agenda, establishes its committees, and appoints their membership, presiding personally over the most important of them. Finally, if the prime minister resigns then the entire government must also resign.

100 So influential is the prime minister today that the late Richard Crossman in 1963, before himself becoming a Cabinet minister, described the British polity as being 'Prime Ministerial Government'. This it certainly is not, but neither is the prime minister only a 'first among equals'. He or she is unquestionably the keystone of the Cabinet arch and the leader of the entire governmental team. The conventional powers of the British prime minister are far greater than those of his or her French counterpart who, under the usage of the Fifth Republic, enjoys no more than that residue of powers which the President chooses to leave to the office and is, at the lowest, no more than the President's parliamentary manager, dispensable as soon as he or she loses either the confidence of the legislature or that of the President: indeed his situation is not dissimilar to that of Lord North under George III. At the same time the powers of the British prime minister are more circumscribed than those of the German Chancellor. For the

German Constitution specifically lays down not only that the Chancellor shall appoint and dismiss governmental colleagues (the *Regierung*) but that only the Chancellor 'shall determine, and be responsible for, the general policy guidelines' (art. 65).

101 *The Cabinet and the Government.* Ministers collectively are sometimes known as 'the government', sometimes as 'the ministry' and sometimes as 'the administration'. However, from all those ministers, the prime minister makes a personal choice of a small number, ranging in recent years from seventeen to twenty-three, to comprise the Cabinet. As with the office of prime minister the composition, power, and status of this body is almost unrecognized in statute law. Only occasional statutes such as the Ministerial Salaries Act 1965, which distinguishes between the salaries of Cabinet and non-Cabinet ministers, and the Parliamentary Commissioner Act 1967, which states that Cabinet records must not be divulged to the Parliamentary Commissioner, even mention the Cabinet.

102 *Ministers.* The law does not say that ministers must be members of one of the Houses of Parliament but does specify that no more than ninety-five ministers may sit and vote in the Commons at any one time (House of Commons Disqualification Act 1975). Furthermore under the Ministerial and Other Salaries Act 1975 a limit is set to the number of ministers who may receive a salary. These salaries can be altered by executive action—not requiring parliamentary approval—by an Order in Council.

103 In practice, however, and in complete contrast to the French constitutional provisions, which make ministerial office incompatible with membership of either House of the French legislature, and similarly to the American Constitution's provisions which go further and do not permit any executive officers, except in limited cases the Vice-President, to conduct any government business in the legislature, the British Cabinet in the normal way is composed exclusively of peers and MPs. It is certainly possible for a minister to head a department even though not an MP, but this situation is remedied either by making a peer of him or her or by trying to arrange election as MP for some conveniently vacated constituency.

104 *The Cabinet.* The Cabinet, as a collective body, is responsible for formulating the policy to be placed before

Parliament and is also the supreme controlling and directing body of the entire executive branch. Its decisions bind all ministers and their officers in the conduct of their departmental business.

105 The Cabinet meets in plenary session once or twice a week, at the prime minister's summons. Most of its work is prepared in advance in its committees and subcommittees. In 1992, the government published details of 26 such committees and subcommittees, but there were, in addition, around 140 *ad hoc* committees between 1987 and 1992, dealing with various policy matters. These committees are serviced, like the Cabinet itself, by the Cabinet secretariat whose head, the Cabinet Secretary, also serves the prime minister as an adviser. Voting in Cabinet is unusual: in contentious matters it is more common for the prime minister to 'collect the voices'.

106 The executive powers of the Cabinet derive from the legal status of its members: these are ministers of the Crown and as such have defined responsibilities to discharge, and what these are can be ascertained from the law relating to the Royal Prerogative and to statute. Its supreme policy-making power, however, is a political matter and it can exercise it only to the extent that the House of Commons permits. For it is in Parliament that, by law, the power to legislate and to tax resides. The Cabinet is generally able to exercise its power freely because in the usual way it consists of the leaders of the majority party in the House of Commons and the support it is likely to receive is the more predictable and stable because of the convention that the Cabinet shall be collectively responsible to the Commons for matters of policy. In consequence it presents a united view, so that its supporters are confronted with the brutal alternatives of either supporting it or turning it out. This convention, or rather this usage, can be dated back to the years 1827 to 1834. The usage was assisted by the increasing ideological solidarity of political parties after 1874 and this, in its turn, was reinforced by the usage. One consequence is that, to quote Lord Salisbury speaking in 1878, 'for all that passes in a Cabinet, each Member of it who does not resign is absolutely and irretrievably responsible';[24] and its corollary is that if such a minister is not willing to accept this responsibility, then he or she must resign.

[24] *Hansard*, 8 Apr. 1878, cols. 1833–4.

107 The consequences of a situation in which there was no usage of collective Cabinet responsibility for policy would be that the Cabinet could be supported for one measure and defeated on another, so that legislative initiative and not executive leadership would prevail. For well over a century the latter has prevailed and the style of British government is therefore not parliamentary government but Cabinet government.

108 There has grown up a belief that 'the collective responsibility of the Cabinet' is a 'convention of the Constitution', meaning that it is a normative rule which it is improper ever to break. This is not true. 'Collective responsibility' has been simply the working practice of Cabinet since at least 1832 and, until 1975, had been breached only once, in the famous—or notorious— 'agreement to differ' of 1932. Even that breach was condoned on the ground that the then government was a coalition. But the principle was waived by Mr Harold Wilson in 1975, again in a 'unique' situation (the European Community Referendum issue), although he headed a single-party government. It was breached again over the European Elections Bill in June 1977. It was on this occasion that it was argued that 'collective responsibility' was a binding rule and that the then prime minister, Mr Callaghan, ought to have followed it although this might have meant his defeat in the Commons and a general election. But this is not our view of this matter. It may be argued that 'the collective responsibility of the Cabinet for a programme decided at the polls depends on its solid party support'. But in 1977 as in 1975, the majority party was split in two, and so was the Cabinet. If a prime minister is prepared to allow Cabinet and party to accept the shame of indecisiveness and the ignominy of disarray in order to cling to office, we know of no historically binding precedent that would compel him or her to insist on solidarity at the certain risk of resignation and a devastating defeat at the polls; while there are a fair number of (admittedly somewhat weak) precedents to support the line that Mr Callaghan took. In short the collective responsibility of the Cabinet for policy has been central to the working of the constitution, but it is a central usage, not a convention.

109 In this connection it is interesting to see if the constitutions of Germany or France offer more specific guidelines. In both, it is clear that the legislature can dismiss the chief executive

and his team of ministers. The French Constitution (art. 20(3)) states that the government is 'responsible to Parliament'. This implies that the government is a collective unity that stands or falls together. The German Constitution merely makes reference to the Chancellor being responsible to the Bundestag (art. 67) but as under art. 65 he or she is the sole author of general policy we have to infer that if he or she resigns his entire team or Regierung must do so also.

110 It remains only to distinguish the British and German models from the American and French models. Generically Britain and Germany may be styled 'parliamentary' or, in the British case, specifically the 'Cabinet' type of government. Their essential feature is that a corporate executive team is responsible to and dismissable by the elected legislature. This type contrasts with the American 'presidential' type: the Congress can frustrate the President's policies but cannot remove him short of treason, bribery, 'or other high Crimes and Misdemeanours' (art. II, section 4) and even then only by the clumsy and arduous process of judicial impeachment. In France, the President can be impeached only on grounds of high treason (art. 68). Impeachment requires an absolute majority of both houses in an open ballot and a trial by the High Court of Justice.

111 The discussion now points to a further and formidable aspect of the responsibility of the collective Cabinet to the legislature: whether or not it has the power to dissolve this and to invoke a new general election. No such power exists in the executive branch in the American Constitution. But both the French and the German constitutions do make provision for the prime minister or the Chancellor respectively to require the President, the head of state, to dissolve the legislature and call new elections. Indeed, there is a unique circumstance in which the German President can dissolve the Bundestag and call new elections (art. 63(4)). In Britain it is the prime minister individually —not the Cabinet collectively—who has the right (by convention) to require the Queen to dissolve Parliament and issue the writs for a new general election.

112 The dissolution power serves the same purpose in all these constitutions: it provides the means whereby a deadlock deriving from a legislative majority hostile to the executive, the Cabinet, can be broken. It is broken by a fresh appeal to the electorate.

Such an appeal brings about the only circumstances in which the parliamentary or Cabinet style of government can work: namely, where the legislative majority and the executive branches are of the same mind.

113 The dissolution power of the chief executives in these parliamentary-style governments has a latent function, as well as the manifest one stated above. It offers the formally dependent executive a weapon to warn or to threaten a hostile legislature.

114 *Ministers Individually.* In their private capacities ministers are responsible to the ordinary courts of law for their personal acts, but the constitutional texts do not always state this specifically. Here we are concerned with the political responsibility of ministers. Whereas the French Constitution does not clearly distinguish the collective responsibilities of the ministers from their individual political responsibilities, the German text does when it states (art. 65) that, within the guidelines laid down by the Chancellor, 'each . . . Minister shall conduct the affairs of his department independently and on his own responsibility'. In practice the French tradition approximates to this, and both cases resemble British practice supposedly governed by a convention, namely, the convention of 'the individual responsibility of Ministers for their departments'. Supposedly, each minister is vicariously accountable to Parliament for all acts of omission or commission by the officials in his department, and a distinction is drawn between a minister's faithful (even if politically objectionable) execution of the policy of the Cabinet, and his or her defective management of the administrative detail under his or her control. This is the purported distinction between 'policy' and 'administration'. For the first, the entire Cabinet must assume responsibility, as we have seen above. For the supposedly purely departmental aspect, the minister alone is held to be accountable and must speak to and answer challenges in the Commons. The supposed convention stipulates that he or she must assume responsibility for all the departmental officials' acts and omissions and, if censured by the Commons on this account, is bound to resign. In fact the convention, such as it is, falls far short of this. For one thing it has been regarded as a sufficient defence for the minister to demonstrate that the acts complained of either took place in such a manner that he or she was physically or materially incapable of knowing them or alternatively were car-

ried out against his or her explicit instructions. For another, the line between what is collective 'policy' and departmental 'administration' has proved to be a fluid one. Again, even on occasions when the action is clearly of the latter departmental type, prime minister and Cabinet have often extended the span of 'collective responsibility' to shelter the delinquent colleague form individual censure. In the end the 'convention' turns out to be the truism that if a minister is not supported by his Cabinet colleagues and/or members of his parliamentary party in the course of debate censuring his conduct, it is highly possible that he or she will face a majority of MPs demanding resignation, and in those circumstances would have little option but to comply.[25]

115 *Government Departments.* In all modern states the executive powers are parcelled out into bundles of duties which are thereupon assigned severally to individual ministers. The office which attends to these duties and of which he or she is the head is, generically, a 'department'. Of the constitutions none specifies the names or even the number of such departments. Clearly then, none of the states concerned nowadays regards the number and names of the government departments as matters of 'constitutional importance', and therefore we may similarly disregard them here.

116 *The Civil Service.* In each of the countries concerned, as in Britain, the day-to-day work of governing is carried out by a corps of permanent, professional officials, in Britain the civil service. In each country, again, these officials are immediately responsible to their respective ministers, who are officially the policy-makers and as such are responsible for the officials' conduct, either to the elected chief executive (as in the USA) or to the legislature (as elsewhere, including Britain). In short, in none of these countries is the civil service directly responsible to the electorate. This point is not stated explicitly in any of the constitutional texts however and, indeed, their references to the civil service are scattered and perfunctory. For the purpose of the present exercise, that is for an explication of the British Constitution against the background of our constitutional texts, all that seems necessary is to outline the bare essentials.

[25] See, for an introduction to the concepts of collective and individual responsibility, Geoffrey Marshall (ed.), *Ministerial Responsibility* (Oxford University Press, 1989).

117 In Britain the Minister for Public Service and Science, an office established in 1992, is responsible for the conduct, the remuneration, and working of the Home Civil Service; while the Secretary of State for Foreign and Commonwealth Affairs plays the same role in respect of the Foreign Service. Both act under the authority of the prime minister. With a few exceptions, nobody may be appointed to a permanent post until his qualifications have been approved by the Civil Service Commission which, in respect to the selection of personnel, is independent of ministers. It is the commission that formulates the regulations concerning recruitment, which provide for open competition. There are, however, an increasing number of exceptions, especially in quasi-autonomous governmental and non-governmental organizations which are outside the civil service proper. The civil servant holds office 'at the pleasure of the Crown'; this means that he or she can be dismissed with no common law remedy for wrongful dismissal. But the courts have recognized that civil servants have some contractual rights, and statutes have given them others. In practice tenure has been permanent, except for personal misconduct, ill health, and—but this is in very exceptional cases—gross inefficiency. However, an increasing number of civil service appointments, generally in the executive agencies established following the Ibbs Report of 1988,[26] are now on the basis of fixed-term contracts.

118 The civil servant is politically neutral. No civil servant may sit as such in the House of Commons. Apart from the grades that are excepted by law, none may even stand as a parliamentary candidate without first resigning from the civil service. Certainly, this is true of all members of the highest grade. For the intermediate grades, special arrangements apply, and it is only members of the industrial and minor grades of the service who are free to stand as candidates. Finally, all except the latter grades are required to act discreetly in discussing any matters relating to public policy.

119 The civil servant answers to the House of Commons only via his minister. Civil servants can be and often are summoned to witness before the major scrutiny committees of the Commons, notably the Public Accounts Committee and the departmentally-

---

[26] *Improving Management in Government: The Next Steps* (HMSO, 1988).

related Select Committees. However, what they are to witness to is held to be 'administration': when matters of 'policy' come up, they explain that these are for Ministers to speak to. The Permanent Secretaries of Whitehall departments are accounting officers for their departments, and as such are directly accountable to Parliament via the Public Accounts Committee. In addition, the written answers of agency chief executives to MPs' questions are printed in Hansard. With the exception of these particular kinds of communications, it remains true that the sole constitutional channel between the Commons and the civil service is the minister of the appropriate department.

THE JUDICIAL BRANCH

120 There are five major points of similarity/dissimilarity between the scope and jurisdiction of the judicial branch of government in Britain and in the other constitutions under discussion here.

121 First, the British courts resemble those of the other countries in that they interpret the laws in force and their interpretation is the law until or unless it is altered by a higher court or by Parliament.

122 Second, British courts resemble those of the USA in that they interpret such law as may be deemed 'constitutional', that is relating to the distribution and allocation of public authority, as well as all other aspects of law. Another way of putting this is to say that in these two countries the interpretation of constitutional law vests in the 'ordinary' courts of the land. In Germany, by contrast, the court that handles these matters is a specially constituted one, the Federal Constitutional Court or *Verfassungsgericht* (art. 93). In France only a limited number of 'constitutional' issues are reviewable, principally, for our present purposes the compatibility of a Bill, already duly enacted by Parliament but not yet promulgated, with the constitution. Furthermore the body that reviews such a matter is not a court at all but a special tribunal called the Constitutional Council.

123 Third, unlike the appropriate court or tribunal for constitutional laws in the USA, Germany, France, and Russia, and subject to what has been said about European Community law,

the British law courts cannot set aside a duly enacted parliamentary statute.

124 Fourth, the British arrangement resembles the American in that both these countries have but one set of courts to deal with all cases, whether these pertain to the executive branch or otherwise. Both France and Germany have a further set of special administrative courts in parallel to the 'ordinary' courts of the country. However, in Britain there are administrative tribunals, separate from the courts, to deal with a wide range of miscellaneous activities.

125 Fifth, Britain differs from France but not from the other countries concerned in that not one legal and judicial system obtains, as in France, but one for England and Wales, another for Scotland, and a third for Northern Ireland.

126 *The Organization of the Judiciary: England and Wales.* For civil cases (except for a small number of such cases handled by the magistrates' courts, as described below), the lowest tier is that of the county courts. Above them stands the High Court, functionally divided into Chancery, Queen's Bench, and Family Divisions. Appeal lies to the Court of Appeal (Civil Division) and thence, with leave, to the House of Lords. For criminal cases the inferior courts are the magistrates' courts, which also handle a limited number of civil cases. Above them stands the Crown Court, established under the Courts Act 1971, with both appellate and original jurisdiction. Appeal lies from this to the Queen's Bench Divisional Court of the High Court or the Court of Appeal (Criminal Division). On a very restricted range of issues, there is further appeal to the House of Lords. After that there would remain, in criminal matters, only the appeal to the Royal Prerogative of Mercy as exercised by the Home Secretary. The death penalty for murder was abolished in 1965, but remains in force for treason and for one or two other miscellaneous offences.

127 *Scotland.* In Scotland, civil jurisdiction is exercised by the Court of Session, divided into an Inner House of two divisions, and an Outer House comprising single judges and the Sheriff Court from which appeals lie to the Inner House and, ultimately, to the House of Lords. Criminal jurisdiction resides in district courts and the Sheriff Court, and appeal lies to the High Court of Justiciary. There is no appeal from this to the House of Lords.

128 *Northern Ireland.* In Northern Ireland civil jurisdiction is exercised by magistrates courts, county courts, the High Court (with Queen's Bench, Chancery, and Family Divisions), and the Court of Appeal. Criminal jurisdiction is exercised by magistrates courts, the Crown Court, the Queen's Bench Division of the High Court, and the Court of Appeal. Civil and criminal appeals from the Court of Appeal and, in specified cases, from the High Court lie to the House of Lords.

129 *The House of Lords as the Highest Court.* This body illustrates a characteristic feature of the UK constitution, namely the gap between form and function. Although bearing the same name as the Upper House of the legislature of which it is theoretically an advisory committee for lawsuits, in fact the House of Lords in its judicial capacity is quite a different entity. It hears civil and criminal appeals from England, Wales, and Northern Ireland, and also in civil (but not criminal) cases originating in Scotland. In theory any peer may sit, uninvited, to hear an appeal. This last happened in 1883, when the intrusive lay peer's opinion was superciliously ignored by the lawyers. In practice its members consist of eleven judges appointed from the Bench of the superior courts or (occasionally) from among the ranks of senior barristers; normally at least two are Scots lawyers. The formal name for these judges is Lords of Appeal in Ordinary, and they are usually called 'the Law Lords'; they are appointed to life peerages on elevation to the highest court. To them may be added the Lord Chancellor, ex-Lord Chancellors and other peers who have held high judicial office. Normally a hearing is held before five Law Lords.

130 *The Judicial Committee of the Privy Council.* There is also a court which in law is a committee of the historic Privy Council (membership of which exceeds 300), which is styled the Judicial Committee of the Privy Council. Its domestic jurisdiction is slight. It hears appeals from tribunals which maintain the professional discipline of various organizations such as those, for instance, of the medical profession. Also, it can be asked to give an advisory opinion on any question in law which the Crown remits to it: for instance in 1958 the Commons sought its opinions on the nature of disqualification from sitting in that House. Its chief function, however, is to act as the Court of Appeal from the courts in the Channel Islands and the Isle of Man, the

remaining colonies, protectorates, and associated states, and from such Commonwealth countries as have so decided. Its quorum is three. Its composition includes the Lord Chancellor and the Lords of Appeal in Ordinary (the Law Lords of the House of Lords). In addition, the Lord President of the Council and former Lords President are also members, but they never sit. Lords Justice of Appeal are also members of the committee. They have sometimes been known to sit, but seldom do so. It also includes some Privy Councillors who are senior judges from other Commonwealth countries. As a matter of formal technicality it does not decide the case before it but tenders advice to the Crown as to whether the appeal should be allowed or dismissed. By convention the Government always follows this advice and issues the appropriate Order in Council.

131 *Judicial Independence.*   The independence of the judiciary from the pressures of both the legislative and the executive branches of government is a cardinal entailment of the doctrine of the separation of powers. In many democracies, including Britain, judges of the high courts and sometimes of all courts (for example, in Britain, France, and Germany) are appointed. In the last three countries mentioned, it is the executive branch that appoints. In the USA it is the President, but by and with the consent of the Senate. Thus, in all these instances the appointment is in the hands of a politically charged body. How then is the 'independence' of the judiciary secured?

132 The answer lies in the respective provisions for payment and for removal. The principle seems to be that though a judge may be appointed by the executive, he or she shall not—or not easily—be removed by it. Thus the German Constitution provides (art. 97) that the judge cannot be dismissed 'except by virtue of a judicial decision', and under this is subsumed removal by the process of impeachment (art. 98). The French Constitution declares that 'Judges shall be irremovable' (art. 64) and that disciplinary proceedings must take place in the Conseil Supérieur de la Magistrature. It must be remembered, however, that in these two countries, as in all 'civil law' countries, judges are civil servants. In the USA, a common law country like Britain, the judges are appointed during 'good behaviour', their salaries may not be tampered with, but they may be impeached before the Senate for misconduct.

133 In Britain judges are not, or rather do not seem to be, Crown agents. Their independence is secured by the conventional and statutory provisions for their appointment, payment, and removal and for their judicial immunities. They are appointed by the Crown, which in practice means by the prime minister or the Lord Chancellor, depending on the status of the court in question. The possibility of appointing for primarily political reasons is mitigated by the statutory provision that only practising lawyers of many years' standing shall be appointed to the Bench. Once appointed, the judges' salaries are charged on the Consolidated Fund (which is not subject to annual review by the Commons) and, furthermore, if changed (which is done by Order in Council) can only be raised, and never lowered. While in office, judges enjoy judicial immunity for all acts said or done within their jurisdiction. They are disqualified from sitting in the House of Commons as MPs.

134 A High Court judge is indeed removable by the Crown but, by convention, only under the procedures laid down in the Act of Settlement (1701) as restated by the Appellate Jurisdiction Act 1875 and the Supreme Court Act 1981. These Acts require removal to take place only on an address to the Crown presented by both Houses of Parliament. The last occasion on which a judge was removed was in 1830. He was an Irish judge, and the reason for his removal was emphatically not political.

ESCAPE CLAUSES AND DISCRETIONARY POWERS

135 Written constitutions have great difficulty in providing for emergency situations. By their nature they impose legal constraints—they prescribe complicated and dilatory procedures. Consequently, they have to provide certain escape clauses to allow the government discretionary powers to cope with emergencies. Examination of these constitutions suggests a double distinction. On the one hand they lay down what may be called the 'circumstances of emergency', that is specifications of the conditions which must prevail for the situation to be regarded as an 'emergency'. On the other, they regulate 'states of emergency', by which is meant the new legal conditions that prevail in these 'circumstances of emergency'.

136 One circumstance that is always provided for is a state of war, although in the German Constitution this is referred to as a 'state of defence'. Another is what the American Constitution refers to as 'domestic violence' and 'insurrection'. The German Constitution refers mysteriously to a 'state of tension' (*Spannungsfall*) without defining this (art. 80a). The French Constitution, at art. 16, stipulates, by way of contrast, a set of highly specific circumstances which constitute the circumstances of emergency.

137 States of emergency may consist of the suspension of the writ of habeas corpus in the American constitution; the declaration of martial law; the declaration of a state of siege; and/or other unspecified powers to take what action the circumstances demand. In every case, the constitution-former's problem is how to permit the executive to take emergency action and yet prevent it from using this permission to subvert the rest of the constitution, as happened to the Weimar Constitution through the use of art. 48, and more recently in India in 1976, where Mrs Gandhi used the emergency powers of the constitution to establish a personal dictatorship and to subvert the guarantees of civil rights contained in the rest of the document. It is in order to escape this dilemma that a constitution such as the French provides that where its emergency art. 16 is invoked, Parliament sits as of right and cannot be dissolved; while the German constitution goes to more elaborate lengths to ensure that the legislature shall meet and above all that the Constitutional Court shall continue to sit and carry out its functions.

138 This dilemma does not exist under the British Constitution. The Queen-in-Parliament is supreme and omnicompetent and in principle can do anything she likes under any circumstances she thinks fit. The problem is reduced to the technical one of providing the executive with the power to act quickly and widely without having to get separate parliamentary approval for each one of its measures: in short to confer decree-making powers on the executive.

139 In Britain the Crown, that is the government, can always call on the police and if necessary the armed forces to repress 'domestic violence' or 'insurrection'. How far it can go without express parliamentary sanction—that is by virtue of the prerogative power alone—is abstruse and not at all clear in law. As far as

martial law is concerned, the last time it was proclaimed in time of war was as far back as the days of Charles I. The proclamation of martial law in times of peace cannot be made simply under prerogative powers. On the contrary, were a state of martial law proclaimed the English courts would recognize it 'in appropriate circumstances'—but this implies that it is a matter for the courts to judge. In practice, martial law was quite extensively used in Ireland before that country became independent in 1921.

140 However, the usual exercise of emergency power nowadays is through the Emergency Powers Act 1920, as amended in 1964. This is a permanent statute. It envisages circumstances where the community or part of it is likely to be deprived of the essentials of life, by reason of interference with the supply of food, water, fuel, light, and transport. If the government considers that this has occurred or is likely to it may, under the authority of this statute, proclaim a state of emergency. This proclamation expires within one month, but can be superseded by a new proclamation—and so on. However, Parliament must be informed immediately and if the Houses are in recess or prorogued they must meet within five days. Once the state of emergency has been proclaimed the government has the authority to make Orders for securing the essentials of life to the community; they must be laid before Parliament and, unless approved by both Houses, expire after seven days. Moreover, the substance of the emergency regulations is circumscribed; they may not impose military or industrial conscription, nor alter the rules of criminal procedure, nor make it an offence to strike or peacefully persuade others to strike.

141 Such states of emergency have been proclaimed quite often in peacetime to deal with situations created or threatened by strikes. In time of war, however, governments have gone to Parliament to secure the grant of much more sweeping powers to make regulations for securing public safety and prosecuting the war. The First World War witnessed the Defence of the Realm Acts 1914 and 1915. In the Second World War the Emergency Powers (Defence) Act 1939 empowered the government to make regulations requiring 'persons . . . to place themselves, their services and their property at the disposal of His Majesty'. This Act, conferring this vast power on the executive branch, was rushed through both Houses of Parliament and received the royal

assent within a few hours. Such safeguard as there was lay in the provision that every Order in Council containing defence regulations had to be laid before Parliament, subject to amendment by either House, within a period of twenty-eight days.

142 Special powers to deal with threats to security in Northern Ireland have been on the statute book in one form or another for most of this century. Currently, the 1991 Northern Ireland (Emergency Provisions) Act confers wide powers on the police and security forces to stop and question people, limits the use of release on bail and of trial by jury, defines a number of offences connected with proscribed organizations, and confers the power (not currently exercised) to detain without trial. A separate statute deals with the effect in Great Britain of the conflict in Northern Ireland. The Prevention of Terrorism (Temporary Provisions) Act 1989 restricts freedom of association on the mainland by allowing certain organizations to be proscribed, and limits freedom of movement by permitting exclusion orders to be issued where they appear expedient to prevent acts of terrorism. In addition the Act confers wide powers of arrest without warrant of persons suspected of being guilty of offences under the Act. Both these statutes are subject to annual renewal by Parliament.

DEFENCE AND EXTERNAL AFFAIRS

143 Who conducts foreign affairs? The Crown, as head of state, acts in this area as the representative of the nation, but the conduct of foreign affairs is in the hands of Ministers, as are almost all other matters. However, the regal power to conduct external affairs is a 'prerogative' matter so that, with certain exceptions to be noted below, what ministers do in this field is legally binding on the nation and does not require parliamentary consent. For instance, the appointment of ambassadors does not require parliamentary approval. For all this the convention of the responsibility of ministers to Parliament for their actions always permits the Commons to question any action by them. Similarly, although declarations of war or peace and the conduct of foreign relations generally are, in law, the province of the executive, they must by convention conform to the wishes of Parliament.

144 Within this general framework it is the Crown, acting through its ministers, that appoints ambassadors and all other diplomatic agents, and receives the credentials of those from other states. The treaty-making power likewise is vested in the Crown, but it is wise for ministers, if not perhaps necessary, to ensure parliamentary approval. Where a treaty imposes taxation or makes a money grant or affects existing law or interferes with the private rights of an individual, the consent of Parliament is positively required if the treaty is to be binding on the subject and enforceable at law.

145 The supreme command of all air, sea, and land forces is vested in the Crown but, again, in all such matters the Crown has to act on the advice of ministers. It is the Secretary of State for Defence (always a member of the Cabinet) who is specifically responsible to Parliament for giving such 'advice'.

146 The abuse or potential abuse of a standing army in peacetime was one of the prime issues in the struggles between Crown and Parliament in the seventeenth and early eighteenth centuries. The navy, in contrast, was never regarded as a threat to liberty. Consequently, the Bill of Rights 1689 expressly forbids the government (the Crown) from maintaining a standing army in time of peace except by the consent of Parliament. The raising and maintenance of the air force, however, is authorized by a permanent Statute (the Air Force (Constitution) Act 1917). The maintenance of a navy requires no statutory authority at all: it is raised and kept up solely by virtue of the common law prerogative of the Crown.

147 In practice parliamentary control of all three services is effectively guaranteed by two devices. The first is financial. The money required to maintain the services is requested by ministers, debated, and granted by Parliament on an annual basis. The second device concerns the discipline of each force. The disciplinary codes of the services, without which neither mutiny nor desertion would be illegal, are made lawful only through statute. The Army and Air Force Acts, and the Naval Discipline Act 1957, run for five years at a stretch before requiring a new statute from Parliament; but they would automatically expire within the five-year period unless Parliament expressly approved an annual Order in Council to permit the renewal of the Act. The requirement for regular approval of the armed forces has enabled the

Commons to scrutinize army discipline regularly by a series of Armed Forces Acts, the last of which was enacted in 1991. In 1971 the Naval Discipline Act 1957 was brought within the same system.

148 *The Commonwealth and the Dependencies.* The Commonwealth 'is the ghost of the British Empire sitting crowned on the grave thereof': and one might say as much about the French community as laid down in the French Constitution. But, like France, Britain still possesses dependencies as well as maintaining links with former dependencies. The topic is one of great complexity and the details are subject to constant change; what follows is a general outline only.

149 The Commonwealth embraces territories that were once dependent in some fashion upon the authority of the British Parliament and/or Crown. Independence from the UK and membership of the Commonwealth are not the same, for admission to the latter depends on both the wishes of the country concerned and the agreement of existing members, although it in practice has never been refused to a colony gaining independence. There is no written constitution of the Commonwealth, nor are there written rules for membership. It comprises independent members and a number of categories of other territories. The landmark statute is the Statute of Westminster 1931 section 4 of which provides that 'No Act of Parliament passed after the commencement of this Act shall extend or be deemed to extend to a Dominion as part of the law of that Dominion unless it is expressly declared in that Act that the Dominion has requested and consented to the enactment thereof'. (The term 'Dominion' has now been dropped in favour of 'full member' or 'independent member' of the Commonwealth.) The effect of this statute has been written into the Acts of the British Parliament which granted independence to former colonies during the period following the Second World War.

150 In 1931 certain tangible links remained between the (now) independent Dominions and the British polity. They all recognized allegiance to the British Crown, and the Judicial Committee of the Privy Council as the highest court of appeal in respect to their own constitutions. This is no longer so. Of the fifty-one members of the Commonwealth, twenty-nine are republics and there are also six indigenous monarchies. Most

members of the Commonwealth have now abolished or greatly restricted the right of appeal from their courts to the Judicial Committee of the Privy Council.

151 There remain, outside the fifty-one independent and fully self-governing members of the Commonwealth, a variety of territories which are not fully independent. These territories may have Governors, representing the Crown, and most have legislative assemblies, some of which may possess the power to make the territory self-governing in internal matters. The constitutions of such territories are embodied either in a British statute or in letters patent or an Order in Council of the British Crown.

152 *International Law.* The question of the relationship between the domestic laws of a country (its 'municipal law') and international law is complex. The German Constitution provides expressly that international law is an integral part of its municipal law (art. 25). The French Constitution states (art. 55) only that duly approved and ratified treaties or agreements shall have an authority superior to domestic legislation on the relevant matters. However, in the preamble to the Constitution of the Fourth Republic 1946, which is adhered to by the 1958 Constitution, it is stipulated that the Republic 'shall conform to the rules of international public law'. The relationship between domestic and international law in the UK is a complex matter. The general principles of the law of nations are taken to be part of the common law of England (and Scotland) but treaties between sovereign states do not as such confer rights or impose duties on British citizens. Since they were made and ratified by the executive, they do not alter the domestic law. For that, the legislature must act, and many statutes are adopted to give effect to international conventions, usually printing the international document as a schedule to the national statute; but the European Convention on Human Rights has not been so incorporated. The particular relationship of national and European Community law, and the supremacy of the latter, were discussed above.

CITIZENS AND THE STATE

153 The constitutions all mention citizens but do not state, or not in any detail, how citizenship is acquired and what constitutes

the distinguishing characteristics of a citizen as contrasted with an alien. A codified constitution for Britain would presumably, like these other constitutions, refer the reader to the ordinary laws of the land. Suffice it to say therefore that citizenship, under the 1981 British Nationality Act, may be acquired in three main ways. The first, corresponding to a highly general, indeed universal, concept, is that citizenship may be acquired by birth in the UK, provided that one of the child's legitimate parents is either a British citizen or is 'settled' in the UK; or by descent if either parent is a British citizen otherwise than by descent. Second—and again, as is almost universal elsewhere—citizenship may be acquired by naturalization, the appropriate minister in this case being the Home Secretary. Applicants must satisfy the Home Secretary that they have lived in the UK for five years, that they are of good character, have sufficient knowledge of English, Welsh, or Gaelic, and if naturalized intend to have their principal home in the UK. Less stringent requirements apply where the applicant is the spouse of a British citizen. Finally, citizenship may also be acquired by registration with the Home Secretary. This process is particularly relevant to such categories as children born in the UK but not acquiring citizenship by birth, and also citizens of British dependent territories overseas and British overseas citizens, that is citizens of the UK and Colonies who do not qualify for either British citizenship or British dependent territories citizenship, who have satisfied a five year residence requirement.

154 *The Electorate.* We have already specified how the electorate is composed. Manifestly, one of the privileges of being a British citizen is the right to vote and to hold parliamentary office. Curiously, and anomalously, this privilege is shared by citizens of the Irish Republic and by citizens of any Commonwealth country, provided they have satisfied the residence requirements.

155 *The Political Parties.* Elections are contested by political parties. Some constitutions, like the German, contain general clauses regulating the status of such organizations. No such provision appears in the American Constitution, and in Britain the laws that relate to parties are rare and parenthetical. Certainly there is no general 'Statute of Parties' concerned with their aims, organization, finances, and procedures. In law they are treated as essentially private bodies.

156 *Rights and Duties of Citizens.* Each of the codified con-

stitutions contains a recitation of the rights (sometimes also of the duties) of citizens—whoever these may be. True, the French Constitution refers to these rights parenthetically, by means of its preamble, which in its turn refers to the preamble to the constitution of 1946 and to the 1789 Declaration of the Rights of Man and the Citizen. Such recitations are usually known nowadays as so many 'Bills of Rights'. No such document exists among the laws of Britain.

157 Yet the British unquestionably enjoy a large number of individual rights in their capacity as citizens of the country. As far as the application of the law is concerned it may fairly be argued that they enjoy much wider personal freedom than in some countries with Bills of Rights. But, while they may appear to enjoy freedoms comparable with those of their American, French, and German counterparts, in the constitutions of these countries the rights are expressed in the written constitution and are enforceable by a court or (in a limited range of circumstances) a specially appointed constitutional tribunal (as in the case of France).

158 The UK, like Germany and France, is a signatory of the European Convention on Human Rights (1950) and in 1966 accepted the compulsory jurisdiction of the European Commission and Court of Human Rights to which, therefore, an aggrieved individual can appeal. From this it may be inferred that the rights of the citizen in either Britain, France, or Germany are all subsumable under the Declaration of Human Rights, since the first seventeen articles of the European Convention are those of the Declaration. But Britain, unlike France or Germany and most of the other signatories, did not choose to incorporate the European Convention into her domestic law.

159 From these equivalences and differences we may deduce the following. First, it is possible to express the rights of British citizens in such general language and subject to so many qualifications and escape clauses that, at a certain level of abstraction, they may appear identical with those of their European neighbours. Second, the detailed and precise import of these generally expressed rights in Britain, *vis-à-vis* Germany and France, can be understood only by examining the specific laws and the judicial decisions thereon in Britain compared with these other countries.

Such a task is beyond the scope of this introduction. A catalogue of rights such as freedom of expression, assembly, petition, association, and election would be too equivocal; a particularization would, conversely, be tantamount to a volume on civil liberties in Britain and would, indeed, take us beyond even that into the fields of judicial procedure, police powers, and of social and economic legislation. Third, the scope and effectiveness of the laws relating to civil liberty are not affected in principle by whether or not they are embodied in a charter which has the force of fundamental and superior law; witness the insubstantiality of rights in the former constitution of the USSR on the one hand and the practical effectiveness of the American Constitution's 'Bill of Rights' on the other.

160 The most that can be done here, therefore, is not to describe the substance of citizens' rights but their status. And the following observations may be made about this:

(1) The rights of the British citizen are not codified into statements of general principle like the clauses in the preamble to the French 1946 constitution, the first twenty articles of the German Constitution, or Amendments I–X, XIV, and XV of the American Constitution. Nor are they guaranteed any greater legal sanctity than that enjoyed by, for example, a Lotteries and Gaming Act. These liberties are founded in the common law of the kingdom, or in statutes, and in either case they are interpreted by the ordinary courts of the country; and both these and subsequent judicial decisions thereon can be overridden or altered by subsequent parliamentary statutes. In a word: the rights of the British citizen are not 'entrenched'.

(2) Furthermore, these rights are residual. To know one's rights is to know what matters or actions the law forbids. Thus citizens are free to express their opinion in speech or writing or other visual means, subject, however, to a long train of restrictions including, *inter alia*, the laws relating to treason, the Official Secrets Act, sedition, defamation, incitement to mutiny or to disaffection, obscene publication, or blasphemy; and to those also that relate to incitement to a criminal offence, or to provoking public discord or incitement to racial hatred. And each of these qualifying restrictions is defined by statute, common law, and the judicial decisions thereon.

(3) Finally, for every wrongful encroachment on the citizens' liberties, there exists a legal remedy, ascertainable and enforceable by the ordinary courts of the land.

161 A number of eminent lawyers have increasingly found this situation unsatisfactory. They have called for a Bill of Rights enshrined in a codified constitution on lines similar to the American or the German constitution. Their dissatisfaction has arisen from recent developments in the parliamentary system. Parliament is sovereign; this is the key axiom of the constitution, and consequently Lord Scarman was able to write: 'Its sovereign power [is] more often than not exercised at the will of an executive sustained by an impregnable majority . . . The less internal control Parliament is prepared to accept, the greater the need for a constitutional settlement protecting entrenched provisions in the field of fundamental human rights'.[27] But to establish such a 'constitutional settlement' is far more easily said than done, especially in the light of the doctrine of the sovereignty of Parliament.

162 It is sometimes argued that the desired result could be brought about by Parliament passing a statute which is, somehow, 'entrenched'. That is to say, the statute would prescribe a procedure for altering itself which is more elaborate than that required for ordinary statutes, for example that it may be amended only by a two-thirds majority, or a two-thirds majority in each House, and/or by a popular referendum. But constitutional lawyers are divided as to whether such entrenchment is legally feasible, that is whether Parliament could not, under its ordinary procedure, simply wipe from the book the 'entrenching' statute.[28]

163 This argument can be taken more widely, too. On the one hand, it seems that the mechanism of the entrenched Bill of Rights plus judicial review operates effectively only in countries whose legislatures have long been habituated to the arrangement: the American experience dates from *Marbury* v. *Madison* (1803), while the German system takes up the centuries-old *Rechtsstaat* tradition. On the other hand, the absence of entrenched clauses

---

[27] Leslie Scarman, *English Law: The New Dimension* (Stevens, 1974), 74–5.

[28] For a brief but powerful statement see the opinion given to the House of Lords Select Committee on a Bill of Rights by D. Rippengal QC, a Clerk of the Lords, HL 176, 1977–8, 1–10.

in the Australian and Canadian constitutions did not restrict civil liberties in those countries as compared with, say, the USA or Germany, and has demonstrably restricted them far less than in the great majority of states which have such entrenched Bills of Rights. In short, there are more ways than one of negating civil liberties and more ways than one of guaranteeing them.

164 In his unpublished lectures on the Comparative Study of Constitutions,[29] Dicey characterized the British constitution as a 'historic' constitution. By this he meant not just that it was an ancient constitution but, more importantly, that it was original and spontaneous, the product not of deliberate design but of historical development. It is the long historical continuity of British institutions that gives the constitution its strength. Indeed, the most striking feature of the constitution is the way in which continuity in the form of institutions has masked a transformation of their function. The monarchy and the House of Lords, for example, have their origins in Anglo-Saxon times, while the House of Commons was born in the mediæval period. Their roles today, however, are quite different from those which they performed even 200 years ago. The Commons no longer makes and unmakes governments, while the House of Lords is now a revising chamber rather than an active legislative body, and the evolution of a limited monarchy has led to royal power being replaced by a constitutional monarchy. Evolutionary change within a framework of unchanging forms has, since the Restoration in 1660, been the hallmark of British constitutional development.

165 The constitution relies, however, more heavily than any of the others analyzed in this book, upon tacitly accepted and agreed conventions. British government, the political scientist Sidney Low declared at the beginning of this century, 'is based upon a system of tacit understandings. But the understandings are not always understood'.[30] The stability of the constitution depends upon some common agreement as to what the conventions of the constitution actually are; it rests on what President de Gaulle, speaking in Westminster Hall in 1960, referred to as 'an unchallengeable general consent'.[31] Were that consent to be

[29] The manuscript of these lectures may be found in the Codrington Library, All Souls College, Oxford.
[30] Sidney Low, *The Governance of England* (T. Fisher Unwin, 1904), 12.
[31] Jean Lacouture, *De Gaulle. The Ruler: 1945–1970* (Collins Harvill, 1991), 352.

withdrawn, then the perpetuation of an uncodified constitution might also come under threat. For, as Gladstone once remarked, the British Constitution 'presumes more boldly than any other, the good faith of those who work it'.[32] That remains as true today as it was when Gladstone wrote it, over 100 years ago.

[32] W. E. Gladstone, *Gleanings of Past Years* (John Murrray, 1879), I, 245.

4

The Constitution of the United States of America 1787

WE THE PEOPLE of the United States, in Order to form a more perfect Union, establish Justice, insure domestic Tranquility, provide for the common defence, promote the general Welfare, and secure the Blessings of Liberty to ourselves and our Posterity, do ordain and establish this Constitution for the United States of America.

ARTICLE I

Section 1. All legislative Powers herein granted shall be vested in a Congress of the United States, which shall consist of a Senate and House of Representatives.

Section 2. [1] The House of Representatives shall be composed of Members chosen every second Year by the People of the several States, and the Electors in each State shall have the Qualifications requisite for Electors of the most numerous Branch of the State Legislature.

[2] No person shall be a Representative who shall not have attained to the Age of twenty five Years, and been seven Years a Citizen of the United States, and who shall not, when elected, be an Inhabitant of that State in which he shall be chosen.

[3] [Representatives and direct Taxes shall be apportioned among the several States which may be included within this Union, according to their respective Numbers, which shall be determined by adding to the whole Number of free Persons, including those bound to Service for a Term of Years, and

Note. This text of the Constitution follows the engrossed copy signed by Gen. Washington and the deputies from twelve States. The superior number preceding the paragraphs designates the number of the clause; it was not in the original.

excluding Indians not taxed, three fifths of all other Persons.].*
The actual Enumeration shall be made within three Years after
the first Meeting of the Congress of the United States, and within
every subsequent Term of ten Years, in such Manner as they
shall by Law direct. The Number of Representatives shall not
exceed one for every thirty Thousand, but each State shall have
at Least one Representative; and until such enumeration shall be
made, the State of New Hampshire shall be entitled to chuse
three, Massachusetts eight, Rhode-Island and Providence Planta-
tions one, Connecticut five, New-York six, New Jersey four,
Pennsylvania eight, Delaware one, Maryland six, Virginia ten,
North Carolina five, South Carolina five, and Georgia three.

4 When vacancies happen in the Representation from any
State, the Executive Authority thereof shall issue Writs of
Election to fill such Vacancies.

5 The House of Representatives shall chuse their Speaker and
other Officers; and shall have the sole Power of Impeachment.

Section 3. 1 The Senate of the United States shall be composed
of two Senators from each State, [chosen by the Legislature
thereof,]† for six Years; and each Senator shall have one Vote.

2 Immediately after they shall be assembled in Consequence of
the first Election, they shall be divided as equally as may be into
three Classes. The Seats of the Senators of the first Class shall be
vacated at the Expiration of the second Year, of the second Class
at the Expiration of the fourth Year, and of the third Class at
the Expiration of the sixth Year, so that one third may be chosen
every second Year; [and if Vacancies happen by Resignation, or
otherwise, during the Recess of the Legislature of any State, the
Executive thereof may make temporary Appointments until the
next Meeting of the Legislature, which shall then fill such
Vacancies].‡

3 No Person shall be a Senator who shall not have attained to
the Age of thirty Years, and been nine Years a Citizen of the
United States, and who shall not, when elected, be an Inhabitant
of that State for which he shall be chosen.

* The part included in square brackets was changed by section 2 of the fourteenth amendment.

† The part included in square brackets was changed by section 1 of the seventeenth amendment.

‡ The part included in square brackets was changed by clause 2 of the seventeenth amendment.

4 The Vice President of the United States shall be President of the Senate, but shall have no Vote, unless they be equally divided.

5 The Senate shall chuse their other Officers, and also a President *pro tempore*, in the Absence of the Vice-President, or when he shall exercise the Office of President of the United States.

6 The Senate shall have the sole Power to try all Impeachments. When sitting for that Purpose, they shall be on Oath or Affirmation. When the President of the United States is tried, the Chief Justice shall preside: And no Person shall be convicted without the Concurrence of two thirds of the Members present.

7 Judgment in Cases of Impeachment shall not extend further than to removal from Office, and disqualification to hold and enjoy any Office of honor, Trust or Profit under the United States: but the Party convicted shall nevertheless be liable and subject to Indictment, Trial, Judgment and Punishment, according to Law.

Section 4. 1 The Times, Places and Manner of holding Elections for Senators and Representatives, shall be prescribed in each State by the Legislature thereof; but the Congress may at any time by Law make or alter such Regulations, except as to the Places of chusing Senators.

2 The Congress shall assemble at least once in every Year, and such Meeting shall [be on the first Monday in December,]* unless they shall by Law appoint a different Day.

Section 5. 1 Each House shall be the Judge of the Elections, Returns and Qualifications of its own Members, and a Majority of each shall constitute a Quorum to do Business; but a smaller Number may adjourn from day to day, and may be authorized to compel the Attendance of absent Members, in such Manner, and under such Penalties as each House may provide.

2 Each House may determine the Rules of its Proceedings, punish its Members for disorderly Behaviour, and, with the Concurrence of two thirds, expel a Member.

3 Each House shall keep a Journal of its Proceedings, and from time to time publish the same, excepting such Parts as may

* The part included in square brackets was changed by section 2 of the twentieth amendment.

in their Judgment require Secrecy; and the Yeas and Nays of the Members of either House on any question shall, at the Desire of one fifth of those Present, be entered on the Journal.

[4] Neither House, during the Session of Congress, shall, without the Consent of the other, adjourn for more than three days, nor to any other Place than that in which the two Houses shall be sitting.

Section 6. [1] The Senators and Representatives shall receive a Compensation for their Services, to be ascertained by Law, and paid out of the Treasury of the United States. They shall in all Cases except Treason, Felony and Breach of the Peace, be privileged from Arrest during their Attendance at the Session of their respective Houses, and in going to and returning from the same; and for any Speech or Debate in either House, they shall not be questioned in any other Place.

[2] No Senator or Representative shall, during the Time for which he was elected, be appointed to any civil Office under the Authority of the United States, which shall have been created, or the Emoluments whereof shall have been encreased during such time; and no Person holding any Office under the United States, shall be a Member of either House during his Continuance in Office.

Section 7. [1] All Bills for raising Revenue shall originate in the House of Representatives; but the Senate may propose or concur with Amendments as on other Bills.

[2] Every Bill which shall have passed the House of Representatives and the Senate, shall, before it become a Law, be presented to the President of the United States; If he approve he shall sign it, but if not he shall return it, with his Objections to that House in which it shall have originated, who shall enter the Objections at large on their Journal, and proceed to reconsider it. If after such Reconsideration two thirds of that House shall agree to pass the Bill, it shall be sent, together with the Objections, to the other House, by which it shall likewise be reconsidered, and if approved by two thirds of that House, it shall become a Law. But in all such Cases the Votes of both Houses shall be determined by Yeas and Nays, and the Names of the Persons voting for and against the Bill shall be entered on the Journal of each House respectively. If any Bill shall not be returned by the President within ten Days (Sundays excepted)

after it shall have been presented to him, the Same shall be a Law, in like Manner as if he had signed it, unless the Congress by their Adjournment prevent its Return, in which Case it shall not be a Law.

3 Every Order, Resolution, or Vote to which the Concurrence of the Senate and House of Representatives may be necessary (except on a question of Adjournment) shall be presented to the President of the United States; and before the Same shall take Effect, shall be approved by him, or being disapproved by him, shall be repassed by two thirds of the Senate and House of Representatives, according to the Rules and Limitations prescribed in the Case of a Bill.

Section 8. 1 The Congress shall have Power To lay and collect Taxes, Duties, Imposts and Excises, to pay the Debts and provide for the common Defence and general Welfare of the United States; but all Duties, Imposts and Excises shall be uniform throughout the United States;

2 To borrow Money on the credit of the United States;

3 To regulate Commerce with foreign Nations, and among the several States, and with the Indian Tribes;

4 To establish an uniform Rule of Naturalization, and uniform Laws on the subject of Bankruptcies throughout the United States;

5 To coin Money, regulate the Value thereof, and of foreign Coin, and fix the Standard of Weights and Measures;

6 To provide for the Punishment of counterfeiting the Securities and current Coin of the United States;

7 To establish Post Offices and post Roads;

8 To promote the Progress of Science and useful Arts, by securing for limited Times to Authors and Inventors the exclusive Right to their respective Writings and Discoveries;

9 To constitute Tribunals inferior to the supreme Court;

10 To define and punish Piracies and Felonies committed on the high Seas, and Offences against the Law of Nations;

11 To declare War, grant Letters of Marque and Reprisal, and make Rules concerning Captures on Land and Water;

12 To raise and support Armies, but no Appropriation of Money to that Use shall be for a longer Term than two Years;

13 To provide and maintain a Navy;

14 To make Rules for the Government and Regulation of the land and naval Forces;

[15] To provide for calling forth the Militia to execute the Laws of the Union, suppress Insurrections and repel Invasions;

[16] To provide for organizing, arming, and disciplining, the Militia, and for governing such Part of them as may be employed in the Service of the United States, reserving to the States respectively, the Appointment of the Officers, and the Authority of training the Militia according to the discipline prescribed by Congress;

[17] To exercise exclusive Legislation in all Cases whatsoever, over such District (not exceeding ten Miles square) as may, by Cession of particular States, and the Acceptance of Congress, become the Seat of the Government of the United States, and to exercise like Authority over all Places purchased by the Consent of the Legislature of the State in which the Same shall be, for the Erection of Forts, Magazines, Arsenals, dock-Yards, and other needful Buildings;—And

[18] To make all Laws which shall be necessary and proper for carrying into Execution the foregoing Powers, and all other Powers vested by this Constitution in the Government of the United States, or in any Department or Officer thereof.

Section 9. [1] The Migration or Importation of such Persons as any of the States now existing shall think proper to admit, shall not be prohibited by the Congress prior to the Year one thousand eight hundred and eight, but a Tax or duty may be imposed on such Importation, not exceeding ten dollars for each Person.

[2] The Privilege of the Writ of Habeas Corpus shall not be suspended, unless when in Cases of Rebellion or Invasion the public Safety may require it.

[3] No Bill of Attainder or ex post facto Law shall be passed.

*[4] No Capitation, or other direct, Tax shall be laid, unless in Proportion to the Census or Enumeration herein before directed to be taken.

[5] No Tax or Duty shall be laid on Articles exported from any State.

[6] No Preference shall be given by any Regulation of Commerce or Revenue to the Ports of one State over those of another: nor shall Vessels bound to, or from, one State, be obliged to enter, clear, or pay Duties in another.

* See also the sixteenth amendment.

[7] No Money shall be drawn from the Treasury, but in Consequence of Appropriations made by Law; and a regular Statement and Account of the Receipts and Expenditures of all public Money shall be published from time to time.

[8] No Title of Nobility shall be granted by the United States: And no Person holding any Office of Profit or Trust under them, shall, without the Consent of the Congress, accept of any present, Emolument, Office, or Title, of any kind whatever, from any King, Prince, or foreign State.

Section 10. [1] No State shall enter into any Treaty, Alliance, or Confederation; grant Letters of Marque and Reprisal; coin Money; emit Bills of Credit; make any Thing but gold and silver Coin a tender in Payment of Debts; pass any Bill of Attainder, *ex post facto* Law, or Law impairing the Obligation of Contracts, or grant any Title of Nobility.

[2] No State shall, without the Consent of the Congress, lay any Imposts or Duties on Imports or Exports, except what may be absolutely necessary for executing its inspection Laws: and the net Produce of all Duties and Imposts, laid by any State on Imports or Exports, shall be for the Use of the Treasury of the United States; and all such Laws shall be subject to the Revision and Controul of the Congress.

[3] No State shall, without the Consent of Congress, lay any duty of Tonnage, keep Troops, or Ships of War in time of Peace, enter into any Agreement or Compact with another State, or with a foreign Power, or engage in War, unless actually invaded, or in such imminent Danger as will not admit of delay.

ARTICLE II

Section 1. [1] The executive Power shall be vested in a President of the United States of America. He shall hold his Office during the Term of four Years, and, together with the Vice-President, chosen for the same Term, be elected, as follows

[2] Each State shall appoint, in such Manner as the Legislature thereof may direct, a Number of Electors, equal to the whole Number of Senators and Representatives to which the State may be entitled in the Congress: but no Senator or Representative, or

Person holding an Office of Trust or Profit under the United States, shall be appointed an Elector.

[The Electors shall meet in their respective States, and vote by Ballot for two Persons, of whom one at least shall not be an Inhabitant of the same State with themselves. And they shall make a List of all the Persons voted for, and of the Number of Votes for each; which List they shall sign and certify, and transmit sealed to the Seat of the Government of the United States, directed to the President of the Senate. The President of the Senate shall, in the Presence of the Senate and House of Representatives, open all the Certificates, and the Votes shall then be counted. The Person having the greatest Number of Votes shall be the President, if such Number be a Majority of the whole Number of Electors appointed; and if there be more than one who have such Majority, and have an equal Number of Votes, then the House of Representatives shall immediately chuse by Ballot one of them for President; and if no Person have a Majority, then from the five highest on the List the said House shall in like Manner chuse the President. But in chusing the President, the Votes shall be taken by States, the Representation from each State having one Vote; A quorum for this Purpose shall consist of a Member or Members from two thirds of the States, and a Majority of all the Senates shall be necessary to a Choice. In every Case, after the Choice of the President, the Person having the greatest Number of Votes of the Electors shall be the Vice-President. But if there should remain two or more who have equal Votes, the Senate shall chuse from them by Ballot the Vice-President.]*

³ The Congress may determine the Time of chusing the Electors, and the Day on which they shall give their Votes; which Day shall be the same throughout the United States.

⁴ No Person except a natural born Citizen, or a Citizen of the United States, at the time of the Adoption of this Constitution, shall be eligible to the Office of President; neither shall any Person be eligible to that Office who shall not have attained to the Age of thirty five Years, and been fourteen Years a Resident within the United States.

⁵ In Case of the Removal of the President from Office, or of

* This paragraph has been superseded by the twelfth amendment.

his Death, Resignation, or Inability to discharge the Powers and Duties of the said Office,* the Same shall devolve on the Vice-President, and the Congress may by Law provide for the Case of Removal, Death, Resignation or Inability, both of the President and Vice-President, declaring what Officer shall then act as President, and such Officer shall act accordingly, until the Disability be removed, or a President shall be elected.

6 The President shall, at stated Times, receive for his Services, a Compensation, which shall neither be encreased nor diminished during the Period for which he shall have been elected, and he shall not receive within that Period any other Emolument from the United States, or any of them.

7 Before he enter on the Execution of his Office, he shall take the following Oath or Affirmation:—'I do solemnly swear (or affirm) that I will faithfully execute the Office of President of the United States, and will to the best of my Ability, preserve, protect and defend the Constitution of the United States.'

Section 2. 1 The President shall be Commander in Chief of the Army and Navy of the United States, and of the Militia of the several States, when called into the actual Service of the United States; he may require the Opinion, in writing, of the principal Officer in each of the executive Departments, upon any Subject relating to the Duties of their respective Offices, and he shall have Power to grant Reprieves and Pardons for Offences against the United States, except in Cases of Impeachment.

2 He shall have Power, by and with the Advice and Consent of the Senate, to make Treaties, provided two thirds of the Senators present concur; and he shall nominate, and by and with the Advice and Consent of the Senate, shall appoint Ambassadors, other public Ministers and Consuls, Judges of the supreme Court, and all other Officers of the United States, whose Appointments are not herein otherwise provided for, and which shall be established by Law: but the Congress may by Law vest the Appointment of such inferior Officers, as they think proper, in the President alone, in the Courts of Law, or in the Heads of Departments.

3 The President shall have Power to fill up all Vacancies that may happen during the Recess of the Senate, by granting Commissions which shall expire at the End of their next Session.

* This provision has been affected by the twenty-fifth amendment.

Section 3. He shall from time to time give to the Congress Information of the State of the Union, and recommend to their Consideration such Measures as he shall judge necessary and expedient; he may, on extraordinary Occasions, convene both Houses, or either of them, and in Case of Disagreement between them, with Respect to the Time of Adjournment, he may adjourn them to such Time as he shall think proper; he shall receive Ambassadors and other public Ministers; he shall take Care that the Laws be faithfully executed, and shall Commission all the Officers of the United States.

Section 4. The President, Vice-President and all civil Officers of the United States, shall be removed from Office on Impeachment for, and Conviction of, Treason, Bribery, or other high Crimes and Misdemeanors.

ARTICLE III

Section 1. The judicial Power of the United States, shall be vested in one supreme Court, and in such inferior Courts as the Congress may from time to time ordain and establish. The Judges, both of the supreme and inferior Courts, shall hold their Offices during good Behaviour, and shall, at stated Times, receive for their Services, a Compensation, which shall not be diminished during their Continuance in Office.

Section 2. [1] The judicial Power shall extend to all Cases, in Law and Equity, arising under this Constitution, the Laws of the United States, and Treaties made, or which shall be made, under their Authority;—to all Cases affecting Ambassadors, other public Ministers and Consuls;—to all Cases of admiralty and maritime Jurisdiction;—to Controversies to which the United States shall be a Party;—to Controversies between two or more States;—between a State and Citizens of another State;*— between Citizens of different States,—between Citizens of the same State claiming Lands under Grants of different States, and between a State, or the Citizens thereof, and foreign States, Citizens or Subjects.

[2] In all Cases affecting Ambassadors, other public Ministers

---

* This clause has been affected by the eleventh amendment.

and Consuls, and those in which a State shall be Party, the supreme Court shall have original Jurisdiction. In all the other Cases before mentioned, the supreme Court shall have appellate Jurisdiction, both as to Law and Fact, with such Exceptions, and under such Regulations as the Congress shall make.

[3] The Trial of all Crimes, except in Cases of Impeachment, shall be by Jury; and such Trial shall be held in the State where the said Crimes shall have been committed; but when not committed within any State, the Trial shall be at such Place or Places as the Congress may by Law have directed.

Section 3. [1] Treason against the United States, shall consist only in levying War against them, or in adhering to their Enemies, giving them Aid and Comfort. No Person shall be convicted of Treason unless on the Testimony of two Witnesses to the same overt Act, or on Confession in open Court.

[2] The Congress shall have Power to declare the Punishment of Treason, but no Attainder of Treason shall work Corruption of Blood, or Forfeiture except during the Life of the Person attained.

ARTICLE IV

Section 1. Full Faith and Credit shall be given in each State to the public Acts, Records, and judicial Proceedings of every other State. And the Congress may by general Laws prescribe the Manner in which such Acts, Records and Proceedings shall be proved, and the Effect thereof.

Section 2. [1] The Citizens of each State shall be entitled to all Privileges and Immunities of Citizens in the several States.

[2] A Person charged in any State with Treason, Felony, or other Crime, who shall flee from Justice, and be found in another State, shall on Demand of the executive Authority of the State from which he fled, be delivered up, to be removed to the State having Jurisdiction of the Crime.

[3] [No Person held to Service or Labour in one State, under the Laws thereof, escaping into another, shall, in Consequence of any Law or Regulation therein, be discharged from such Service or Labour, but shall be delivered up on Claim of the Party to whom such Service or Labour may be due.]*

* This paragraph has been superseded by the thirteenth amendment.

Section 3. [1] New States may be admitted by the Congress into this Union; but no new State shall be formed or erected within the Jurisdiction of any other State; nor any State be formed by the Junction of two or more States, or Parts of States, without the Consent of the Legislatures of the States concerned as well as of the Congress.

[2] The Congress shall have Power to dispose of and make all needful Rules and Regulations respecting the Territory or other Property belonging to the United States; and nothing in this Constitution shall be so construed as to Prejudice any Claims of the United States, or of any particular State.

Section 4. The United States shall guarantee to every State in this Union a Republican Form of Government, and shall protect each of them against Invasion; and on Application of the Legislature, or of the Executive (when the Legislature cannot be convened) against domestic Violence.

ARTICLE V

The Congress, whenever two thirds of both Houses shall deem it necessary, shall propose Amendments to this Constitution, or, on the Application of the Legislatures of two thirds of the several States, shall call a Convention for proposing Amendments, which, in either Case, shall be valid to all Intents and Purposes, as Part of this Constitution, when ratified by the Legislatures of three fourths of the several States, or by Conventions in three fourths thereof, as the one or the other Mode of Ratification may be proposed by the Congress; Provided [that no Amendment which may be made prior to the Year One thousand eight hundred and eight shall in any Manner affect the first and fourth Clauses in the Ninth Section of the first Article; and]* that no State, without its Consent, shall be deprived of its equal Suffrage in the Senate.

ARTICLE VI

[1] All Debts contracted and Engagements entered into, before the Adoption of this Constitution, shall be as valid against the

* Obsolete.

United States under this Constitution, as under the Confederation.

² This Constitution, and the Laws of the United States which shall be made in Pursuance thereof; and all Treaties made, or which shall be made, under the Authority of the United States, shall be the supreme Law of the Land; and the Judges in every State shall be bound thereby, any Thing in the Constitution or Laws of any State to the Contrary notwithstanding.

³ The Senators and Representatives before mentioned, and the Members of the several State Legislatures, and all executive and judicial Officers, both of the United States and of the several States, shall be bound by Oath or Affirmation, to support this Constitution; but no religious Test shall ever be required as a Qualification to any Office or public Trust under the United States.

ARTICLE VII

The Ratification of the Conventions of nine States, shall be sufficient for the Establishment of this Constitution between the States so ratifying the Same.

DONE in Convention by the Unanimous Consent of the States present the Seventeenth Day of September in the Year of our Lord one thousand seven hundred and Eighty seven and of the Independence of the United States of America, the Twelfth, IN WITNESS whereof We have hereunto subscribed our Names.

GEORGE WASHINGTON,
President and deputy from Virginia

[Signed also by the deputies of twelve States:]
New Hampshire. John Langdon, Nicholas Gilman
Massachusetts. Nathaniel Gorham, Rufus King
Connecticut. Wm. Saml. Johnson, Roger Sherman
New York. Alexander Hamilton
New Jersey. Wil. Livingston, David Brearley, Wm. Paterson, Jona. Dayton
Pennsylvania. B. Franklin, Robt. Morris, Thos. FitzSimons, James Wilson, Thomas Mifflin, Geo. Clymer, Jared Ingersoll, Gouv. Morris

Delaware. Geo. Read, John Dickinson, Jaco. Broom, Gunning Bedford, jun., Richard Bassett

Maryland. James McHenry, Danl. Carroll, Dan. of St Thos. Jenifer

Virginia. John Blair, James Madison Jr.

North Carolina. Wm. Blount, Hu. Williamson, Rich'd. Dobbs Spaight

South Carolina. J. Rutledge, Charles Pinckney, Charles Cotesworth Pinckney, Pierce Butler

Georgia. William Few, Abr. Baldwin

Attest: William Jackson, *Secretary*

RATIFICATION OF THE CONSTITUTION

The Constitution was adopted by a convention of the States on 17 September 1787, and was subsequently ratified by the several States, on the following dates: Delaware, 7 December 1787; Pennsylvania, 12 December 1787; New Jersey, 18 December 1787; Georgia, 2 January 1788; Connecticut, 9 January 1788; Massachusetts, 6 February 1788; Maryland, 28 April 1788; South Carolina, 23 May 1788; New Hampshire, 21 June 1788.

Ratification was completed on 21 June 1788.

The Constitution was subsequently ratified by Virginia, 25 June 1788; New York, 26 July 1788; North Carolina, 21 November 1789; Rhode Island, 29 May 1790; and Vermont, 10 January 1791.

ARTICLES IN ADDITION TO, AND IN AMENDMENT OF, THE CONSTITUTION OF THE UNITED STATES OF AMERICA, PROPOSED BY CONGRESS, AND RATIFIED BY THE LEGISLATURES OF THE SEVERAL STATES PURSUANT TO THE FIFTH ARTICLE OF THE ORIGINAL CONSTITUTION

ARTICLE [I]*[1]

Congress shall make no law respecting an establishment of religion, or prohibiting the free exercise thereof; or abridging the freedom of speech, or of the press; or the right of the people peaceably to assemble, and to petition the Government for a redress of grievances.

ARTICLE [II]

A well regulated Militia, being necessary to the security of a free State, the right of the people to keep and bear Arms, shall not be infringed.

ARTICLE [III]

No Soldier shall, in time of peace be quartered in any house, without the consent of the Owner, nor in time of war, but in a manner to be prescribed by law.

ARTICLE [IV]

The right of the people to be secure in their persons, houses, papers, and effects, against unreasonable searches and seizures,

---

* Only the 13th, 14th, 15th and 16th articles of amendment had numbers assigned to them at the time of ratification.
[1] The first ten amendments were duly ratified, thus becoming effective in 1791.

shall not be violated, and no Warrants shall issue, but upon probable cause, supported by Oath or affirmation, and particularly describing the place to be searched, and the persons or things to be seized.

No person shall be held to answer for a capital, or otherwise infamous crime, unless on a presentment or indictment of a Grand Jury, except in cases arising in the land or naval forces, or in the Militia, when in actual service in time of War or public danger; nor shall any person be subject for the same offence to be twice put in jeopardy of life or limb; nor shall be compelled in any criminal case to be a witness against himself, nor be deprived of life, liberty, or property, without due process of law; nor shall private property be taken for public use without just compensation.

In all criminal prosecutions, the accused shall enjoy the right to a speedy and public trial, by an impartial jury of the State and district wherein the crime shall have been committed, which district shall have been previously ascertained by law, and to be informed of the nature and cause of the accusation; to be confronted with the witnesses against him; to have compulsory process for obtaining Witnesses in his favor, and to have the assistance of counsel for his defence.

In Suits at common law, where the value in controversy shall exceed twenty dollars, the right of trial by jury shall be preserved, and no fact tried by a jury, shall be otherwise reexamined in any Court of the United States, than according to the rules of the common law.

ARTICLE [VIII]

Excessive bail shall not be required, nor excessive fines imposed, nor cruel and unusual punishments inflicted.

ARTICLE [IX]

The enumeration in the Constitution, of certain rights, shall not be construed to deny or disparage others retained by the people.

ARTICLE [X]

The powers not delegated to the United States by the Constitution, nor prohibited by it to the States, are reserved to the States respectively, or to the people.

ARTICLE [XI][2]

The Judicial power of the United States shall not be construed to extend to any suit in law or equity, commenced or prosecuted against one of the United States by Citizens of another State, or by Citizens or Subjects of any Foreign State.

ARTICLE [XII][3]

The electors shall meet in their respective states and vote by ballot for President and Vice-President, one of whom, at least, shall not be an inhabitant of the same state with themselves; they shall name in their ballots the person voted for as President, and in distinct ballots the person voted for as Vice-President, and they shall make distinct lists of all persons voted for as President, and of all persons voted for as Vice-President, and of the number

[2] 1795.   [3] 1804.

of votes for each, which lists they shall sign and certify, and transmit sealed to the seat of the government of the United States, directed to the President of the Senate;—The President of the Senate shall, in the presence of the Senate and House of Representatives, open all the certificates and the votes shall then be counted;—The person having the greatest number of votes for President, shall be the President, if such number be a majority of the whole number of Electors appointed; and if no person have such majority, then from the persons having the highest numbers not exceeding three on the list of those voted for as President, the House of Representatives shall choose immediately, by ballot, the President. But in choosing the President, the votes shall be taken by states, the representation from each state having one vote; a quorum for this purpose shall consist of a member or members from two-thirds of the states, and a majority of all the states shall be necessary to a choice. [And if the House of Representatives shall not choose a President whenever the right of choice shall devolve upon them, before the fourth day of March next following, then the Vice-President shall act as President, as in the case of the death or other constitutional disability of the President.]* The person having the greatest number of votes as Vice-President, shall be the Vice-President, if such number be a majority of the whole number of Electors appointed, and if no person have a majority, then from the two highest numbers on the list, the Senate shall choose the Vice-President; a quorum for the purpose shall consist of two-thirds of the whole number of Senators, and a majority of the whole number shall be necessary to a choice. But no person constitutionally ineligible to the office of President shall be eligible to that of Vice-President of the United States.

ARTICLE XIII[4]

Section 1. Neither slavery nor involuntary servitude, except as a punishment for crime whereof the party shall have been duly convicted, shall exist within the United States, or any place subject to their jurisdiction.

* The part included in square brackets has been superseded by section 3 of the twentieth amendment.
4 1865.

Section 2. Congress shall have power to enforce this article by appropriate legislation.

Section 1. All persons born or naturalized in the United States, and subject to the jurisdiction thereof, are citizens of the United States and of the State wherein they reside. No State shall make or enforce any law which shall abridge the privileges or immunities of citizens of the United States; nor shall any State deprive any person of life, liberty, or property, without due process of law; nor deny to any person within its jurisdiction the equal protection of the laws.

Section 2. Representatives shall be apportioned among the several States according to their respective numbers, counting the whole number of persons in each State, excluding Indians not taxed. But when the right to vote at any election for the choice of electors for President and Vice-President of the United States, Representatives in Congress, the Executive and Judicial officers of a State, or the members of the Legislature thereof, is denied to any of the male inhabitants of such State, being twenty-one years of age, and citizens of the United States, or in any way abridged, except for participation in rebellion, or other crime, the basis of representation therein shall be reduced in the proportion which the number of such male citizens shall bear to the whole number of male citizens twenty-one years of age in such State.

Section 3. No person shall be a Senator or Representative in Congress, or elector of President and Vice-President, or hold any office, civil or military, under the United States, or under any State, who, having previously taken an oath, as a member of Congress, or as an officer of the United States, or as a member of any State legislature, or as an executive or judicial officer of any State, to support the Constitution of the United States, shall have engaged in insurrection or rebellion against the same, or given aid or comfort to the enemies thereof. But Congress may by a vote of two-thirds of each House, remove such disability.

Section 4. The validity of the public debt of the United States,

[5] 1868.

authorized by law, including debts incurred for payment of pensions and bounties for services in suppressing insurrection or rebellion, shall not be questioned. But neither the United States nor any State shall assume or pay any debt or obligation incurred in aid of insurrection or rebellion against the United States, or any claim for the loss or emancipation of any slave; but all such debts, obligations and claims shall be held illegal and void.

Section 5. The Congress shall have power to enforce, by appropriate legislation, the provisions of this article.

ARTICLE XV[6]

Section 1. The right of citizens of the United States to vote shall not be denied or abridged by the United States or by any State on account of race, color, or previous condition of servitude.

Section 2. The Congress shall have power to enforce this article by appropriate legislation.

ARTICLE XVI[7]

The Congress shall have power to lay and collect taxes on incomes, from whatever source derived, without apportionment among the several States, and without regard to any census or enumeration.

ARTICLE [XVII][8]

The Senate of the United States shall be composed of two Senators from each State, elected by the people thereof, for six years; and each Senator shall have one vote. The electors in each State shall have the qualifications requisite for electors of the most numerous branch of the State legislatures.

When vacancies happen in the representation of any State in

---

[6] 1870.   [7] 1913.   [8] 1913.

the Senate, the executive authority of such State shall issue writs of election to fill such vacancies: *Provided*, That the legislature of any State may empower the executive thereof to make temporary appointments until the people fill the vacancies by election as the legislature may direct.

This amendment shall not be so construed as to affect the election or term of any Senator chosen before it becomes valid as part of the Constitution.

ARTICLE [XVIII][9]

[Section 1. After one year from the ratification of this article the manufacture, sale, or transportation of intoxicating liquors within, the importation thereof into, or the exportation thereof from the United States and all territory subject to the jurisdiction thereof for beverage purposes is hereby prohibited.

[Section 2. The Congress and the several States shall have concurrent power to enforce this article by appropriate legislation.

[Section 3. This article shall be inoperative unless it shall have been ratified as an amendment to the Constitution by the legislatures of the several States, as provided in the Constitution, within seven years from the date of the submission hereof to the States by the Congress.]*

ARTICLE [XIX][10]

The right of citizens of the United States to vote shall not be denied or abridged by the United States or by any State on account of sex.

Congress shall have power to enforce this article by appropriate legislation.

ARTICLE [XX][11]

Section 1. The terms of the President and Vice-President shall end at noon on the 20th day of January, and the terms of

---

* Repealed by section 1 of the twenty-first amendment.
[9] 1919.   [10] 1919.   [11] 1933.

Senators and Representatives at noon on the 3d day of January, of the years in which such terms would have ended if this article had not been ratified; and the terms of their successors shall then begin.

Section 2. The Congress shall assemble at least once in every year, and such meetings shall begin at noon on the 3d day of January, unless they shall by law appoint a different day.

Section 3. * If, at the time fixed for the beginning of the term of the President, the President elect shall have died, the Vice-President elect shall become President. If a President shall not have been chosen before the time fixed for the beginning of his term, or if the President elect shall have failed to qualify, then the Vice-President elect shall act as President until a President shall have qualified; and the Congress may by law provide for the case wherein neither a President elect nor a Vice-President elect shall have qualified, declaring who shall then act as President, or the manner in which one who is to act shall be selected, and such person shall act accordingly until a President or Vice-President shall have qualified.

Section 4. The Congress may by law provide for the case of the death of any of the persons from whom the House of Representatives may choose a President whenever the right of choice shall have devolved upon them, and for the case of the death of any of the persons from whom the Senate may choose a Vice-President whenever the right of choice shall have devolved upon them.

Section 5. Sections 1 and 2 shall take effect on the 15th day of October following the ratification of this article.

Section 6. This article shall be inoperative unless it shall have been ratified as an amendment to the Constitution by the legislatures of three-fourths of the several States within seven years from the date of its submission.

ARTICLE [XXI][12]

Section 1. The eighteenth article of amendment to the Constitution of the United States is hereby repealed.

* See, the twenty-fifth amendment.
[12] 1933.

Section 2. The transportation or importation into any State, Territory, or possession of the United States for delivery or use therein of intoxicating liquors, in violation of the laws thereof, is hereby prohibited.

Section 3. This article shall be inoperative unless it shall have been ratified as an amendment to the Constitution by conventions in the several States, as provided in the Constitution, within seven years from the date of the submission hereof to the States by the Congress.

ARTICLE [XXII][13]

Section 1. No person shall be elected to the office of the President more than twice, and no person who has held the office of President, or acted as President, for more than two years of a term to which some other person was elected President shall be elected to the office of the President more than once. But this Article shall not apply to any person holding the office of President when this Article was proposed by the Congress, and shall not prevent any person who may be holding the office of President, or acting as President, during the term within which this Article becomes operative from holding the office of President or acting as President during the remainder of such term.

Section 2. This article shall be inoperative unless it shall have been ratified as an amendment to the Constitution by the legislatures of three-fourths of the several States within seven years from the date of its submission to the States by the Congress.

ARTICLE [XXIII][14]

Section 1. The District constituting the seat of Government of the United States shall appoint in such manner as the Congress may direct:

A number of electors of President and Vice-President equal to the whole number of Senators and Representatives in Congress to which the District would be entitled if it were a State, but in no event more than the least populous State; they shall be in

[13] 1951.   [14] 1960.

addition to those appointed by the States, but they shall be considered, for the purposes of the election of President and Vice-President, to be electors appointed by a State; and they shall meet in the District and perform such duties as provided by the twelfth article of amendment.

Section 2. The Congress shall have power to enforce this article by appropriate legislation.

ARTICLE [XXIV][15]

Section 1. The right of citizens of the United States to vote in any primary or other election for President or Vice-President, for electors for President or Vice-President, or for Senator or Representative in Congress, shall not be denied or abridged by the United States or any State by reason of failure to pay any poll tax or other tax.

Section 2. The Congress shall have power to enforce this article by appropriate legislation.

ARTICLE [XXV][16]

Section 1. In case of the removal of the President from office or of his death or resignation, the Vice-President shall become President.

Section 2. Whenever there is a vacancy in the office of the Vice-President, the President shall nominate a Vice-President who shall take office upon confirmation by a majority vote of both Houses of Congress.

Section 3. Whenever the President transmits to the President *pro tempore* of the Senate and the Speaker of the House of Representatives his written declaration that he is unable to discharge the powers and duties of his office, and until he transmits to them a written declaration to the contrary, such powers and duties shall be discharged by the Vice-President as Acting President.

Section 4. Whenever the Vice-President and a majority of either the principal officers of the executive departments or of such other body as Congress may by law provide, transmit to the

[15] 1964.   [16] 1967.

President *pro tempore* of the Senate and the Speaker of the House of Representatives their written declaration that the President is unable to discharge the powers and duties of his office, the Vice-President shall immediately assume the powers and duties of the office as Acting President.

Thereafter, when the President transmits to the President *pro tempore* of the Senate and the Speaker of the House of Representatives his written declaration that no inability exists, he shall resume the powers and duties of his office unless the Vice-President and a majority of either the principal officers of the executive department or of such other body as Congress may by law provide, transmit within four days to the President *pro tempore* of the Senate and the Speaker of the House of Representatives their written declaration that the President is unable to discharge the powers and duties of his office. Thereupon Congress shall decide the issue, assembling within forty-eight hours for that purpose if not in session. If the Congress, within twenty-one days after receipt of the latter written declaration, or, if Congress is not in session, within twenty-one days after Congress is required to assemble, determines by two-thirds vote of both Houses that the President is unable to discharge the powers and duties of his office, the Vice-President shall continue to discharge the same as Acting President; otherwise, the President shall resume the powers and duties of his office.

ARTICLE [XXVI][17]

Section 1. The right of citizens of the United States, who are eighteen years of age or older, to vote shall not be denied or abridged by the United States or by any State on account of age.

Section 2. The Congress shall have power to enforce this article by appropriate legislation.

ARTICLE [XXVII][18]

No law varying the compensation for the services of the Senators and Representatives shall take effect until an election of Representatives shall have intervened.

[17] 1971.   [18] 1992.

5

Basic Law for the Federal Republic of Germany of 23 May 1949

The Parliamentary Council, meeting in public session at Bonn am Rhein on 23 May 1949, confirmed the fact that the Basic Law for the Federal Republic of Germany, which was adopted by the Parliamentary Council on 8 May 1949, was ratified in the week of 16 to 22 May 1949 by the parliaments of more than two thirds of the participating constituent states (Länder).

By virtue of this fact the Parliamentary Council, represented by its Presidents, has signed and promulgated the Basic Law.

The Basic Law is hereby published in the Federal Law Gazette pursuant to paragraph (3) of Article 145.[1]

PREAMBLE[2]

Conscious of their responsibility before God and men,

Animated by the resolve to serve world peace as an equal part in a united Europe, the German People have adopted, by virtue of their constituent power, this Basic Law.

The Germans in the Länder of Baden-Württemberg, Bavaria, Berlin, Brandenburg, Bremen, Hamburg, Hesse, Lower Saxony, Mecklenburg-Western Pomerania, North Rhine-Westphalia, Rhineland-Palatinate, Saarland, Saxony, Saxony-Anhalt, Schleswig-Holstein and Thuringia have achieved the unity and freedom of Germany in free self-determination. This Basic Law is thus valid for the entire German People.

---

[1] The above notice of publication appeared in the first issue of the *Federal Law Gazette* dated 23 May 1949.

[2] Amended by the Unification Treaty of 31 Aug. 1990 and federal statute of 23 Sept. 1990.

Article 1 (Protection of human dignity)

(1) The dignity of man shall be inviolable. To respect and protect it shall be the duty of all state authority.

(2) The German people therefore acknowledge inviolable and inalienable human rights as the basis of every community, of peace and of justice in the world.

(3)[3] The following basic rights shall bind the legislature, the executive and the judiciary as directly enforceable law.

Article 2 (Rights of liberty)

(1) Everyone shall have the right to the free development of his personality in so far as he does not violate the rights of others or offend against the constitutional order or against morality.

(2) Everyone shall have the right to life and to physical integrity. The liberty of the individual shall be inviolable. Intrusion on these rights may only be made pursuant to a statute.

Article 3 (Equality before the law)

(1) All persons shall be equal before the law.

(2) Men and women shall have equal rights.

(3) No one may be disadvantaged or favoured because of his sex, his parentage, his race, his language, his homeland and origin, his faith, or his religious or political opinions.

Article 4 (Freedom of faith, of conscience and of creed)

(1) Freedom of faith, of conscience, and freedom to profess a religion or a particular philosophy (*Weltanschauung*) shall be inviolable.

(2) The undisturbed practice of religion shall be guaranteed.

(3) No one may be compelled against his conscience to render war service involving the use of arms. Details shall be regulated by a federal statute.

[3] As amended by federal statute of 19 Mar. 1956.

Article 5 (Freedom of expression)

(1) Everyone shall have the right freely to express and disseminate his opinion in speech, writing and pictures and freely to inform himself from generally accessible sources. Freedom of the press and freedom of reporting by means of broadcasts and films shall be guaranteed. There shall be no censorship.

(2) These rights are subject to limitations in the provisions of general statutes, in statutory provisions for the protection of youth, and in the right to respect for personal honour.

(3) Art and science, research and teaching shall be free. Freedom of teaching shall not release anybody from his allegiance to the constitution.

Article 6 (Marriage and family, illegitimate children)

(1) Marriage and family shall enjoy the special protection of the state.

(2) The care and upbringing of children shall be a natural right of and a duty primarily incumbent on the parents. The state shall watch over their endeavours in this respect.

(3) Children may not be separated from their families against the will of the persons entitled to bring them up, except, pursuant to a statute, where those so entitled fail in their duties or the children are otherwise threatened with serious neglect.

(4) Every mother shall be entitled to the protection and care of the community.

(5) Illegitimate children shall be provided by legislation with the same opportunities for their physical and mental development and for their place in society as are enjoyed by legitimate children.

Article 7 (Education)

(1) The entire schooling system shall be under the supervision of the state.

(2) The persons entitled to bring up a child shall have the right to decide whether the child shall attend religion classes.

(3) Religion classes shall form part of the ordinary curriculum in state schools, except in secular (*bekenntnisfrei*) schools. With-

out prejudice to the state's right of supervision, religious instruction shall be given in accordance with the tenets of the religious communities. No teacher may be obliged against his will to give religious instruction.

(4) The right to establish private schools shall be guaranteed. Private schools, as a substitute for state schools, shall require the approval of the state and shall be subject to the statutes of the Länder. Such approval shall be given where private schools are not inferior to the state schools in their educational aims, their facilities and the professional training of their teaching staff, and where segregation of pupils according to the means of the parents is not encouraged thereby. Approval shall be withheld where the economic and legal position of the teaching staff is not sufficiently assured.

(5) A private elementary school shall be permitted only where the education authority finds that it serves a special pedagogic interest, or where, on the application of persons entitled to bring up children, it is to be established as an interdenominational school or as a denominational school or as a school based on a particular philosophical persuasion (*Weltanschauungsschule*) and a state elementary school of this type does not exist in the commune (*Gemeinde*).

(6) Preliminary schools (*Vorschulen*) shall remain abolished.

Article 8 (Freedom of assembly)

(1) All Germans shall have the right to assemble peaceably and unarmed without prior notification or permission.

(2) With regard to open-air meetings, this right may be restricted by or pursuant to a statute.

Article 9 (Freedom of association)

(1) All Germans shall have the right to form associations, partnerships and corporations.

(2) Associations, the purposes or activities of which conflict with criminal statutes or which are directed against the constitutional order or the concept of international understanding, shall be prohibited.

(3) The right to form associations to safeguard and improve

working and economic conditions shall be guaranteed to everyone and to all occupations. Agreements which restrict or seek to impair this right shall be null and void; measures directed to this end shall be illegal. Measures taken pursuant to Article 12a, to paragraphs (2) and (3) of Article 35, to paragraph (4) of Article 87a, or to Article 91 may not be directed against any industrial conflicts engaged in by associations within the meaning of the first sentence of this paragraph in order to safeguard and improve working and economic conditions.[4]

Article 10[5] (Privacy of letters, posts and telecommunications)

(1) Privacy of letters, posts and telecommunications shall be inviolable.

(2) Restrictions may only be ordered pursuant to a statute. Where a restriction serves to protect the free democratic basic order or the existence or security of the Federation, the statute may stipulate that the person affected shall not be informed of such restriction and that recourse to the courts shall be replaced by a review of the case by bodies and auxiliary bodies appointed by Parliament.

Article 11 (Freedom of movement)

(1) All Germans shall enjoy freedom of movement throughout the federal territory.

(2) This right may be restricted only by or pursuant to a statute, and only in cases in which an adequate basis for personal existence is lacking and special burdens would result therefrom for the community, or in which such restriction is necessary to avert an imminent danger to the existence or the free democratic basic order of the Federation or a Land, to combat the danger of epidemics, to deal with natural disasters or particularly grave accidents, to protect young people from neglect or to prevent crime.

---

[4] Last sentence inserted by federal statute of 24 June 1968.
[5] As amended by federal statute of 24 June 1968.

Article 12⁶ (Right to choose an occupation, prohibition of forced labour)

(1) All Germans shall have the right freely to choose their occupation, their place of work and their place of study or training. The practice of an occupation may be regulated by or pursuant to a statute.

(2) No person may be forced to perform work of a particular kind except within the framework of a traditional compulsory community service that applies generally and equally to all.

(3) Forced labour may be imposed only on persons deprived of their liberty by court sentence.

Article 12a⁷ (Liability to military and other service)

(1) Men who have attained the age of eighteen years may be required to serve in the Armed Forces, in the Federal Border Guard, or in a civil defence organization.

(2) A person who refuses, on grounds of conscience, to render war service involving the use of arms may be required to render a substitute service. The duration of such substitute service shall not exceed the duration of military service. Details shall be regulated by a statute which shall not interfere with freedom to take a decision based on conscience and shall also provide for the possibility of a substitute service not connected with units of the Armed Forces or of the Federal Border Guard.

(3) Persons liable to military service who are not required to render service pursuant to paragraph (1) or (2) of this Article may, during a state of defence (*Verteidigungsfall*), be assigned by or pursuant to a statute to an employment involving civilian services for defence purposes, including the protection of the civilian population; it shall, however, not be permissible to assign persons to an employment subject to public law except for the purpose of discharging police functions or such other functions of public administration as can only be discharged by persons employed under public law. Persons may be assigned to an employment— as referred to in the first sentence of this paragraph—with the Armed Forces, including the supplying and servicing of the latter,

---

⁶ As amended by federal statutes of 19 Mar. 1956 and 24 June 1968.
⁷ Inserted by federal statute of 24 June 1968.

or with public administrative authorities; assignments to employment connected with supplying and servicing the civilian population shall not be permissible except in order to meet their vital requirements or to guarantee their safety.

(4) Where, during a state of defence, civilian service requirements in the civilian health system or in the stationary military hospital organization cannot be met on a voluntary basis, women between eighteen and fifty-five years of age may be assigned to such services by or pursuant to a statute. They may on no account render service involving the use of arms.

(5) Prior to the existence of a state of defence, assignments under paragraph (3) of this Article may only be made where the requirements of paragraph (1) of Article 80a are satisfied. It shall be admissible to require persons by or pursuant to a statute to attend training courses in order to prepare them for the performance of such services in accordance with paragraph (3) of this Article as require special knowledge or skills. To this extent, the first sentence of this paragraph shall not apply.

(6) Where, during a state of defence, staffing requirements for the purposes referred to in the second sentence of paragraph (3) of this Article cannot be met on a voluntary basis, the right of a German to quit the pursuit of his occupation or quit his place of work may be restricted by or pursuant to a statute in order to meet these requirements. The first sentence of paragraph (5) of this Article shall apply mutatis mutandis prior to the existence of a state of defence.

Article 13 (Inviolability of the home)

(1) The home shall be inviolable.

(2) Searches may be ordered only by a judge or, in the event of danger resulting in any delay in taking action, by other organs as provided by statute and may be carried out only in the form prescribed by law.

(3) Intrusions and restrictions may otherwise only be made to avert a public danger or a mortal danger to individuals, or, pursuant to a statute, to prevent substantial danger to public safety and order, in particular to relieve a housing shortage, to combat the danger of epidemics or to protect juveniles who are exposed to a moral danger.

Article 14 (Property, right of inheritance, taking of property)

(1) Property and the right of inheritance shall be guaranteed. Their content and limits shall be determined by statute.

(2) Property imposes duties. Its use should also serve the public weal.

(3) The taking of property shall only be permissible in the public weal. It may be effected only by or pursuant to a statute regulating the nature and extent of compensation. Such compensation shall be determined by establishing an equitable balance between the public interest and the interests of those affected. In case of dispute regarding the amount of compensation, recourse may be had to the courts of ordinary jurisdiction.

Article 15 (Socialization)

Land, natural resources and means of production may for the purpose of socialization be transferred to public ownership or other forms of collective enterprise for the public benefit by a statute regulating the nature and extent of compensation. In respect of such compensation the third and fourth sentences of paragraph (3) of Article 14 shall apply *mutatis mutandis*.

Article 16[8] (Deprivation of citizenship, extradition)

(1) German citizenship may not be withdrawn. Loss of citizenship may occur only pursuant to a statute, and may be lost against the will of the person concerned only if such person does not thereby become stateless.

(2) No German may be extradited to a foreign country.

Article 16a[9] (Right of Asylum)

(1) Persons persecuted on political grounds shall enjoy the right of asylum.

(2) Paragraph 1 may not be invoked by a person entering from a Member State of the European Community, or from a third State in which the application of the Convention on the

---

[8] Amended by federal statute of 28 June 1993.
[9] Inserted by federal statute of 28 June 1993.

Legal Status of Refugees and of the Convention on the Protection of Human Rights and Fundamental Freedoms is ensured. Those states outside the European Community to which the provisions of the preceding sentence apply will be specified by a statute requiring the consent of the Bundesrat. In the cases covered by the first sentence of this paragraph, residence curtailment measures may be enforced although an appeal be pending against them.

(3) A statute requiring the consent of the Bundesrat may determine those States in which, by reason of the legal situation, the application of the law and the general political circumstances, it appears to be guaranteed that there is neither political persecution nor inhuman or humiliating punishment or treatment. An alien from such a state does not count as a person subject to political persecution unless he puts forward facts demonstrating that, contrary to this presumption, he is subject to political persecution.

(4) In the cases falling under paragraph (3) hereof and in other cases which are or are deemed to be obviously unfounded, the enforcement of residence curtailment measures may be suspended by the courts only when there is serious doubt as to the lawfulness of the measures in question. The examination of the issue may be restricted in range, and tardy pleadings need not be considered. Details shall be regulated by statute.

(5) Paragraphs (1) to (4) hereof are without prejudice to the international agreements of the Member States of the European Communities among themselves and with third States which, subject to those duties arising from the Convention on the Legal Status of Refugees and the Convention on the Protection of Human Rights and Fundamental Freedoms whose application is to be ensured in all the contracting States, deal with the jurisdictional rules for the examination of asylum seekers including the mutual recognition of decisions on asylum.

Article 17 (Right of petition)

Everyone shall have the right individually or jointly with others to address written requests or complaints to the competent agencies and to parliaments.

Article 17a[10] (Restriction of individual basic rights through legislation enacted for defence purposes and concerning substitute service)

(1) Statutes concerning military service and substitute service may, by provisions applying to members of the Armed Forces and of the substitute services during their period of military or substitute service, restrict the basic right freely to express and to disseminate opinions in speech, writing and pictures (first half-sentence of paragraph (1) of Article 5), the basic right of assembly (Article 8), and the right of petition (Article 17) in so far as this right permits the submission of requests or complaints jointly with others.

(2) Statutes serving defence purposes including the protection of the civilian population may provide for the restriction of the basic rights of freedom of movement (Article 11) and inviolability of the home (Article 13).

Article 18 (Forfeiture of basic rights)[11]

Whoever abuses freedom of expression of opinion, in particular freedom of the press (paragraph (1) of Article 5), freedom of teaching (paragraph (3) of Article 5), freedom of assembly (Article 8), freedom of association (Article 9), privacy of letters, posts and telecommunications (Article 10), property (Article 14), or the right of asylum (Article 16a) in order to combat the free democratic basic order shall forfeit these basic rights. Such forfeiture and the extent thereof shall be determined by the Federal Constitutional Court.

Article 19 (Restriction of basic rights)

(1) In so far as a basic right may, under this Basic Law, be restricted by or pursuant to a statute, such statute shall apply generally and not solely to an individual case. Furthermore, such statute shall name the basic right, indicating the Article concerned.

(2) In no case may the essence of a basic right be encroached upon.

---

[10] Inserted by federal statute of 19 Mar. 1956.
[11] Amended by federal statute of 28 June 1993.

(3) The basic rights shall apply also to domestic juristic persons to the extent that the nature of such rights permits.

(4) Should any person's rights be violated by public authority, recourse to the court shall be open to him. In so far as no other jurisdiction has been established, recourse shall be to the courts of ordinary jurisdiction. The second sentence of paragraph (2) of Article 10 shall not be affected by the provisions of this paragraph.[12]

II. THE FEDERATION AND THE STATES (LÄNDER)

Article 20 (Basic principles of state order, right to resist)

(1) The Federal Republic of Germany shall be a democratic and social federal state.

(2) All state authority shall emanate from the people. It shall be exercised by the people through elections and voting and by specific organs of the legislature, the executive power, and the judiciary.

(3) Legislation shall be subject to the constitutional order; the executive and the judiciary shall be bound by law and justice.

(4)[13] All Germans shall have the right to resist any person seeking to abolish this constitutional order, should no other remedy be possible.

Article 21[14] (Political parties)

(1) The political parties shall participate in the forming of the political will of the people. They may be freely established. Their internal organization shall conform to democratic principles. They shall publicly account for the sources and use of their funds and for their assets.

(2) Parties which, by reason of their aims or the behaviour of their adherents, seek to impair or abolish the free democratic basic order or to endanger the existence of the Federal Republic

[12] Last sentence inserted by federal statute of 24 June 1968.
[13] Inserted by federal statute of 24 June 1968.
[14] As amended by federal statute of 21 Dec. 1983.

of Germany shall be unconstitutional. The Federal Constitutional Court shall decide on the question of unconstitutionality.

(3) Details shall be regulated by federal statutes.

Article 22 (Federal flag)

The federal flag shall be black, red and gold.

Article 23[15] (Participation in the development of the European Union)

(1) For the realization of a united Europe, the Federal Republic of Germany participates in the development of the European Union which is bound to democratic, law-governed, social, and federative principles and to the principle of subsidiarity, and which guarantees a protection of basic rights essentially comparable to that of this Basic Law. By a statute enacted with the consent of the Bundesrat, the Republic may transfer to it sovereign powers (*Hoheitsrechte*). Article 79(2) and (3) governs the foundation of the European Union as well as amendments to its Treaty bases and similar rules whereby this Basic Law according to its terms may be amended or supplemented or such amendments or additions may be made possible.

(2) The Bundestag and, through the Bundesrat, the Länder participate in the affairs of the European Union. The Federal Government must furnish comprehensive and timely information to the Bundestag and Bundesrat.

(3) Before participating in legal measures of the European Union, the Federal Government shall afford the Bundestag the opportunity for comment thereon. In negotiations, the Federal Government shall take the Bundestag's comments into account. Details shall be regulated by statute.

(4) In so far as it has to participate in a relevant internal measure or in so far as the Länder have internal powers, the Bundesrat is to participate in the Federation's formation of policy.

(5) In any area of exclusive competence of the Federation, to the extent that the interests of the Länder are affected or in so far as otherwise the Federation has the right to legislate, the

---

[15] Old art. 23 repealed by the Unification Treaty of 31 Aug. 1990 and federal statute of 23 Sept. 1990. New text inserted by federal statute of 21 Dec. 1992.

Federal Government shall take into account the comments of the Bundesrat. Where the issue affects the legislative powers of the Länder, the structure of their authorities or their administrative procedure, the Bundesrat's opinion is to be considered authoritative in the policy formation of the Federation; in this regard the overall responsibility of the Federation is to be maintained. The Federal Government's consent is required for all matters which may lead to an increase in expenditure or decrease in revenue for the Federation.

(6) Where the issue affects the exclusive legislative powers of the Länder, the exercise of rights vested in the Federal Republic of Germany as a Member State of the European Union shall be transferred from the Federation to a representative of the Länder nominated by the Bundesrat. The exercise of rights occurs with the participation of and in coordination with the Federal Government; in this regard the overall responsibility of the Federation is to be preserved.

(7) Details relevant to paragraphs 4 to 6 shall be regulated by a statute requiring the consent of the Bundesrat.

Article 24 (Entry into a collective security system)

(1) The Federation may by legislation transfer sovereign powers to intergovernmental institutions.

(1a)[16] In so far as the Länder have competence for the exercise of state powers and the performance of state functions they may, with the consent of the Federal Government, transfer sovereign powers to neighbouring institutions.

(2) For the maintenance of peace, the Federation may enter a system of mutual collective security; in doing so it shall consent to such limitations upon its rights of sovereignty as will bring about and secure a peaceful and lasting order in Europe and among the nations of the world.

(3) For the settlement of disputes between states, the Federation shall accede to agreements concerning international arbitration of a general, comprehensive and obligatory nature.

---

[16] Inserted by federal statute of 21 Dec. 1992.

Article 25 (Public international law and federal law)

The general rules of public international law shall be an integral part of federal law. They shall take precedence over statutes and shall directly create rights and duties for the inhabitants of the federal territory.

Article 26 (Ban on preparing a war of aggression)

(1) Acts tending to and undertaken with intent to disturb the peaceful relations between nations, especially to prepare for war of aggression, shall be unconstitutional. They shall be made a criminal offence.

(2) Weapons designed for warfare may not be manufactured, transported or marketed except with the permission of the Federal Government. Details shall be regulated by a federal statute.

Article 27 (Merchant fleet)

All German merchant vessels shall form one merchant fleet.

Article 28 (Federal guarantee concerning Länder constitutions, guarantee of self-government for local authorities)

(1) The constitutional order in the Länder shall conform to the principles of the republic, democratic and social state under the rule of law (*Rechtsstaat*), within the meaning of this Basic Law. In each of the Länder, counties (*Kreise*), and communes (*Gemeinden*), the people shall be represented by a body chosen in general, direct, free, equal and secret elections. Citizens of other Member States of the European Community may, in accordance with the law of the European Community, vote and be candidates in county and commune elections.[17] In the communes the communal assembly may take the place of an elected body.

(2) The communes shall be guaranteed the right to regulate, on their own responsibility, all the affairs of the local community within the limits set by statute. Within the framework of their

[17] Inserted by federal statute of 21 Dec. 1992.

statutory functions, the associations of communes (*Gemeinde-verbände*) shall also have such right to self-government as may be provided by statute.

(3) The Federation shall ensure that the constitutional order of the Länder conforms to the basic rights and to the provisions of paragraphs (1) and (2) of this Article.

Article 29[18] (New delimitation of Länder boundaries)

(1) A new delimitation of federal territory may be made to ensure that the Länder by their size and capacity are able effectively to fulfil the functions incumbent upon them. Due regard shall be given to regional, historical and cultural ties, economic expediency, and the requirements of regional policy and planning.

(2) Measures for a new delimitation of federal territory shall be effected by federal statutes which shall require confirmation by referendum. The Länder thus affected shall be consulted.

(3) A referendum shall be held in the Länder from whose territories or partial territories a new Land or a Land with redefined boundaries is to be formed (affected Länder). The referendum shall be held on the question whether the affected Länder are to remain within their existing boundaries or whether the new Land or Land with redefined boundaries should be formed. The referendum shall be deemed to be in favour of the formation of a new Land or of a Land with redefined boundaries where approval is given to the change by a majority in the future territory of such Land and by a majority in all the territories or partial territories of an affected Land whose assignment to a Land is to be changed in the same sense. The referendum shall be deemed not to be in favour where in the territory of one of the affected Länder a majority reject the change; such rejection shall, however, be of no consequence where in one part of the territory whose assignment to the affected Land is to be changed a majority of two-thirds approve of the change, unless in the entire territory of the affected Land a majority of two-thirds reject the change.

(4) Where in a clearly definable area of interconnected popula-

---

[18] As amended by federal statutes of 19 Aug. 1969 and of 23 Aug. 1976.

tion and economic settlement, the parts of which lie in several Länder and which has a population of at least one million, one tenth of those of its population entitled to vote in Bundestag elections petition by popular initiative for the assignment of that area to one Land, provision shall be made within two years in a federal statute determining whether the delimitation of the affected Länder shall be changed pursuant to paragraph (2) of this Article or determining that a plebiscite shall be held in the affected Länder.

(5) The plebiscite shall establish whether approval is given to a change of Länder delimitation to be proposed in the statute. The statute may put forward different proposals, not exceeding two in number, for the plebiscite. Where approval is given by a majority to a proposed change of Länder delimitation, provision shall be made within two years in a federal statute determining whether the delimitation of the Länder concerned shall be changed pursuant to paragraph (2) of this Article. Where approval is given, in accordance with the third and fourth sentences of paragraph (3) of this Article, to a proposal put forward for the plebiscite, a federal statute providing for the formation of the proposed Land shall be enacted within two years of the plebiscite and shall no longer require confirmation by referendum.

(6) A majority in a referendum or in a plebiscite shall consist of a majority of the votes cast, provided that they amount to at least one quarter of the population entitled to vote in Bundestag elections. Other detailed provisions concerning referendums, popular petitions and plebiscites (*Volksentscheide, Volksbegehren, Volksbefragungen*) shall be made in a federal statute; such statute may also provide that popular petitions may not be repeated within a period of five years.

(7) Other changes concerning the territory of the Länder may be effected by state agreements between the Länder concerned or by a federal statute with the approval of the Bundesrat where the territory which is to be the subject of a new delimitation does not have more than 10,000 inhabitants. Detailed provision shall be made in a federal statute requiring the approval of the Bundesrat and the majority of the members of the Bundestag. It shall make provision for the affected communes and districts to be heard.

Article 30 (Distribution of competence between the Federation and the Länder)

Except as otherwise provided or permitted by this Basic Law, the exercise of governmental powers and the discharge of governmental functions shall be incumbent on the Länder.

Article 31 (Precedence of federal law)

Federal law shall take precedence over Land law.

Article 32 (Foreign relations)

(1) Relations with foreign states shall be conducted by the Federation.

(2) Before the conclusion of a treaty affecting the special circumstances of a Land, that Land shall be consulted in sufficient time.

(3) In so far as the Länder have power to legislate, they may, with the consent of the Federal Government, conclude treaties with foreign states.

Article 33 (Equal political status of all Germans, professional civil service)

(1) Every German shall have in every Land the same political (*staatsbürgerlich*) rights and duties.

(2) Every German shall be equally eligible for any public office according to his aptitude, qualifications and professional achievements.

(3) Enjoyment of civil and political rights, eligibility for public office, and rights acquired in the public service shall be independent of religious denomination. No one may suffer any disadvantage by reason of his adherence or non-adherence to a denomination or to a philosophical persuasion.

(4) The exercise of state authority as a permanent function shall, as a rule, be entrusted to members of the public service whose status, service and loyalty are governed by public law.

(5) The law of the public service shall be regulated with due regard to the traditional principles of the professional civil service.

Article 34 (Liability in the event of a breach of official duty)

Where any person, in the exercise of a public office entrusted to him, violates his official obligations to a third party, liability shall rest in principle on the state or the public body which employs him. In the event of wilful intent or gross negligence, the right of recourse against the holder of a public office shall be reserved. In respect of the claim for compensation or the right of recourse, the jurisdiction of the ordinary courts shall not be excluded.

Article 35[19] (Legal and administrative assistance, assistance during disasters)

(1) All federal and Land authorities shall render each other legal and administrative assistance.

(2) In order to maintain or to restore public security or order, a Land may, in cases of particular importance, call upon forces and facilities of the Federal Border Guard to assist its police where without this assistance the police could not, or only with considerable difficulty, fulfil a task. In order to deal with a natural disaster or an especially grave accident, a Land may request the assistance of the police forces of other Länder or of forces and facilities of other administrative authorities or of the Federal Border Guard or the Armed Forces.[20]

(3) Where the natural disaster or the accident endangers a region larger than a Land, the Federal Government may, in so far as this is necessary to effectively deal with such danger, instruct the Land governments to place their police forces at the disposal of other Länder, and may use units of the Federal Border Guard or the Armed Forces to support the police forces. Measures taken by the Federal Government pursuant to the first sentence of this paragraph shall be revoked at any time at the demand of the Bundesrat, and otherwise immediately upon removal of the danger.

---

[19] As amended by federal statute of 24 June 1968.
[20] As amended by federal statute of 28 July 1972.

Article 36 (Personnel of the federal authorities)

(1) Civil servants employed in the highest federal authorities shall be drawn from all Länder in appropriate proportion. Persons employed in other federal authorities should, as a rule, be drawn from the Land in which they serve.

(2)[21] Military laws shall, *inter alia*, take into account both the division of the Federation into Länder and the regional ties of their populations.

Article 37 (Federal coercion)

(1) Where a Land fails to comply with its obligations of a federal character imposed by this Basic Law or another federal statute, the Federal Government may, with the consent of the Bundesrat, take the necessary measures to enforce such compliance by the Land by way of federal coercion.

(2) For the purpose of exercising such federal coercion, the Federal Government or its commissioner shall have the right to give instructions to all Länder and their authorities.

III. THE FEDERAL PARLIAMENT (BUNDESTAG)

Article 38 (Elections)

(1) The deputies to the German Bundestag shall be elected in general, direct, free, equal and secret elections. They shall be representatives of the whole people, not bound by orders and instructions, and shall be subject only to their conscience.

(2)[22] Anyone who has attained the age of eighteen years shall be entitled to vote; anyone who has attained majority shall be eligible for election.

(3) Details shall be regulated by a federal statute.

---

[21] Inserted by federal statute of 19 Mar. 1956.
[22] As amended by federal statute of 31 July 1970.

Article 39 (Assembly and legislative term)

(1)[23] The Bundestag shall be elected for a four-year term. Its legislative term shall end with the assembly of a new Bundestag. The new election shall be held forty-five months at the earliest, and forty-seven months at the latest after the beginning of the legislative term. Where the Bundestag is dissolved, the new election shall be held within sixty days.

(2) The Bundestag shall assemble, at the latest, on the thirtieth day after the election.

(3) The Bundestag shall determine the termination and resumption of its meetings. The President of the Bundestag may convene it at an earlier date. He shall do so where one third of its members or the Federal President or the Federal Chancellor so demand.

Article 40 (President, rules of procedure)

(1) The Bundestag shall elect its President, vice presidents and secretaries. It shall draw up its rules of procedure.

(2) The President shall exercise proprietary and police powers in the Bundestag building. No search or seizure may take place on the premises of the Bundestag without his permission.

Article 41 (Scrutiny of elections)

(1) The scrutiny of elections shall be the responsibility of the Bundestag. It shall also decide whether a deputy has lost his seat in the Bundestag.

(2) Complaints against such decisions of the Bundestag may be lodged with the Federal Constitutional Court.

(3) Details shall be regulated by a federal statute.

Article 42 (Proceedings, voting)

(1) The debates of the Bundestag shall be public. Upon a motion of one tenth of its members, or upon a motion of the Federal Government, the public may be excluded by a two-thirds

---

[23] As amended by federal statute of 23 Aug. 1976.

majority. The decision on the motion shall be taken at a meeting not open to the public.

(2) Decisions of the Bundestag shall require a majority of the votes cast unless this Basic Law provides otherwise. The rules of procedure may provide for exceptions in respect of elections to be conducted by the Bundestag.

(3) True and accurate reports on the public meetings of the Bundestag and of its committees shall not give rise to any liability.

Article 43 (Presence of members of the Federal Government and of the Bundesrat)

(1) The Bundestag and its committees may demand the presence of any member of the Federal Government.

(2) The members of the Bundesrat and of the Federal Government as well as persons commissioned by them shall have access to all meetings of the Bundestag and its committees. They shall be heard at any time.

Article 44 (Committees of investigation)

(1) The Bundestag shall have the right, and upon the motion of one quarter of its members the duty, to set up a committee of investigation, which shall take the requisite evidence at public hearings. The public may be excluded.

(2) The rules of criminal procedure shall apply *mutatis mutandis* to the taking of evidence. The privacy of letters, posts and telecommunications shall remain unaffected.

(3) Courts and administrative authorities shall be bound to render legal and administrative assistance.

(4) The decisions of committees of investigation shall not be subject to judicial consideration. The courts shall be free to evaluate and judge the facts on which the investigation is based.

Article 45[24] (Federal Committee for European Union affairs)

The Bundestag shall appoint a committee for European Union affairs. It may empower the committee to exercise the rights

[24] Old art. repealed by federal statute of 23 Aug. 1976. New text inserted by federal statute of 21 Dec. 1992.

which, under article 23, the Bundestag enjoys as against the Federal Government.

Article 45a[25] (Committees on Foreign Affairs and Defence)

(1)[26] The Bundestag shall appoint a Committee on Foreign Affairs and a Committee on Defence.

(2) The Committee on Defence shall also have the rights of a committee of investigation. Upon the motion of one quarter of its members it shall have the duty to make a specific matter the subject of investigation.

(3) Paragraph (1) of Article 44 shall not apply to defence matters.

Article 45b[27] (Defence Commissioner of the Bundestag)

A Defence Commissioner of the Bundestag shall be appointed to safeguard the basic rights and to assist the Bundestag in exercising parliamentary control. Details shall be regulated by a federal statute.

Article 45c (Petitions Committee)

(1) The Bundestag shall appoint a Petitions Committee to deal with requests and complaints addressed to the Bundestag pursuant to Article 17.

(2) The powers of the Committee to consider complaints shall be regulated by a federal statute.

Article 46 (Indemnity and immunity of deputies)

(1) A deputy may not at any time be subjected to court proceedings or disciplinary action or otherwise called to account outside the Bundestag for a vote cast or a statement made by him in the Bundestag or in any of its committees. This shall not apply to defamatory insults.

(2) A deputy may not be called to account or arrested for a

---

[25] Inserted by federal statute of 19 Mar. 1956.
[26] Second sentence deleted by federal statute of 23 Aug. 1976.
[27] Inserted by federal statute of 15 July 1975.

punishable offence except by permission of the Bundestag, unless he is apprehended during commission of the offence or in the course of the following day.

(3) The permission of the Bundestag shall also be necessary for any other restriction of the personal liberty of a deputy or for the initiation of proceedings against a deputy under Article 18.

(4) Any criminal proceedings or any proceedings under Article 18 against a deputy, any detention or any other restriction of his personal liberty shall be suspended at the demand of the Bundestag.

Article 47 (Right of deputies to refuse to give evidence)

Deputies may refuse to give evidence concerning persons who have confided facts to them in their capacity as deputies, or to whom they have confided facts in such capacity, as well as evidence concerning these facts themselves. To the extent that this right of refusal to give evidence exists, no seizure of documents shall be permissible.

Article 48 (Entitlements of deputies)

(1) Any candidate for election to the Bundestag shall be entitled to the leave necessary for his election campaign.

(2) No one may be prevented from accepting and exercising the office of deputy. He may not be given notice of dismissal nor dismissed from employment on this ground.

(3) Deputies shall be entitled to adequate remuneration ensuring their independence. They shall be entitled to the free use of all state-owned means of transport. Details shall be regulated by a federal statute.

Article 49[28] (Repealed)

[28] Amended by federal statute of 19 Mar. 1956; repealed by federal statute of 23 Aug. 1976.

IV. THE FEDERAL COUNCIL (BUNDESRAT)

Article 50[29] (Functions)

The Länder shall participate through the Bundesrat in the legislation and administration of the Federation and in the affairs of the European Union.

Article 51 (Composition)

(1) The Bundesrat shall consist of members of the Land governments which appoint and recall them. Other members of such governments may act as substitutes.

(2)[30] Each Land shall have at least three votes; Länder with more than two million inhabitants shall have four, Länder with more than six million inhabitants five, and Länder with more than seven million inhabitants six votes.

(3) Each Land may delegate as many members as it has votes. The votes of each Land may be cast only as a block vote and only by members present or their substitutes.

Article 52 (President, rules of procedure)

(1) The Bundesrat shall elect its President for one year.

(2) The President shall convene the Bundesrat. He shall convene the Bundesrat where delegates from at least two Länder or the Federal Government so demand.

(3) The Bundesrat shall take its decisions with at least the majority of its votes. It shall draw up its rules of procedure. Its meetings shall be public. The public may be excluded.

(3a)[31] For European Union affairs the Bundesrat may form a Europe Chamber whose decisions count as those of the Bundesrat; article 51(2) and (3) second sentence applies *mutatis mutandis.*

(4) Other members of or persons commissioned by Land governments may serve on the committees of the Bundesrat.

---

[29] Amended by the federal statute of 21 Dec. 1992.
[30] Amended by the Unification Treaty of 31 Aug. 1990 and federal statute of 23 Sept. 1990.
[31] Amended by the federal statute of 21 Dec. 1992.

Article 53 (Presence of members of the Federal Government)

The members of the Federal Government shall have the right, and on demand the duty, to attend the meetings of the Bundesrat and of its committees. They shall have the right to be heard at any time. The Bundesrat shall be kept informed by the Federal Government as regards the conduct of affairs.

IVa.[32] THE JOINT COMMITTEE

Article 53a (Composition, rules of procedure, right to information)

(1) Two thirds of the members of the Joint Committee shall be deputies of the Bundestag and one third shall be members of the Bundesrat. The Bundestag shall delegate its deputies in proportion to the relative strength of its parliamentary groups; deputies shall not be members of the Federal Government. Each Land shall be represented by a Bundesrat member of its choice; these members shall not be bound by instructions. The establishment of the Joint Committee and its procedures shall be regulated by rules of procedure to be adopted by the Bundestag and requiring the consent of the Bundesrat.

(2) The Federal Government shall inform the Joint Committee about its plans in respect of a state of defence. The rights of the Bundestag and its committees under paragraph (1) of Article 43 shall remain unaffected by the provision of this paragraph.

V. THE FEDERAL PRESIDENT

Article 54 (Election)

(1) The Federal President shall be elected, without debate, by the Federal Convention (*Bundesversammlung*). Every German who is entitled to vote in Bundestag elections and has attained the age of forty years shall be eligible for election.

(2) The term of office of the Federal President shall last five

---

[32] Inserted by federal statute of 24 June 1968.

years. Re-election for a consecutive term shall be permitted only once.

(3) The Federal Convention shall consist of the members of the Bundestag and an equal number of members elected by the parliaments of the Länder according to the principles of proportional representation.

(4) The Federal Convention shall meet not later than thirty days before the expiration of the term of office of the Federal President or, in the case of premature termination, not later than thirty days after that date. It shall be convened by the President of the Bundestag.

(5) After the expiration of a legislative term, the period specified in the first sentence of paragraph (4) of this Article shall begin with the first meeting of the Bundestag.

(6) The person receiving the votes of the majority of the members of the Federal Convention shall be elected. Where such majority is not obtained by any candidate in two ballots, the candidate who receives the largest number of votes in the next ballot shall be elected.

(7) Details shall be regulated by a federal statute.

Article 55 (Incompatibilities)

(1) The Federal President may not be a member of the government nor of a legislative body of the Federation or of a Land.

(2) The Federal President may not hold any other salaried office, nor engage in an occupation, nor belong to the management or the board of directors of an enterprise carried on for profit.

Article 56 (Oath of office)

On assuming his office, the Federal President shall take the following oath before the assembled members of the Bundestag and the Bundesrat:

I swear that I will dedicate my efforts to the well-being of the German people, enhance their benefits, avert harm from them, uphold and defend the Basic Law and the statutes of the Federation, fulfil my duties conscientiously, and do justice to all. So help me God.

The oath may also be taken without religious affirmation.

Article 57 (Representation)

Where the Federal President is prevented from acting, or where his office falls prematurely vacant, his powers shall be exercised by the President of the Bundesrat.

Article 58 (Countersignature)

Orders and directions of the Federal President shall require, for their validity, the countersignature of the Federal Chancellor or the appropriate Federal Minister. This shall not apply to the appointment and dismissal of the Federal Chancellor, the dissolution of the Bundestag under Article 63 and a request made under paragraph (3) of Article 69.

Article 59 (Authority to represent the Federation in its international relations)

(1) The Federal President shall represent the Federation in its international relations. He shall conclude treaties with foreign states on behalf of the Federation. He shall accredit and receive envoys.

(2) Treaties which regulate the political relations of the Federation or relate to matters of federal legislation shall require the consent or participation, in the form of a federal statute, of the bodies competent in any specific case for such federal legislation. As regards administrative agreements, the provisions concerning the federal administration shall apply *mutatis mutandis*.

Article 59a[33] (Repealed)

Article 60 (Appointment and dismissal of federal judges, federal civil servants and soldiers; right of pardon)

(1)[34] The Federal President shall appoint and dismiss the federal judges, the federal civil servants, the officers and non-commissioned officers, except as may otherwise be provided for by statute.

[33] Inserted by federal statute of 19 Mar. 1956 and repealed by federal statute of 24 June 1968.

[34] As amended by federal statute of 19 Mar. 1956.

(2) He shall exercise the right of pardon in individual cases on behalf of the Federation.

(3) He may delegate these powers to other authorities.

(4) Paragraphs (2) to (4) of Article 46 shall apply *mutatis mutandis* to the Federal President.

Article 61 (Impeachment before the Federal Constitutional Court)

(1) The Bundestag or the Bundesrat may impeach the Federal President before the Federal Constitutional Court for wilful violation of this Basic Law or any other federal statute. The motion of impeachment shall be tabled by at least one quarter of the members of the Bundestag or one quarter of the votes of the Bundesrat. A decision to impeach shall require a majority of two thirds of the members of the Bundestag or of two thirds of the votes of the Bundesrat. The impeachment shall be pleaded by a person commissioned by the impeaching body.

(2) Where the Federal Constitutional Court finds the Federal President guilty of a wilful violation of this Basic Law or of another federal statute, it may declare him to have forfeited his office. After impeachment, it may issue an interim order preventing the Federal President from exercising his functions.

VI. THE FEDERAL GOVERNMENT

Article 62 (Composition)

The Federal Government shall consist of the Federal Chancellor (*Bundeskanzler*) and the Federal Ministers.

Article 63 (Election and appointment of the Federal Chancellor)

(1) The Federal Chancellor shall be elected, without debate, by the Bundestag upon the proposal of the Federal President.

(2) The person obtaining the votes of the majority of the members of the Bundestag shall be elected. The person elected shall be appointed by the Federal President.

(3) Where the person proposed is not elected, the Bundestag

may elect within fourteen days of the ballot a Federal Chancellor by more than one half of its members.

(4) Where no candidate has been elected within this period, a new ballot shall take place without delay in which the person obtaining the largest number of votes shall be elected. Where the person elected has obtained the votes of the majority of the members of the Bundestag, the Federal President shall appoint him within seven days of the election. Where the person elected did not obtain such a majority, the Federal President shall, within seven days, either appoint him or dissolve the Bundestag.

Article 64 (Appointment of Federal Ministers)

(1) The Federal Ministers shall be appointed and dismissed by the Federal President upon the proposal of the Federal Chancellor.

(2) The Federal Chancellor and the Federal Ministers, on assuming office, shall take before the Bundestag the oath provided for in Article 56.

Article 65 (Powers exercised in the Federal Government)

The Federal Chancellor shall determine and be responsible for the general policy guidelines. Within the limits set by these guidelines, each Federal Minister shall conduct the affairs of his department independently and on his own responsibility. The Federal Government shall decide on differences of opinion between Federal Ministers. The Federal Chancellor shall conduct the affairs of the Federal Government in accordance with rules of procedure adopted by it and approved by the Federal President.

Article 65a[35] (Power of command over the Armed Forces)

Power of command in respect of the Armed Forces shall be vested in the Federal Minister of Defence.

---

[35] Inserted by federal statute of 19 Mar. 1956 and amended by federal statute of 24 June 1968.

Article 66 (Incompatibilities)

The Federal Chancellor and the Federal Ministers may not hold any other salaried office, nor engage in an occupation, nor belong to the management or, without the consent of the Bundestag, to the board of directors of an enterprise carried on for profit.

Article 67 (Constructive vote of no confidence)

(1) The Bundestag can express its lack of confidence in the Federal Chancellor only by electing a successor with the majority of its members and by requesting the Federal President to dismiss the Federal Chancellor. The Federal President shall comply with the request and appoint the person elected.

(2) Forty-eight hours shall elapse between the motion and the election.

Article 68 (Vote of confidence, dissolution of the Bundestag)

(1) Where a motion of the Federal Chancellor for a vote of confidence is not carried by the majority of the members of the Bundestag, the Federal President may, upon the proposal of the Federal Chancellor, dissolve the Bundestag within twenty-one days. The right of dissolution shall lapse as soon as the Bundestag elects another Federal Chancellor with the majority of its members.

(2) Forty-eight hours shall elapse between the motion and the vote thereon.

Article 69 (Deputy Federal Chancellor, tenure of office of members of the Federal Government)

(1) The Federal Chancellor shall appoint a Federal Minister as his deputy.

(2) The tenure of office of the Federal Chancellor or a Federal Minister shall end in any event on the assembly of a new Bundestag; the tenure of office of a Federal Minister shall also end on any other termination of the Federal Chancellor's tenure of office.

(3) At the request of the Federal President the Federal Chancellor, or at the request of the Federal Chancellor or of the Federal President a Federal Minister, shall be bound to continue to manage the affairs of his office until the appointment of a successor.

VII. LEGISLATIVE POWERS OF THE FEDERATION

Article 70 (Legislation of the Federation and the Länder)

(1) The Länder shall have the right to legislate in so far as this Basic Law does not confer legislative power on the Federation.

(2) The division of competence between the Federation and the Länder shall be determined by the provisions of this Basic Law concerning exclusive and concurrent legislative powers.

Article 71 (Exclusive legislative power of the Federation, definition)

In matters within the exclusive legislative power of the Federation, the Länder shall have power to legislate only where and to the extent that they are given such explicit authorization by a federal statute.

Article 72 (Concurrent legislative power of the Federation, definition)

(1) In matters within the concurrent legislative power, the Länder shall have power to legislate as long as and to the extent that the Federation does not exercise its right to legislate.

(2) The Federation shall have the right to legislate in these matters to the extent that a need for regulation by federal legislation exists because:

1. a matter cannot be effectively regulated by the legislation of individual Länder, or
2. the regulation of a matter by a Land statute might prejudice the interests of other Länder or of the whole body politic, or
3. the maintenance of legal or economic unity, especially the maintenance of uniformity of living conditions beyond the territory of any one Land, necessitates such regulation.

Article 73 (Exclusive legislative power, catalogue)

The Federation shall have exclusive power to legislate in the
following matters:

1.[36] foreign affairs and defence, including the protection of
    the civilian population;
2. citizenship in the Federation;
3. freedom of movement, passport matters, immigration,
    emigration and extradition;
4. currency, money and coinage, weights and measures, as
    well as the determination of standards of time;
5. the unity of the customs and trading area, treaties on
    commerce and on navigation, the freedom of move-
    ment of goods, and the exchange of goods and pay-
    ments with foreign countries, including customs and
    other frontier protection;
6. federal railroads and air transport;
7. postal and telecommunication services;
8. the legal status of persons employed by the Federation
    and by federal corporate bodies under public law;
9. industrial property rights, copyrights and publishing
    law;
10.[37] co-operation between the Federation and the Länder
    concerning
    (a) criminal police,
    (b) protection of the free democratic basic order, of the
        existence and the security of the Federation or of a
        Land (protection of the constitution) and
    (c) protection against activities in the federal territory
        which, through the use of force or actions in prepa-
        ration for the use of force, endanger the foreign
        interests of the Federal Republic of Germany,
    as well as the establishment of a Federal Criminal
    Police Office and the international control of crime;
11. statistics for federal purposes.

---

[36] As amended by federal statutes of 26 Mar. 1954 and 24 June 1968.
[37] As amended by federal statute of 28 July 1972.

Article 74 (Concurrent legislation, catalogue)

Concurrent legislative powers shall cover the following matters:

1. civil law, criminal law and execution of sentences, the organization and procedure of courts, the legal profession, notaries and legal advice (*Rechtsberatung*);
2. registration of births, deaths and marriages;
3. the law of association and assembly;
4. the law relating to residence and settlement of aliens;
4a.[38] the law relating to weapons and explosives;
5. the protection of German cultural assets against migration abroad;
6. refugee and expellee matters;
7. public welfare;
8. citizenship in the Länder;
9. war damage and reparations;
10.[39] benefits to war-disabled persons and to dependants of those killed in the war as well as assistance to former prisoners of war;
10a.[40] war graves of soldiers, graves of other victims of war and of victims of despotism;
11. the law relating to economic matters (mining, industry, supply of power, crafts, trades, commerce, banking, stock exchanges and private insurance);
11a.[41] the production and utilization of nuclear energy for peaceful purposes, the construction and operation of installations serving such purposes, protection against hazards arising from the release of nuclear energy or from ionizing radiation, and the disposal of radioactive substances;
12. labour law, including the legal organization of enterprises, protection of workers, employment exchanges and agencies, as well as social insurance, including unemployment insurance;

[38] Inserted by federal statute of 28 July 1972 and amended by federal statute of 23 Aug. 1976.
[39] As amended by federal statute of 16 June 1965.
[40] Inserted by federal statute of 16 June 1965.
[41] Inserted by federal statute of 23 Dec. 1959.

13.[42]   the regulation of educational and training grants
and the promotion of scientific research;

14.   the law regarding expropriation, to the extent that
matters enumerated in Articles 73 and 74 are concerned;

15.   transfer of land, natural resources and means of production to public ownership or other forms of collective enterprise for the public benefit;

16.   prevention of the abuse of economic power;

17.   promotion of agricultural production and forestry,
securing the supply of food, the importation and
exportation of agricultural and forestry products,
deep-sea and coastal fishing, and preservation of the
coasts;

18.   real estate transactions, land law and matters concerning agricultural leases, as well as housing, settlement and homestead matters;

19.   measures against human and animal diseases that
are communicable or otherwise endanger public
health, admission to the medical profession and to
other medical occupations or practices, as well as
trade in medicines, curatives, narcotics and poisons;

19a.[43] the economic viability of hospitals and the regulation of hospitalization fees;

20.[44]   protection regarding the marketing of food, drink
and tobacco, of necessities of life, fodder, agricultural and forest seeds and seedlings, and protection
of plants against diseases and pests, as well as the
protection of animals;

21.   ocean and coastal shipping, as well as sea marks,
inland navigation, meteorological services, sea routes,
and inland waterways used for general traffic;

22.[45]   road traffic, motor transport, construction and maintenance of long-distance highways, as well as the collection of charges for the use of public highways by
vehicles and the allocation of revenue therefrom;

[42] As amended by federal statute of 12 May 1969.
[43] Inserted by federal statute of 12 May 1969.
[44] As amended by federal statute of 18 Mar. 1971.
[45] As amended by federal statute of 12 May 1969.

23.   non-federal railroads, except mountain railroads;
24.[46] waste disposal, air pollution control and noise abatement.

Article 74a[47] (Concurrent legislative power of the Federation, remuneration and pensions of members of the public service)

(1) Concurrent legislative power shall further extend to the remuneration and pensions of members of the public service whose service and loyalty are governed by public law, in so far as the Federation does not have exclusive power to legislate pursuant to item 8 of Article 73.

(2) Federal statutes enacted pursuant to paragraph (1) of this Article shall require the consent of the Bundesrat.

(3) Federal statutes enacted pursuant to item 8 of Article 73 shall likewise require the consent of the Bundesrat, in so far as they prescribe for the structure and assessment of remuneration and pensions, including the rating of posts, criteria or minimum or maximum rates other than those provided for in federal statutes enacted pursuant to paragraph (1) of this Article.

(4) Paragraphs (1) and (2) of this Article shall apply *mutatis mutandis* to the remuneration and pensions of judges in the Länder. Paragraph (3) of this Article shall apply *mutatis mutandis* to statutes enacted pursuant to paragraph (1) of Article 98.

Article 75[48] (Power of the Federation to pass framework legislation, catalogue)

Subject to the conditions laid down in Article 72, the Federation shall have the right to enact framework legislation concerning:

1.[49]   the legal status of persons in the public service of the Länder, communes or other corporate bodies under public law, in so far as Article 74a does not provide otherwise;
1a.[50] the general principles governing higher education;

---

[46] As amended by federal statute of 12 Apr. 1972.
[47] Inserted by federal statute of 18 Mar. 1971.
[48] As amended by federal statute of 12 May 1969.
[49] As amended by federal statute of 18 Mar. 1971.
[50] Inserted by federal statute of 12 May 1969.

2.   the general legal status of the press and the film industry;
3.   hunting, nature conservation and landscape management;
4.   land distribution, regional planning and the management of water resources;
5.   matters relating to the registration of residence or domicile (*Meldewesen*) and to identity cards.

Article 76 (Bills)

(1) Bills shall be introduced in the Bundestag by the Federal Government or by members of the Bundestag or by the Bundesrat.

(2)[51] Bills of the Federal Government shall first be submitted to the Bundesrat. The Bundesrat shall be entitled to state its position on such bills within six weeks. A bill which, on submission to the Bundesrat, is exceptionally specified by the Federal Government to be particularly urgent may be submitted by the latter to the Bundestag three weeks later, even though the Federal Government may not yet have received the statement of the Bundesrat's position; upon receipt, such statement shall be transmitted to the Bundestag by the Federal Government without delay.

(3)[52] Bills of the Bundesrat shall be submitted to the Bundestag by the Federal Government within three months. In doing so, the Federal Government shall state its own view.

Article 77 (Legislative procedure)

(1) Federal statutes shall be enacted by the Bundestag. Upon their adoption they shall, without delay, be transmitted to the Bundesrat by the President of the Bundestag.

(2)[53] The Bundesrat may, within three weeks of the receipt of the adopted bill, demand that a committee for joint consideration of bills, composed of members of the Bundestag and members of the Bundesrat, be convened. The composition and the procedure of this committee shall be regulated by rules of procedure to be adopted by the Bundestag and requiring the consent of the

[51] As amended by federal statute of 15 Nov. 1968.
[52] As amended by federal statute of 17 July 1969.
[53] As amended by federal statute of 15 Nov. 1968.

Bundesrat. The members of the Bundesrat on this committee shall not be bound by instructions. Where the consent of the Bundesrat is required for a bill to become a statute, the Bundestag and the Federal Government may also demand that the committee be convened. Should the committee propose any amendment to the adopted bill, the Bundestag shall again vote on the bill.

(3) In so far as the consent of the Bundesrat is not required for a bill to become a statute, the Bundesrat may, when the proceedings under paragraph (2) of this Article are completed, enter an objection within two weeks against a bill adopted by the Bundestag. The period for entering an objection shall begin, in the case of the last sentence of paragraph (2) of this Article, on the receipt of the bill as readopted by the Bundestag, and in all other cases on the receipt of a communication from the chairman of the committee provided for in paragraph (2) of this Article to the effect that the committee's proceedings have been concluded.

(4) Where the objection was adopted with the majority of the votes of the Bundesrat, it can be rejected by a decision of the majority of the members of the Bundestag. Where the Bundesrat adopted the objection with a majority of at least two thirds of its votes, its rejection by the Bundestag shall require a majority of two thirds, including at least the majority of the members of the Bundestag.

Article 78 (Passage of federal statutes)

A bill adopted by the Bundestag shall become a statute where the Bundesrat consents to it, or fails to make a demand pursuant to paragraph (2) of Article 77, or fails to enter an objection within the period stipulated in paragraph (3) of Article 77, or withdraws such objection, or where the objection is overridden by the Bundestag.

Article 79 (Amendment of the Basic Law)

(1) This Basic Law can be amended only by statutes which expressly amend or supplement the text thereof. In respect of international treaties, the subject of which is a peace settlement, the preparation of a peace settlement or the phasing out of an

occupation regime, or which are intended to serve the defence of the Federal Republic, it shall be sufficient, for the purpose of clarifying that the provisions of this Basic Law do not preclude the conclusion and entry into force of such treaties, to effect a supplementation of the text of this Basic Law confined to such clarification.[54]

(2) Any such statute shall require the consent of two thirds of the members of the Bundestag and two thirds of the votes of the Bundesrat.

(3) Amendments of this Basic Law affecting the division of the Federation into Länder, the participation on principle of the Länder in legislation, or the basic principles laid down in Articles 1 and 20 shall be inadmissible.

Article 80 (Issue of ordinances)

(1) The Federal Government, a Federal Minister or the Land governments may be authorized by statute to issue ordinances (*Rechtsverordnungen*). The content, purpose and scope of the authorization so conferred shall be laid down in the statute concerned. This legal basis shall be stated in the ordinance. Where a statute provides that such authorization may be delegated, such delegation shall require another ordinance.

(2) The consent of the Bundesrat shall be required, unless otherwise provided by federal legislation, for ordinances issued by the Federal Government or a Federal Minister concerning basic rules for the use of facilities of the federal railroads and of postal and telecommunication services, or charges thereof, or concerning the construction and operation of railroads, as well as for ordinances issued pursuant to federal statutes that require the consent of the Bundesrat or that are executed by the Länder as agents of the Federation or as matters of their own concern.

Article 80a[55] (Application of legal provisions in a state of tension)

(1) Where this Basic Law or a federal statute on defence, including the protection of the civilian population, stipulates that legal provisions may only be applied in accordance with this

---

[54] Second sentence inserted by federal statute of 26 Mar. 1954.
[55] Inserted by federal statute of 24 June 1968.

Article, their application shall, except in a state of defence, be admissible only after the Bundestag has determined that a state of tension (*Spannungsfall*) exists or where it has specifically approved such application. In respect of the cases mentioned in the first sentence of paragraph (5) and the second sentence of paragraph (6) of Article 12a, such determination of a state of tension and such specific approval shall require a two-thirds majority of the votes cast.

(2) Any measures taken by virtue of legal provisions enacted under paragraph (1) of this Article shall be revoked whenever the Bundestag so demands.

(3) In derogation of paragraph (1) of this Article, the application of such legal provisions shall also be admissible by virtue of and in accordance with a decision taken with the consent of the Federal Government by an international body within the framework of a treaty of alliance. Any measures taken pursuant to this paragraph shall be revoked whenever the Bundestag so demands with the majority of its members.

Article 81 (State of legislative emergency)

(1) Should, in the circumstances of Article 68, the Bundestag not be dissolved, the Federal President may, at the request of the Federal Government and with the consent of the Bundesrat, declare a state of legislative emergency with respect to a bill, where the Bundestag rejects the bill although the Federal Government has declared it to be urgent. The same shall apply where a bill has been rejected although the Federal Chancellor had combined with it the motion under Article 68.

(2) Where, after a state of legislative emergency has been declared, the Bundestag again rejects the bill or adopts it in a version stated to be unacceptable to the Federal Government, the bill shall be deemed to have become a statute to the extent that the Bundesrat consents to it. The same shall apply where the bill is not passed by the Bundestag within four weeks of its reintroduction.

(3) During the term of office of a Federal Chancellor, any other bill rejected by the Bundestag may become a statute in accordance with paragraphs (1) and (2) of this Article within a period of six months after the first declaration of a state of leg-

islative emergency. After the expiration of this period, a further declaration of a state of legislative emergency shall be inadmissible during the term of office of the same Federal Chancellor.

(4) This Basic Law may not be amended nor repealed nor suspended in whole or in part by a statute enacted pursuant to paragraph (2) of this Article.

Article 82 (Promulgation and effective date of legal provisions)

(1) Statutes enacted in accordance with the provisions of this Basic Law shall, after countersignature, be signed by the Federal President and promulgated in the *Federal Law Gazette.* Ordinances shall be signed by the agency which issues them and, unless otherwise provided by the statute, shall be promulgated in the *Federal Law Gazette (Bundesgesetzblatt).*

(2) Every statute or every ordinance should specify its effective date. In the absence of such a provision, it shall take effect on the fourteenth day after the end of the day on which the *Federal Law Gazette* containing it was published.

VIII. THE EXECUTION OF FEDERAL STATUTES AND THE FEDERAL ADMINISTRATION

Article 83 (Distribution of competences between the Federation and the Länder)

The Länder shall execute federal statutes as matters of their own concern in so far as this Basic Law does not otherwise provide or permit.

Article 84 (Land execution and Federal Government supervision)

(1) Where the Länder execute federal statutes as matters of their own concern, they shall provide for the establishment of the requisite authorities and the regulation of administrative procedures in so far as federal statutes consented to by the Bundesrat do not otherwise provide.

(2) The Federal Government may, with the consent of the Bundesrat, issue general administrative rules.

(3) The Federal Government shall exercise supervision to ensure that the Länder execute the federal statutes in accordance with applicable law. For this purpose the Federal Government may send commissioners to the highest Land authorities and, with their consent or, where such consent is refused, with the consent of the Bundesrat, also to subordinate authorities.

(4) Should any shortcomings which the Federal Government has found to exist in the execution of federal statutes in the Länder not be corrected, the Bundesrat shall decide, at the request of the Federal Government or the Land concerned, whether such Land has violated the law. The decision of the Bundesrat may be challenged in the Federal Constitutional Court.

(5) With a view to the execution of federal statutes, the Federal government may be authorized by a federal statute requiring the consent of the Bundesrat to issue individual instructions for particular cases. They shall be addressed to the highest Land authorities unless the Federal Government considers the matter urgent.

Article 85 (Execution by the Länder as agents of the Federation)

(1) Where the Länder execute federal statutes as agents of the Federation, the establishment of the requisite authorities shall remain the concern of the Länder, except in so far as federal statutes consented to by the Bundesrat otherwise provide.

(2) The Federal Government may, with the consent of the Bundesrat, issue general administrative rules. It may regulate the uniform training of civil servants (*Beamte*) and other salaried public employees (*Angestellte*). The heads of authorities at the intermediate level shall be appointed with its agreement.

(3) The Land authorities shall be subject to the instructions of the competent highest federal authorities. Such instructions shall be addressed to the highest Land authorities unless the Federal Government considers the matter urgent. Execution of the instructions shall be ensured by the highest Land authorities.

(4) Federal supervision shall cover the lawfulness and appropriateness of execution. The Federal Government may, for this purpose, require the submission of reports and documents and send commissioners to all authorities.

Article 86 (Direct federal administration)

Where the Federation executes statutes by means of direct federal administration or by federal corporate bodies or institutions under public law, the Federal Government shall, in so far as the statute concerned contains no special provision, issue pertinent general administrative rules. The Federal Government shall provide for the establishment of the requisite authorities in so far as the statute concerned does not otherwise provide.

Article 87[56] (Matters for direct federal administration)

(1) The foreign service, the federal finance administration, the federal railroads, the federal postal service and, in accordance with the provisions of Article 89, the administration of federal waterways and of shipping shall be conducted as matters of direct federal administration with their own administrative substructures.

Federal legislation may be enacted to establish Federal Border Guard authorities and central offices for police information and communications, for the criminal police and for the compilation of data for the purposes of protection of the constitution and of protection against activities on federal territory which, through the use of force or acts preparatory to the use of force, endanger the foreign interests of the Federal Republic of Germany.

(2) Social insurance institutions whose sphere of competence extends beyond the territory of one Land shall be administered as federal corporate bodies under public law.

(3) In addition, independent federal higher authorities as well as new federal corporate bodies and institutions under public law may be established by federal legislation for matters on which the Federation has the power to legislate. Where new functions arise for the Federation in matters on which it has the power to legislate, federal authorities at the intermediate and lower levels may be established, in case of urgent need, with the consent of the Bundesrat and of the majority of the members of the Bundestag.[57]

---

[56] Inserted by federal statute of 19 Mar. 1956 and amended by federal statute of 24 June 1968.

[57] As amended by federal statute of 28 July 1972.

Article 87a[58] (Establishment and powers of the Armed Forces)

(1) The Federation shall establish Armed Forces for defence purposes. Their numerical strength and general organizational structure shall be shown in the budget.

(2) Apart from defence, the Armed Forces may only be used in so far as explicitly permitted by this Basic Law.

(3) While a state of defence or a state of tension exists, the Armed Forces shall have the power to protect civilian property and discharge functions of traffic control in so far as this is necessary for the performance of their defence mission. Moreover, the Armed Forces may, when a state of defence or a state of tension exists, be entrusted with the protection of civilian property also in support of police measures; in this event the Armed Forces shall cooperate with the competent authorities.

(4) In order to avert any imminent danger to the existence or to the free democratic basic order of the Federation or a Land, the Federal Government may, should conditions as envisaged in paragraph (2) of Article 91 obtain and the police forces and the Federal Border Guard be inadequate, use the Armed Forces to support the police and the Federal Border Guard in the protection of civilian property and in combating organized and militarily armed insurgents. Any such use of the Armed Forces shall be discontinued whenever the Bundestag or the Bundesrat so demands.

Article 87b[59] (Administration of the Federal Armed Forces)

(1) The Federal Armed Forces Administration shall be conducted as a direct federal administration with its own administrative substructure. Its function shall be to administer personnel matters and directly to meet the material requirements of the Armed Forces. Tasks connected with benefits to disabled persons or with construction work shall not be assigned to the Federal Armed Forces Administration except by federal legislation requiring the consent of the Bundesrat. Such consent shall also be required for any statutes to the extent that they empower the Federal Armed Forces Administration to interfere with rights of

---

[58] Inserted by federal statute of 19 Mar. 1956.
[59] Inserted by federal statute of 19 Mar. 1956,

third parties; this shall, however, not apply in the case of statutes concerning personnel matters.

(2) Moreover, federal statutes concerning defence, including recruitment for military service and protection of the civilian population, may, with the consent of the Bundesrat, provide that they shall be executed, wholly or in part, either by means of direct federal administration having its own administrative substructure or by the Länder acting as agents of the Federation. Where such statutes are executed by the Länder acting as agents of the Federation, they may, with the consent of the Bundesrat, provide that the powers vested in the Federal Government or appropriate highest federal authorities by virtue of Article 85 shall be transferred wholly or in part to higher federal authorities; in such an event it may be enacted that these authorities shall not require the consent of the Bundesrat in issuing general administrative rules as referred to in the first sentence of paragraph (2) of Article 85.

Article 87c[60] (Administration in the field of nuclear energy)

Statutes enacted under item 11a of Article 74 may, with the consent of the Bundesrat, provide that they shall be executed by the Länder acting as agents of the Federation.

Article 87d[61] (Aviation administration)

(1) Aviation administration shall be conducted as a direct federal administration. Its public- or private-law form of organization shall be settled by a Federal statute.

(2) Through federal legislation requiring the consent of the Bundesrat, functions of aviation administration may be transferred to the Länder acting as agents of the Federation.

Article 88[62] (Federal Bank)

The Federation shall establish a note-issuing and currency bank as the Federal Bank (Bundesbank). Its functions and competences

[60] Inserted by federal statute of 23 Dec. 1959.
[61] Inserted by federal statute of 6 Feb. 1961 and amended by federal statute of 14 July 1992.
[62] Amended by federal statute of 21 Dec. 1992.

may within the framework of the European Union be transferred to a European Central Bank which is independent and bound to the primary aim of ensuring price stability.

Article 89 (Federal waterways)

(1) The Federation shall be the owner of the former Reich waterways.

(2) The Federation shall administer the federal waterways through its own authorities. It shall exercise those governmental functions relating to inland shipping which extend beyond the territory of one Land, and those governmental functions relating to maritime shipping which are conferred on it by statute. Upon request, the Federation may transfer the administration of federal waterways, in so far as they lie within the territory of one Land, to that Land as its agent. Where a waterway touches the territories of several Länder, the Federation may delegate one Land to be its agent where so requested by the Länder concerned.

(3) In the administration, development and new construction of waterways, the needs of land improvement and of water economy shall be safeguarded in agreement with the Länder.

Article 90 (Federal highways)

(1) The Federation shall be the owner of the former Reich motorways (*Reichsautobahnen*) and Reich highways.

(2) The Länder, or such self-governing corporate bodies as are competent under Land law, shall administer as agents of the Federation the federal motorways and other federal highways used for long-distance traffic.

(3) At the request of a Land, the Federation may place federal motorways and other federal highways used for long-distance traffic under direct federal administration in so far as they lie within the territory of that Land.

Article 91[63] (Internal emergency)

(1) In order to avert any imminent danger to the existence or to the free democratic basic order of the Federation or a Land, a

---

[63] As amended by federal statute of 24 June 1968.

Land may request the services of the police forces of other Länder, or of the forces[64] and facilities of other administrative authorities and of the Federal Border Guard.

(2) Where the Land where such danger is imminent is not itself willing or able to combat the danger, the Federal Government may place the police in that Land and the police forces of other Länder under its own instructions and use units of the Federal Border Guard. The order for this shall be rescinded after the removal of the danger or else at any time at the demand of the Bundesrat. Where the danger extends to a region larger than a Land, the Federal Government may, in so far as is necessary for effectively combating such danger, issue instructions to the Land governments; the first and second sentences of this paragraph shall not be affected by this provision.

VIIIa. JOINT TASKS[65]

Article 91a (Participation of the Federation by virtue of federal legislation)

(1) The Federation shall participate, in the following sectors, in the discharge of responsibilities of the Länder, provided that such responsibilities are important to society as a whole and that federal participation is necessary for the improvement of living conditions (joint tasks):

1.[66] extension and construction of institutions of higher education, including university clinics;
2. improvement of regional economic structures;
3. improvement of the agrarian structure and of coast preservation.

(2) Joint tasks shall be defined in detail by a federal statute requiring the consent of the Bundesrat. Such legislation should include general principles governing the discharge of joint tasks.

(3) Such legislation shall provide for the procedure and the institutions required for joint overall planning. The inclusion of a

---

[64] e.g. civil defence corps, emergency civil engineering corps, fire brigades.
[65] Inserted by federal statute of 12 May 1969.
[66] As amended by federal statute of 31 July 1970.

project in the overall planning shall require the consent of the Land in which it is to be carried out.

(4) In cases to which items 1 and 2 of paragraph (1) of this Article apply, the Federation shall meet one half of the expenditure in each Land. In cases to which item 3 of paragraph (1) of this Article applies, the Federation shall meet at least one half of the expenditure, and such proportion shall be the same for all the Länder. Details shall be regulated by statute. Provision of funds shall be subject to appropriation in the budgets of the Federation and the Länder.

(5) The Federal Government and the Bundesrat shall be informed about the execution of joint tasks, should they so demand.

Article 91b⁶⁷ (Co-operation of the Federation and the Länder by virtue of agreements made)

The Federation and the Länder may, pursuant to agreements, co-operate in educational planning and in the promotion of institutions and projects of scientific research of supraregional importance. The apportionment of costs shall be regulated in the relevant agreements.

IX. THE ADMINISTRATION OF JUSTICE

Article 92⁶⁸ (Court organization)

Judicial power shall be vested in the judges; it shall be exercised by the Federal Constitutional Court, by the federal courts provided for in this Basic Law, and by the courts of the Länder.

Article 93 (Federal Constitutional Court, jurisdiction)

(1) The Federal Constitutional Court shall decide:
1.   on the interpretation of this Basic Law in the event of disputes concerning the extent of the rights and duties of a highest federal body or of other parties concerned

---

⁶⁷ Inserted by federal statute of 12 May 1969.
⁶⁸ As amended by federal statute of 18 June 1968.

who have been vested with rights of their own by this Basic Law or by rules of procedure of a highest federal body;

2. in case of differences of opinion or doubts on the formal and material compatibility of federal law or Land law with this Basic Law, or on the compatibility of Land law with other federal law, at the request of the Federal Government, of a Land government or of one third of the Bundestag members;

3. in case of differences of opinion on the rights and duties of the Federation and the Länder, particularly in the execution of federal law by the Länder and in the exercise of federal supervision;

4. on other disputes involving public law, between the Federation and the Länder, between different Länder or within a Land, unless recourse to another court exists;

4a.[69] on complaints of unconstitutionality, which may be entered by any person who claims that one of his basic rights or one of his rights under paragraph (4) of Article 20 or under Article 33, 38, 101, 103 or 104 has been violated by public authority;

4b. on complaints of unconstitutionality entered by communes or associations of communes on the ground that their right to self-government under Article 28 has been violated by a statute other than a Land statute open to complaint to the respective Land constitutional court;

5. in the other cases provided for in this Basic Law.

(2) The Federal Constitutional Court shall also act in such other cases as are assigned to it by federal legislation.

Article 94 (Federal Constitutional Court, composition)

(1) The Federal Constitutional Court shall consist of federal judges and other members. Half of the members of the Federal Constitutional Court shall be elected by the Bundestag and half by the Bundesrat. They may not be members of the Bundestag,

---

[69] Inserted by federal statute of 29 Jan. 1969.

the Bundesrat, the Federal Government, nor of any of the corresponding bodies of a Land.

(2) The constitution and procedure of the Federal Constitutional Court shall be regulated by a federal statute which shall specify in what cases its decisions shall have the force of law.[70] Such statute may require that all other legal remedies must have been exhausted before a complaint of unconstitutionality can be entered, and may make provision for a special procedure as to admissibility.

Article 95[71] (Highest courts of justice of the Federation, Joint Panel)

(1) For the purposes of ordinary, administrative, fiscal, labour and social jurisdiction, the Federation shall establish as highest courts of justice the Federal Court of Justice, the Federal Administrative Court, the Federal Finance Court, the Federal Labour Court and the Federal Social Court.

(2) The judges of each of these courts shall be selected jointly by the competent Federal Minister and a committee for the selection of judges consisting of the competent Land ministers and an equal number of members elected by the Bundestag.

(3) In order to preserve uniformity of decisions, a Joint Panel (*Senat*) of the courts specified in paragraph (1) of this Article shall be set up. Details shall be regulated by a federal statute.

Article 96[72] (Other federal courts, exercise of federal jurisdiction by courts of the Länder)

(1) The Federation may establish a federal court for matters concerning industrial property rights.

(2) The Federation may establish military criminal courts for the Armed Forces as federal courts. They may only exercise criminal jurisdiction while a state of defence exists, and otherwise only over members of the Armed Forces serving abroad or on

[70] Inserted by federal statute of 29 Jan. 1969.
[71] As amended by federal statute of 18 June 1968.
[72] The original Art. 96 was repealed by federal statute of 18 June 1968. The present Art. 96 is the former Art. 96a as inserted by federal statute of 19 Mar. 1956 and amended by federal statutes of 6 Mar. 1961, 18 June 1968, 12 May 1969, and 26 Aug. 1969.

board warships. Details shall be regulated by federal statute. These courts shall be within the competence of the Federal Minister of Justice. Their full-time judges shall be persons qualified to hold judicial office.

(3) The highest court of justice for appeals from the courts mentioned in paragraphs (1) and (2) of this Article shall be the Federal Court of Justice.

(4)[73] The Federation may establish federal courts for disciplinary proceedings against, and for proceedings in pursuance of complaints by, persons in the federal public service.

(5)[74] In respect of criminal proceedings under paragraph (1) of Article 26 or involving the protection of the State, a federal statute requiring the consent of the Bundesrat may provide that Land courts shall exercise federal jurisdiction.

Article 96a

Article 97 (Independence of the judges)

(1) The judges shall be independent and subject only to the law.

(2) Judges appointed permanently on a full-time basis in established positions cannot, against their will, be dismissed or permanently or temporarily suspended from office or given a different posting or retired before the expiration of their term of office except by virtue of a judicial decision and only on the grounds and in the form provided for by statute. Legislation may set age limits for the retirement of judges appointed for life. In the event of changes in the structure of courts or in their districts, judges may be transferred to another court or removed from office, provided they retain their full salary.

Article 98[75] (Legal status of judges in the Federation and the Länder)

(1) The legal status of the federal judges shall be regulated by a special federal statute.

[73] As amended by federal statute of 12 May 1969.
[74] Inserted by federal statute of 26 Aug. 1969.
[75] As amended by federal statute of 18 Mar. 1971.

(2) Where a federal judge, in his official capacity or unofficially, infringes the principles of this Basic Law or the constitutional order of a Land, the Federal Constitutional Court may decide by a two-thirds majority, upon the request of the Bundestag, that the judge be given a different office or retired. In a case of intentional infringement, his dismissal may be ordered.

(3) The legal status of the judges in the Länder shall be regulated by special Land statutes. The Federation may enact outline provisions, in so far as paragraph (4) of Article 74a does not provide otherwise.

(4) The Länder may provide that the Land Minister of Justice together with a committee for the selection of judges shall decide on the appointment of judges in the Länder.

(5) The Länder may, in respect of Land judges, enact provisions corresponding to those of paragraph (2) of this Article. Existing Land constitutional law shall remain unaffected. The decision in a case of impeachment of a judge shall rest with the Federal Constitutional Court.

Article 99[76] (Decision by the Federal Constitutional Court and the highest courts of the Federation in disputes concerning Land law)

The decision on constitutional disputes within a Land may be assigned by Land legislation to the Federal Constitutional Court, and the decision at last instance in matters involving the application of a Land law to the highest courts of justice referred to in paragraph (1) of Article 95.

Article 100 (Compatibility of statutory law with the Basic Law)

(1) Where a court considers that a statute on whose validity the court's decision depends is unconstitutional, the proceedings shall be stayed, and a decision shall be obtained from the Land court with jurisdiction over constitutional disputes where the constitution of a Land is held to be violated, or from the Federal Constitutional Court where this Basic Law is held to be violated. This shall also apply where this Basic Law is held to be violated by Land law or where a Land statute is held to be incompatible with a federal statute.

[76] As amended by federal statute of 18 June 1968.

(2) Where, in the course of litigation, doubt exists whether a rule of public international law is an integral part of federal law and whether such rule directly creates rights and duties for the individual (Article 25), the court shall obtain a decision from the Federal Constitutional Court.

(3)[77] Where the constitutional court of a Land, in interpreting this Basic Law, intends to deviate from a decision of the Federal Constitutional Court or of the constitutional court of another Land, it shall obtain a decision from the Federal Constitutional Court.

Article 101 (Ban on extraordinary courts)

(1) Extraordinary courts shall be inadmissible. No one may be removed from the jurisdiction of his lawful judge.

(2) Courts for special fields of law may be established only by legislation.

Article 102 (Abolition of capital punishment)

Capital punishment shall be abolished.

Article 103 (Hearing in accordance with the law, ban on retroactive criminal legislation and on repeated punishment)

(1) In the courts everyone shall be entitled to a hearing in accordance with the law.

(2) An act can be punished only where it constituted a criminal offence under the law before the act was committed.

(3) No one may be punished for the same act more than once under general criminal legislation.

Article 104 (Legal guarantees in the event of deprivation of liberty)

(1) The liberty of the individual may be restricted only by virtue of a formal statute and only in compliance with the forms prescribed therein. Detained persons may not be subjected to mental or to physical ill-treatment.

---

[77] As amended by federal statute of 18 June 1968.

(2) Only judges may decide on the admissibility or continuation of any deprivation of liberty. Where such deprivation is not based on the order of a judge, a judicial decision shall be obtained without delay. The police may hold no one on their own authority in their own custody longer than the end of the day after the day of apprehension. Details shall be regulated by legislation.

(3) Any person provisionally detained on suspicion of having committed an offence shall be brought before a judge not later than the day following the day of apprehension; the judge shall inform him of the reasons for the detention, examine him and give him an opportunity to raise objections. The judge shall, without delay, either issue a warrant of arrest setting forth the reasons therefor or order his release from detention.

(4) A relative or a person enjoying the confidence of the person detained shall be notified without delay of any judicial decision imposing or ordering the continuation of his deprivation of liberty.

X. FINANCE

Article 104a[78] (Apportionment of expenditure between the Federation and the Länder)

(1) The Federation and the Länder shall separately meet the expenditure resulting from the discharge of their respective tasks in so far as this Basic Law does not provide otherwise

(2) Where the Länder act as agents of the Federation, the Federation shall meet the resulting expenditure.

(3) Federal statutes to be executed by the Länder and granting money payments may make provision for such payments to be met wholly or in part by the Federation. Where any such statute provides that the Federation shall meet one half of the expenditure or more, it shall be implemented by the Länder as agents of the Federation. Where any such statute provides that the Länder shall meet one quarter of the expenditure or more, it shall require the consent of the Bundesrat.

---

[78] Inserted by federal statute of 12 May 1969.

(4) The Federation may grant the Länder financial assistance for particularly important investments by the Länder or communes or associations of communes, provided that such investments are necessary to avert a disturbance of the overall economic equilibrium or to equalize differences of economic capacities within the federal territory or to promote economic growth. Details, especially concerning the kinds of investments to be promoted, shall be regulated by a federal statute requiring the consent of the Bundesrat or by administrative arrangements under the federal budget law.

(5) The Federation and the Länder shall meet the administrative expenditure incurred by their respective authorities and shall be responsible to each other for ensuring proper administration. Details shall be regulated by a federal statute requiring the consent of the Bundesrat.

Article 105 (Legislative powers)

(1) The Federation shall have exclusive power to legislate on customs duties and fiscal monopolies.

(2)[79] The Federation shall have concurrent power to legislate on all other taxes the revenue from which accrues to it wholly or in part or where the conditions provided for in paragraph (2) of Article 72 apply.

(2a)[80] The Länder shall have power to legislate on local excise taxes as long and in so far as they are not identical with taxes imposed by federal legislation.

(3) Federal laws relating to taxes the receipts from which accrue wholly or in part to the Länder or communes or associations of communes shall require the consent of the Bundesrat.

Article 106[81] (Apportionment of tax revenue)

(1) The yield of fiscal monopolies and the revenue from the following taxes shall accrue to the Federation:
1. customs duties;

---

[79] As amended by federal statute of 12 May 1969.
[80] Inserted by federal statute of 12 May 1969.
[81] As amended by federal statutes of 23 Dec. 1955, of 24 Dec. 1956, and of 12 May 1969.

2. excise taxes in so far as they do not accrue to the Länder pursuant to paragraph (2) of this Article, or jointly to the Federation and the Länder in accordance with paragraph (3) of this Article, or to the communes in accordance with paragraph (6) of this Article;
3. road freight tax;
4. capital transaction taxes, the insurance tax and the bill of exchange tax;
5. non-recurrent levies on property, and contributions imposed for the purpose of implementing the equalization of burdens (*Lastenausgleich*) legislation;[82]
6. income and corporation surtaxes;
7. charges imposed within the framework of the European Communities.

(2) Revenue from the following taxes shall accrue to the Länder:
1. wealth tax;
2. inheritance tax;
3. motor vehicle tax;
4. such taxes on transactions as do not accrue to the Federation pursuant to paragraph (1) of this Article or jointly to the Federation and the Länder pursuant to paragraph (3) of this Article;
5. beer tax;
6. gaming casinos levy.

(3) Revenue from income taxes, corporation taxes and turnover taxes shall accrue jointly to the Federation and the Länder (joint taxes) to the extent that the revenue from the income tax is not allocated to the communes pursuant to paragraph (5) of this Article. The Federation and the Länder shall share equally the revenues from income taxes and corporation taxes. The respective shares of the Federation and the Länder in the revenue from the turnover tax shall be determined by a federal statute requiring the consent of the Bundesrat. Such determination shall be based on the following principles:
1. The Federation and the Länder shall have an equal claim to coverage from current revenues of their respective necessary expenditures. The extent of such expenditures shall

---

[82] i.e. contributions imposed on persons having suffered no war damage and used to indemnify persons having suffered such damage.

be determined having due regard to financial planning for several years ahead.

2. The coverage requirements of the Federation and of the Länder shall be co-ordinated in such a way that a fair balance is struck, any overburdening of taxpayers precluded, and uniformity of living conditions in the federal territory ensured.

(4) The respective shares of the Federation and the Länder in the revenue from the turnover tax shall be apportioned anew whenever the relation of revenues to expenditures in the Federation develops substantially differently from that of the Länder. Where federal legislation imposes additional expenditures on or withdraws revenue from the Länder, the additional burden may be compensated for by allocation of federal grants under a federal statute requiring the consent of the Bundesrat, provided such additional burden is limited to a short period of time. Such statutes shall lay down the principles for calculating such grants and distributing them among the Länder.

(5) A share of the revenue from the income tax shall accrue to the communes, to be passed on by the Länder to their communes on the basis of income taxes paid by the inhabitants of the latter. Details shall be regulated by a federal statute requiring the consent of the Bundesrat. Such statute may provide that communes shall assess the rate which shall be applicable to this communal share.

(6) Revenue from taxes on real estate and on local industry and trade shall accrue to the communes; revenue from local excise taxes shall accrue to the communes or, as may be provided for by Land legislation, to associations of communes. Communes shall be authorized to assess, within the framework of the relevant statutes, the rates at which the taxes on real estate and on local industry and trade are levied locally. Where there are no communes in a Land, revenue from taxes on real estate and on local industry and trade as well as from local excise taxes shall accrue to the Land. The Federation and the Länder may participate by virtue of an apportionment, in the revenue from the tax on local industry and trade. Details regarding such apportionment shall be regulated by a federal statute requiring the consent of the Bundesrat. In accordance with Land legislation, taxes on real estate and on local industry and trade as well as the

communes' share of revenue from the income tax may be taken as a basis for calculating the amount of apportionment.

(7) An overall percentage, to be determined by Land legislation, of the Land share of total revenue from joint taxes shall accrue to the communes or associations of communes. In all other respects Land legislation shall determine whether and to what extent revenue from Land taxes shall accrue to communes or associations of communes.

(8) Where in individual Länder or communes or associations of communes the Federation causes special facilities to be provided which directly result in an increase of expenditure or a loss of revenue (special burden) to these Länder or communes or associations of communes, the Federation shall grant the necessary compensation where and in so far as such Länder or communes or associations of communes cannot reasonably be expected to bear such special burden. In granting such compensation, due account shall be taken of third-party indemnities and financial benefits accruing to the Länder or communes or associations of communes concerned as a result of provision for such facilities.

(9) For the purpose of this Article, revenues and expenditures of communes or associations of communes shall be deemed to be Land revenues and expenditures.

Article 107[83] (Financial equalization)

(1) Revenue from Land taxes and the Land share of revenue from income and corporation taxes shall accrue to the individual Länder to the extent that such taxes are collected by revenue authorities within their respective territories (local revenue). A federal statute requiring the consent of the Bundesrat may provide in detail for the delimitation as well as the manner and scope of allotment of local revenue from corporation and wage taxes. Such statute may also provide for the delimitation and allotment of local revenue from other taxes. The Land share of revenue from the turnover tax shall accrue to the individual Länder on a per capita basis; a federal statute requiring the consent of the Bundesrat may provide for supplementary shares not

[83] As amended by federal statutes of 23 Dec. 1955 and of 12 May 1969.

exceeding one quarter of a Land share to be granted to Länder whose per capita revenue from Land taxes and from the income and corporation taxes is below the average of all the Länder combined.

(2) Such statute shall ensure a reasonable equalization between financially strong and financially weak Länder, due account being taken of the financial capacity and financial requirements of communes or associations of communes. Such statute shall specify the conditions governing equalization claims of Länder entitled to equalization payments and equalization liabilities of Länder owing equalization payments as well as the criteria for determining the amounts of equalization payments. Such statute may also provide for grants to be made by the Federation from federal funds to financially weak Länder in order to complement the coverage of their general financial requirements (supplementary grants).

Article 108[84] (Revenue administration)

(1) Customs duties, fiscal monopolies, excise taxes subject to federal legislation, including the import turnover tax, and charges imposed within the framework of the European Communities shall be administered by federal revenue authorities. The organization of these authorities shall be regulated by federal statute. The heads of authorities at the intermediate level shall be appointed in consultation with the respective Land governments.

(2) All other taxes shall be administered by Land revenue authorities. The organization of these authorities and the uniform training of their civil servants may be regulated by a federal statute requiring the consent of the Bundesrat. The heads of authorities at the intermediate level shall be appointed in agreement with the Federal Government.

(3) To the extent that taxes accruing wholly or in part to the Federation are administered by Land revenue authorities, those authorities shall act as agents of the Federation. Paragraphs (3) and (4) of Article 85 shall apply, the Federal Minister of Finance, however, being substituted for the Federal Government.

(4) In respect of the administration of taxes, a federal statute

---

[84] As amended by federal statute of 12 May 1969.

requiring the consent of the Bundesrat may provide for collaboration between federal and Land revenue authorities, or in the case of taxes under paragraph (1) of this Article for their administration by Land revenue authorities, or in the case of other taxes for their administration by federal revenue authorities, where and to the extent that the execution of revenue statutes is substantially improved or facilitated thereby. As regards taxes the revenue from which accrues exclusively to communes or associations of communes, their administration may wholly or in part be transferred by the Länder from the appropriate Land revenue authorities to communes or associations of communes.

(5) The procedure to be applied by federal revenue authorities shall be laid down by federal legislation. The procedure to be applied by Land revenue authorities or, as envisaged in the second sentence of paragraph (4) of this Article, by communes or associations of communes may be laid down by a federal statute requiring the consent of the Bundesrat.

(6) The jurisdiction of revenue courts shall be uniformly regulated by federal legislation.

(7) The Federal Government may issue appropriate general administrative rules which, to the extent that administration is entrusted to Land revenue authorities or communes or associations of communes, shall require the consent of the Bundesrat.

Article 109[85] (Budget management in the Federation and the Länder)

(1) The Federation and the Länder shall be autonomous and independent of each other in their budget management.

(2) The Federation and the Länder shall have due regard in their budget management to the requirements of overall economic equilibrium.

(3)[86] Through federal legislation requiring the consent of the Bundesrat, principles applicable to both the Federation and the Länder may be established governing budgetary law, responsiveness of budget management to economic trends, and financial planning to cover several years ahead.

(4) With a view to averting disturbances of the overall eco-

[85] As amended by federal statute of 8 June 1967.
[86] As amended by federal statute of 12 May 1969.

nomic equilibrium, federal legislation requiring the consent of the Bundesrat may be enacted providing for:

1. maximum amounts, terms and timing of loans to be raised by territorial entities (*Gebietskörperschaften*) or special purpose associations (*Zweckverbände*), and

2. an obligation on the part of the Federation and the Länder to maintain interest-free deposits at the Deutsche Bundesbank (reserves for counterbalancing economic trends).

Authorizations to issue the relevant ordinances may be conferred on the Federal Government only. Such ordinances shall require the consent of the Bundesrat. They shall be repealed in so far as the Bundestag may so demand; details shall be regulated by federal legislation.

Article 110[87] (Budget and budget law of the Federation)

(1) All revenues and expenditures of the Federation shall be included in the budget; in respect of federal enterprises and special assets, only allocations thereto or remittances therefrom need be included. The budget shall be balanced as regards revenue and expenditure.

(2) The budget shall be laid down in a statute covering one year or several fiscal years separately before the beginning of the first of those fiscal years. Provision may be made for parts of the budget to apply to periods of different duration, but divided into fiscal years.

(3) Bills within the meaning of the first sentence of paragraph (2) of this Article as well as bills to amend the budget statute and the budget shall be submitted simultaneously to the Bundesrat and to the Bundestag; the Bundesrat shall be entitled to state its position on such bills within six weeks or, in the case of amending bills, within three weeks.

(4) The budget statute may contain only such provisions as apply to revenues and expenditures of the Federation and to the period for which the budget statute is being enacted. The budget statute may stipulate that these provisions shall cease to apply only upon the promulgation of the next budget statute or, in the event of an authorization pursuant to Article 115, at a later date.

[87] As amended by federal statute of 12 May 1969.

Article 111 (Interim budget management)

(1) Where, by the end of a fiscal year, the budget for the following year has not been laid down by statute, the Federal Government may, until such statute comes into force, make all payments which are necessary:

(a) to maintain statutory institutions and to carry out measures authorized by statute;

(b) to meet the Federation's legal obligations;

(c) to continue building projects, procurements and other services, or to continue to grant subsidies for these purposes, provided that amounts have already been appropriated in the budget of a previous year.

(2) To the extent that revenues provided by specific legislation and derived from taxes or duties or any other sources, or the working capital reserves, do not cover the expenditures referred to in paragraph (1) of this Article, the Federal Government may borrow the funds necessary for the conduct of current operations up to a maximum of one quarter of the total amount of the previous budget.

Article 112[88] (Expenditures in excess of budgetary estimates)

Expenditures in excess of budgetary appropriations and extra-budgetary expenditures shall require the consent of the Federal Minister of Finance. Such consent may be given only in the case of an unforeseen and compelling necessity. Details may be regulated by federal legislation.

Article 113 (Consent of the Federal Government to increases in expenditures or decreases in revenue)

(1) Statutes increasing the budget expenditures proposed by the Federal Government or involving or likely in future to cause new expenditures shall require the consent of the Federal Government. This shall also apply to statutes involving or likely in future to cause decreases in revenue. The Federal Government may demand that the Bundestag postpone its vote on such bills.

---

[88] As amended by federal statute of 12 May 1969.

In this case the Federal Government shall state its position to the Bundestag within six weeks.

(2) Within four weeks after the Bundestag has adopted such a bill, the Federal Government may demand that it votes on that bill again.

(3) Where the bill has become a statute pursuant to Article 78, the Federal Government may withhold its consent only within six weeks and only after having initiated the procedure provided for in the third and fourth sentences of paragraph (1) or in paragraph (2) of the present Article. Upon the expiry of this period such consent shall be deemed to have been given.

Article 114[89] (Rendering and auditing of accounts)

(1) The Federal Minister of Finance shall, on behalf of the Federal Government, submit annually to the Bundestag and to the Bundesrat for their approval an account, covering the preceding fiscal year, of all revenues and expenditures as well as of property and debt.

(2) The Federal Audit Office, the members of which shall enjoy judicial independence, shall audit the account and examine the management of the budget and the conduct of business as to economy and correctness. The Federal Audit Office shall submit an annual report directly to the Federal Government as well as to the Bundestag and to the Bundesrat. In all other respects the powers of the Federal Audit Office shall be regulated by federal legislation.

Article 115 (Procurement of credit)

(1) The borrowing of funds and the assumption of pledges, guarantees or other commitments, as a result of which expenditure may be incurred in future fiscal years, shall require federal legislative authorization indicating, or permitting computation of, the maximum amounts involved. Revenue obtained by borrowing shall not exceed the total of expenditures for investments provided for in the budget; exceptions shall be permissible only to avert a disturbance of the overall economic equilibrium. Details shall be regulated by federal legislation.

[89] As amended by federal statute of 12 May 1969.

(2) In respect of special assets of the Federation, exceptions to the provisions of paragraph (1) of this Article may be authorized by federal legislation.

xa.[90] STATE OF DEFENCE

Article 115a (Concept and determination of a state of defence)

(1) The determination that federal territory is being attacked by armed force or that such an attack is directly imminent (state of defence) shall be made by the Bundestag with the consent of the Bundesrat. Such determination shall be made at the request of the Federal Government and shall require a two-thirds majority of the votes cast, which shall include at least the majority of the members of the Bundestag.

(2) Where the situation imperatively calls for immediate action and where insurmountable obstacles prevent the timely assembly of the Bundestag, or where there is no quorum in the Bundestag, the Joint Committee shall make this determination with a two-thirds majority of the votes cast, which shall include at least the majority of its members.

(3) The determination shall be promulgated in the *Federal Law Gazette* by the Federal President pursuant to Article 82. Where this cannot be done in time, the promulgation shall be effected in another manner; it shall subsequently be printed in the *Federal Law Gazette* as soon as circumstances permit.

(4) Where the federal territory is being attacked by armed force and where the competent bodies of the Federation are not in a position at once to make the determination provided for in the first sentence of paragraph (1) of this Article, such determination shall be deemed to have been made and promulgated at the time the attack began. The Federal President shall announce such time as soon as circumstances permit.

(5) Where the determination of the existence of a state of defence has been promulgated and where the federal territory is being attacked by armed force, the Federal President may, with the consent of the Bundestag, issue declarations under international law regarding the existence of such state of defence. Where

---

[90] Entire Sect. Xa inserted by federal statute of 24 June 1968.

the conditions mentioned in paragraph (2) of this Article apply, the Joint Committee shall act in substitution for the Bundestag.

Article 115b (Transfer of command to the Federal Chancellor)

Upon the promulgation of a state of defence, the power of command over the Armed Forces shall pass to the Federal Chancellor.

Article 115c (Extension of legislative powers of the Federation)

(1) The Federation shall have the right to legislate concurrently in respect of a state of defence even on matters within the legislative powers of the Länder. Such statutes shall require the consent of the Bundesrat.

(2) Federal legislation to be applicable upon the occurrence of a state of defence to the extent required by conditions obtaining while such state of defence exists may make:

    1. preliminary provision for compensation to be made in the event of property being taken, in derogation of the second sentence of paragraph (3) of Article 14;

    2. provision for a time-limit other than that referred to in the third sentence of paragraph (2) and the first sentence of paragraph (3) of Article 104 in respect of deprivations of liberty, but not exceeding four days at the most, in a case where no judge has been able to act within the time-limit applying in normal times.

(3)[91] Federal legislation to be applicable upon the occurrence of a state of defence to the extent required for averting an existing or directly imminent attack may, subject to the consent of the Bundesrat, regulate the administration and the financial system of the Federation and the Länder in derogation of Sections VIII, VIIIa and X, provided that the viability of the Länder, communes and associations of communes is safeguarded, particularly in financial matters.

(4) Federal statutes enacted pursuant to paragraph (1) or subparagraph 1 of paragraph (2) of this Article may, for the purpose of preparing for their enforcement, be applied even prior to the occurrence of a state of defence.

[91] As amended by federal statute of 12 May 1969.

Article 115d (Legislative process in the case of urgent bills)

(1) While a state of defence exists, the provisions of paragraphs (2) and (3) of this Article shall apply in respect of federal legislation, in derogation of the provisions of paragraph (2) of Article 76, the second sentence of paragraph (1) and paragraphs (2) to (4) of Article 77, Article 78, and paragraph (1) of Article 82.

(2) Bills submitted as urgent by the Federal Government shall be forwarded to the Bundesrat at the same time as they are submitted to the Bundestag. The Bundestag and the Bundesrat shall debate such bills together without delay. In so far as the consent of the Bundesrat is necessary, the majority of its votes shall be required for any such bill to become a statute. Details shall be regulated by rules of procedure adopted by the Bundestag and requiring the consent of the Bundesrat.

(3) The second sentence of paragraph (3) of Article 115a shall apply *mutatis mutandis* in respect of the promulgation of such statutes.

Article 115e[92] (Powers of the Joint Committee)

(1) Where, in a state of defence, the Joint Committee determines with a two-thirds majority of the votes cast, which shall include at least the majority of its members, that insurmountable obstacles prevent the timely assembly of the Bundestag or that there is no quorum in the Bundestag, the Joint Committee shall have the status of both the Bundestag and the Bundesrat and shall exercise their rights as one body.

(2) The Joint Committee may not enact any statute to amend this Basic Law or to deprive it of effect or application either in whole or in part. The Joint Committee shall not be authorized to enact statutes pursuant to the second sentence of paragraph (1) of Article 23, to paragraph (1) of Article 24 or to Article 29.

Article 115f (Powers of the Federal Government)

(1) In a state of defence, the Federal Government may, to the extent necessitated by circumstances:

---

[92] Amended by the federal statute of 21 Dec. 1992.

1. use the Federal Border Guard throughout the federal territory;
2. issue instructions not only to federal administrative authorities but also to Land governments and, where it deems the matter urgent, to Land authorities, and may delegate this power to members of Land governments to be designated by it.

(2) The Bundestag, the Bundesrat and the Joint Committee shall be informed without delay of the measures taken in accordance with paragraph (1) of this Article.

Article 115g (Status and functions of the Federal Constitutional Court)

The constitutional status and the performance of the constitutional functions of the Federal Constitutional Court and its judges shall not be impaired. The Federal Constitutional Court Act may not be amended by a statute enacted by the Joint Committee except in so far as such amendment is required, also in the opinion of the Federal Constitutional Court, to maintain the capability of the Court to function. Pending the enactment of such a statute, the Federal Constitutional Court may take such measures as are necessary to maintain the capability of the Court to carry out its work. Any decisions by the Federal Constitutional Court in pursuance of the second and third sentences of this Article shall require a two-thirds majority of the judges present.

Article 115h (Functioning capability of constitutional organs)

(1) Any legislative terms of the Bundestag or of Land parliaments due to expire while a state of defence exists shall end six months after the termination of such state of defence. A term of office of the Federal President due to expire while a state of defence exists, and the exercise of his functions by the President of the Bundesrat in case of the premature vacancy of the Federal President's office, shall end nine months after the termination of such state of defence. The term of office of a member of the Federal Constitutional Court due to expire while a state of defence exists shall end six months after the termination of such state of defence.

(2) Should the necessity arise for the Joint Committee to elect a new Federal Chancellor, the Committee shall do so with the majority of its members; the Federal President shall propose a candidate to the Joint Committee. The Joint Committee can express its lack of confidence in the Federal Chancellor only by electing a successor with a two-thirds majority of its members.

(3) The Bundestag shall not be dissolved while a state of defence exists.

Article 115i (Powers of the Land governments)

(1) Where the competent federal bodies are incapable of taking the measures necessary to avert the danger, and where the situation imperatively calls for immediate independent action in individual parts of the federal territory, the Land governments or the authorities or commissioners designated by them shall be authorized to take, within their respective spheres of competence, the measures provided for in paragraph (1) of Article 115f.

(2) Any measures taken in accordance with paragraph (1) of the present Article may be revoked at any time by the Federal Government, or, in relation to Land authorities and subordinate federal authorities, by Land minister-presidents.

Article 115k (Duration of validity of extraordinary legal provisions)

(1) Statutes enacted in accordance with Articles 115c, 115e and 115g, as well as ordinances issued by virtue of such statutes, shall, for the duration of their applicability, suspend law which is inconsistent with such statutes or ordinances. This shall not apply to earlier legislation enacted by virtue of Articles 115c, 115e or 115g.

(2) Statutes adopted by the Joint Committee, as well as ordinances issued by virtue of such statutes, shall cease to have effect not later than six months after the termination of a state of defence.

(3)[93] Statutes containing provisions that diverge from Articles 91a, 91b, 104a, 106 and 107 shall apply no longer than the end of the second fiscal year following upon the termination of a

---

[93] As amended by federal statute of 12 May 1969.

state of defence. After such termination they may, with the consent of the Bundesrat, be amended by federal legislation so as to return to the provisions made in Sections VIIIa and X.

Article 115l (Repeal of extraordinary statutes and measures, termination of a state of defence, conclusion of peace)

(1) The Bundestag, with the consent of the Bundesrat, may at any time repeal statutes enacted by the Joint Committee. The Bundesrat may demand that the Bundestag make a decision on such matter. Any measures taken by the Joint Committee or the Federal Government to avert a danger shall be revoked where the Bundestag and the Bundesrat so decide.

(2) The Bundestag, with the consent of the Bundesrat, may at any time declare a state of defence terminated by a decision to be promulgated by the Federal President. The Bundesrat may demand that the Bundestag make a decision on such matter. A state of defence shall, without delay, be declared terminated where the prerequisites for the determination thereof no longer exist.

(3) The conclusion of peace shall be the subject of a federal statute.

XI. TRANSITIONAL AND CONCLUDING PROVISIONS

Article 116 (Definition of 'a German', regranting of citizenship)

(1) Unless otherwise provided by statute, a German within the meaning of this Basic Law is a person who possesses German citizenship or who has been admitted to the territory of the German Reich within the frontiers of 31 December 1937 as a refugee or expellee of German ethnic origin (*Volkszugehörigkeit*) or as the spouse or descendant of such a person.

(2) Former German citizens who, between 30 January 1933 and 8 May 1945, were deprived of their citizenship on political, racial or religious grounds, and their descendants, shall be regranted German citizenship on application. They shall be considered as not having been deprived of their German citizenship where they have established their residence (*Wohnsitz*) in Germany after 8 May 1945 and have not expressed a contrary intention.

Article 117 (Temporary ruling for Article 3 paragraph (2) and Article 11)

(1) Law which is inconsistent with paragraph (2) of Article 3 shall remain in force until adapted to that provision of this Basic Law, but not beyond 31 March 1953.

(2) Statutes which restrict the right of freedom of movement in view of the present housing shortage shall remain in force until repealed by federal legislation.

Article 118 (New delimitation of the Länder of Baden, Württemberg-Baden and Württemberg-Hohenzollern)

A new delimitation of the territory comprising the Länder of Baden, Württemberg-Baden and Württemberg-Hohenzollern may be effected, in derogation of the provisions of Article 29, by agreement between the Länder concerned. Where no agreement is reached, the reorganization shall be effected by federal legislation which shall provide for a plebiscite.

Article 119 (Ordinances having statutory effect in matters relating to refugees and expellees)

In matters relating to refugees and expellees, in particular as regards their distribution among the Länder, the Federal Government may, with the consent of the Bundesrat, issue ordinances having statutory effect, pending the settlement of the matter by federal legislation. The Federal Government may in this matter be authorized to issue individual instructions for particular cases. Except where there is danger resulting in any delay in taking action, such instructions shall be addressed to the highest Land authorities.

Article 120[94] (Occupation costs and burdens resulting from the war)

(1)[95] The Federation shall meet the expenditure for occupation costs and the other internal and external burdens caused by the war, as regulated in detail by federal legislation. To the extent

---

[94] As amended by federal statutes of 30 July 1965 and of 28 July 1969.
[95] As amended by federal statute of 28 July 1969.

that these costs and other burdens have been regulated by federal legislation on or before 1 October 1969, the Federation and the Länder shall meet such expenditure between them in accordance with such federal legislation. In so far as expenditures for such of these costs and burdens as neither have been nor will be regulated by federal legislation have been met on or before 1 October 1965 by Länder, communes, associations of communes or other entities performing functions of the Länder or the communes, the Federation shall not be obliged to meet expenditure of that nature even where it arises after that date. The Federation shall pay the subsidies towards the burdens of social insurance institutions, including unemployment insurance and public assistance to the unemployed. The distribution between the Federation and the Länder of costs and other burdens caused by the war, as regulated in this paragraph, shall not affect any statutory regulation of claims for indemnification in respect of the consequences of the war.

(2) Revenue shall pass to the Federation at the same time as the latter assumes responsibility for the expenditure referred to in this Article.

Article 120a[96] (Implementation of equalization of burdens legislation)

(1) Statutes serving to implement the equalization of burdens may, with the consent of the Bundesrat, stipulate that they shall be executed, as regards equalization benefits, partly by the Federation and partly by the Länder acting as agents of the Federation, and that the relevant powers vested in the Federal Government and the competent highest federal authorities by virtue of Article 85 shall be wholly or partly delegated to the Federal Equalization Office. In exercising these powers, the Federal Equalization Office shall not require the consent of the Bundesrat; with the exception of urgent cases, its instructions shall be given to the highest Land authorities (Land Equalization Offices).

(2) The provisions of the second sentence of paragraph (3) of Article 87 shall not be affected hereby.

[96] Inserted by federal statute of 14 Aug. 1952.

Article 121 (Definition of 'majority of the members')

Within the meaning of this Basic Law, a majority of the members of the Bundestag and a majority of the members of the Federal Convention (*Bundesversammlung*) shall be the majority of the respective statutory number of their members.

Article 122 (Transfer of legislative powers hitherto existing)

(1) From the date of the assembly of the Bundestag, statutes shall be enacted exclusively by the legislative bodies recognized in this Basic Law.

(2) Legislative bodies as well as those bodies participating in legislation in an advisory capacity, whose competence ends by virtue of paragraph (1) of this Article, shall be dissolved with effect from that date.

Article 123 (Continued validity of old law and previous treaties)

(1) Law in force before the first assembly of the Bundestag shall remain in force in so far as it does not conflict with this Basic Law.

(2) Subject to all rights and objections of the interested parties, the treaties concluded by the German Reich concerning matters which, under this Basic Law, shall be within the legislative competence of the Länder, shall remain in force, provided they are and continue to be valid in accordance with general principles of law, until new treaties are concluded by the agencies competent under this Basic Law, or until they are in any other way terminated pursuant to their provisions.

Article 124 (Applicability as federal law within the sphere of exclusive legislative power)

Law affecting matters subject to the exclusive legislative power of the Federation shall become federal law in the area in which it applies.

Article 125 (Applicability as federal law within the sphere of concurrent legislative power)

Law affecting matters subject to the concurrent legislative power of the Federation shall become federal law in the area in which it applies:
1. in so far as it applies uniformly within one or more zones of occupation;
2. in so far as it is law by which former Reich law has been amended after 8 May 1945.

Article 126 (Differences of opinion regarding the applicability of law as federal law)

Differences of opinion regarding the applicability of law as federal law shall be settled by the Federal Constitutional Court.

Article 127 (Legislation of the Bizonal Economic Administration)

Within one year of the promulgation of this Basic Law the Federal Government may, with the consent of the governments of the Länder concerned, extend to the Länder of Baden, Greater Berlin, Rhineland-Palatinate and Württemberg-Hohenzollern any legislation of the Bizonal Economic Administration, in so far as it continues to be in force as federal law under Article 124 or 125.

Article 128 (Continuance of powers to give instructions)

In so far as law continuing in force provides for powers to give instructions within the meaning of paragraph (5) of Article 84, these powers shall remain in existence until otherwise provided by statute.

Article 129 (Applicability of authorizations)

(1) In so far as legal provisions which continue in force as federal law contain authorizations to issue ordinances or to issue general administrative rules or to perform administrative acts, such authorizations shall pass to the agencies henceforth competent in

the matter. In cases of doubt, the Federal Government shall decide in agreement with the Bundesrat; such decisions shall be published.

(2) In so far as legal provisions which continue in force as Land law contain such authorizations, they shall be exercised by the agencies competent under Land law.

(3) In so far as legal provisions within the meaning of paragraphs (1) and (2) of this Article authorize their amendment or supplementation or the issue of legal instead of statutory provisions, such authorizations shall be deemed to have expired.

(4) The provisions of paragraphs (1) and (2) of this Article shall apply *mutatis mutandis* where legal provisions refer to regulations no longer valid or to institutions no longer in existence.

Article 130 (Control over existing institutions)

(1) Administrative agencies and other institutions which serve the public administration or the administration of justice and are not based on Land law or treaties between Länder, as well as the Administrative Union of South West German Railroads and the Administrative Council for the Postal Services and Telecommunications of the French Zone of Occupation, shall be placed under the control of the Federal Government. The Federal Government shall provide, with the consent of the Bundesrat, for their transfer, dissolution or liquidation.

(2) The highest disciplinary superior of the personnel of these administrative bodies and institutions shall be the appropriate Federal Minister.

(3) Corporate bodies and institutions under public law not directly subordinate to a Land nor based on treaties between Länder shall be under the supervision of the competent highest federal authority.

Article 131 (Legal position of persons formerly employed in the public service)

Federal legislation shall be passed to regulate the legal position of persons, including refugees and expellees, who, on 8 May 1945, were employed in the public service, have left the service for reasons other than those arising from civil service regulations or collective agreement rules, and have not until now been reinstated or are employed in a position not corresponding to their former one. The same shall apply *mutatis mutandis* to persons, including refugees and expellees, who, on 8 May 1945, were entitled to a pension and who no longer receive any such pension or any commensurate pension for reasons other than those arising from civil service regulations or collective agreement rules. Until the pertinent federal statute comes into force, no legal claims can be made, unless otherwise provided by Land legislation.

Article 132 (Temporary revocation of rights of persons employed in the public service)

(1) Civil servants and judges who, when this Basic Law comes into force, are appointed for life, may, within six months after the first assembly of the Bundestag, be retired or temporarily retired or be given a different office with lower remuneration where they lack the personal or professional aptitude for their present office. This provision shall apply *mutatis mutandis* also to salaried public employees, other than civil servants or judges, whose service cannot be terminated by notice. Where, however, such service can be terminated by notice, periods of notice in excess of the periods fixed by collective agreement rules may be cancelled within the six months referred to above.

(2) The preceding provision shall not apply to members of the public service who are not affected by the provisions regarding the 'Liberation from National Socialism and Militarism' or who are recognized victims of National Socialism, except on important grounds relating to themselves as individuals.

(3) Those affected may have recourse to the courts in accordance with paragraph (4) of Article 19.

(4) Details shall be specified by an ordinance of the Federal Government requiring the consent of the Bundesrat.

Article 133 (Bizonal Economic Administration, succession to rights and obligations)

The Federation shall succeed to the rights and obligations of the Bizonal Economic Administration.

Article 134 (Reich property to become federal property)

(1) Reich property shall in principle become federal property.

(2) In so far as such property was originally intended to be used predominantly for administrative tasks which, under this Basic Law, are not administrative tasks of the Federation, it shall be transferred without compensation to the agencies now charged with such tasks, and to the Länder in so far as it is being used at present, and not merely temporarily, for administrative tasks which under this Basic Law are now within the administrative competence of the Länder. The Federation may also transfer other property to the Länder.

(3) Property which was placed at the disposal of the Reich by Länder or communes or associations of communes without compensation shall again become the property of such Länder or communes or associations of communes, in so far as it is not required by the Federation for its own administrative tasks.

(4) Details shall be regulated by a federal statute requiring the consent of the Bundesrat.

Article 135 (Succession to property of previously existing Länder and corporate bodies)

(1) Where after 8 May 1945 and before the coming into force of this Basic Law an area has passed from one Land to another, the Land to which the area now belongs shall be entitled to the property located therein of the Land to which it belonged.

(2) Property of Länder or corporate bodies or institutions under public law which no longer exist shall pass, in so far as it was originally intended to be used predominantly for administrative tasks or is being used at present, and not merely temporarily, predominantly for administrative tasks, to the Land or the corporate body or institution under public law which now discharges these tasks.

(3) Real estate of Länder which no longer exist, including appurtenances, shall pass to the Land within which it is located, in so far as it is not included among property within the meaning of paragraph (1) of this Article.

(4) Where an overriding interest of the Federation or the particular interest of an area so requires, a settlement other than in

paragraphs (1) to (3) of this Article may be effected by federal legislation.

(5) In all other respects, the succession in title and the settlement of the property, in so far as it has not been effected before 1 January 1952 by agreement between the Länder or corporate bodies or institutions under public law concerned, shall be regulated by federal legislation requiring the consent of the Bundesrat.

(6) Interests of the former Land of Prussia in enterprises under private law shall pass to the Federation. A federal statute, which may also diverge from this provision, shall regulate details.

(7) In so far as property which on the coming into force of this Basic Law would devolve upon a Land or a corporate body or institution under public law pursuant to paragraphs (1) to (3) of this Article has been disposed of through or by virtue of a Land law or in any other manner by the party thus entitled, the transfer of the property shall be deemed to have taken place before such disposition.

Article 135a[97] (Old liabilities)

(1) The legislation reserved to the Federation in paragraph (4) of Article 134 and in paragraph (5) of Article 135 may also stipulate that the following liabilities shall not be discharged, or not to their full extent:

1. liabilities of the Reich or liabilities of the former Land of Prussia or liabilities of such corporate bodies and institutions under public law as no longer exist;
2. such liabilities of the Federation or corporate bodies and institutions under public law as are connected with the transfer of properties pursuant to Article 89, 90, 134 or 135, and such liabilities of these entities as arise from measures taken by the entities mentioned under item 1;
3. such liabilities of Länder or communes or associations of communes as have arisen from measures taken by these legal entities before 1 August 1945 within the framework of administrative functions incumbent upon or delegated by the Reich to comply with regulations of occupying

---

[97] Inserted by federal statute of 22 Oct. 1957.

powers or to put an end to a state of emergency due to the war.

(2)[98] Paragraph 1 above shall be applied *mutatis mutandis* to liabilities of the German Democratic Republic or its legal entities as well as to liabilities of the Federation or other corporate bodies and institutions under public law which are connected with the transfer of properties of the German Democratic Republic to the Federation, Länder and communes (*Gemeinden*), and to liabilities arising from measures taken by the German Democratic Republic or its legal entities.

Article 136 (First assembly of the Bundesrat)

(1) The Bundesrat shall assemble for the first time on the day of the first assembly of the Bundestag.

(2) Until the election of the first Federal President, his powers shall be exercised by the President of the Bundesrat. He shall not have the right to dissolve the Bundestag.

Article 137 (Right of civil servants to stand for election)

(1)[99] The right of civil servants, of other salaried public employees, of professional soldiers, of temporary volunteer soldiers or of judges to stand for election in the Federation, in the Länder or in the communes may be restricted by legislation.

(2) The electoral statute to be adopted by the Parliamentary Council shall apply to the election of the first Bundestag, of the first Federal Convention and of the first Federal President of the Federal Republic.

(3) The function of the Federal Constitutional Court pursuant to paragraph (2) of Article 41 shall, pending its establishment, be exercised by the German High Court for the Combined Economic Area, which shall decide in accordance with its rules of procedure.

---

[98] Inserted by the Unification Treaty of 31 Aug. 1990 and federal statute of 23 Sept. 1990.
[99] As amended by federal statute of 19 Mar. 1956.

Article 138 (Southern German notaries)

Changes in notarial institutions as presently existing in the Länder of Baden, Bavaria, Württemberg-Baden and Württemberg-Hohenzollern shall require the consent of the governments of these Länder.

Article 139 (Continued validity of denazification provisions)

The legislation enacted for the 'Liberation of the German People from National Socialism and Militarism' shall not be affected by the provisions of this Basic Law.

Article 140 (Law of religious bodies)

The provisions of Articles 136, 137, 138, 139 and 141 of the German Constitution of 11 August 1919 shall be integral parts of this Basic Law.[100]

Article 141 ('Bremen Clause')

The first sentence of paragraph (3) of Article 7 shall not be applied in any Land in which different provisions of Land law were in force on 1 January 1949.

Article 142 (Basic rights in Land constitutions)

Notwithstanding the provision of Article 31, such provisions of Land constitutions shall also remain in force as guarantee basic rights in conformity with Articles 1 to 18 of this Basic Law.

Article 142a[101] (Repealed)

Article 143[102]

(1) Law in the territory specified in Article 3 of the Unification Treaty may deviate from provisions of this Basic Law for a period not extending beyond 31 December 1992 in so far as and

[100] See below following art. 146.

[101] Inserted by federal statute of 26 Mar. 1954 and repealed by federal statute of 24 June 1968.

[102] Inserted by the Unification Treaty of 31 Aug. 1990 and federal statute of 23 Sept. 1990.

as long as no complete adjustment to the order of the Basic Law can be achieved as a consequence of the different conditions. Deviations must not violate Article 19 (2) and must be compatible with the principles set out in Article 79 (3).

(2) Deviations from Sections II, VIII, VIIIa, IX, X and XI are permissible for a period not extending beyond 31 December 1995.

(3) Notwithstanding paragraphs 1 and 2 above, Article 41 of the Unification Treaty and the rules for its implementation shall remain valid in so far as they provide for the irreversibility of intrusion on property in the territory specified in Article 3 of the said Treaty.

Article 144 (Ratification of the Basic Law)

(1) This Basic Law shall require ratification by the parliaments of two thirds of the German Länder in which it is for the time being to apply.

(2) In so far as the applications of this Basic Law are subject to restrictions in any Land listed in Article 23 or in any part thereof, such Land or part thereof shall have the right to send representatives to the Bundestag in accordance with Article 38 and to the Bundesrat in accordance with Article 50.

Article 145 (Promulgation of the Basic Law)

(1) The Parliamentary Council shall confirm in public session, with the participation of the deputies of Greater Berlin, the fact of ratification of this Basic Law and shall sign and promulgate it.

(2) This Basic Law shall come into force at the end of the day of promulgation.

(3) It shall be published in the *Federal Law Gazette*.

Article 146[103] (Duration of validity of the Basic Law)

This Basic Law, which is valid for the entire German people following the achievement of the unity and freedom of Germany, shall cease to be in force on the day on which a constitution adopted by a free decision of the German people comes into force.

[103] Amended by the Unification Treaty of 31 Aug. 1990 and federal statute of 23 Sept. 1990.

EXTRACT FROM THE GERMAN CONSTITUTION OF 11
AUGUST 1919 (WEIMAR CONSTITUTION)[104]

Article 136 (Weimar Constitution)

(1) Civil and political rights and duties shall be neither dependent on nor restricted by the exercise of the freedom of religion.

(2) Enjoyment of civil and political rights and eligibility for public office shall be independent of religious denomination.

(3) No one shall be bound to disclose his religious convictions. The authorities shall not have the right to inquire into a person's membership of a religious body except to the extent that rights or duties depend thereon or that a statistical survey ordered by law makes it necessary.

(4) No one may be compelled to perform any religious act or ceremony or to participate in religious exercises or to use a religious form of oath.

Article 137 (Weimar Constitution)

(1) There shall be no state church.

(2) Freedom of association to form religious bodies shall be guaranteed. The union of religious bodies within the territory of the Reich shall not be subject to any restrictions.

(3) Every religious body shall regulate and administer its affairs autonomously within the limits of the law valid for all. It shall confer its offices without the participation of the state or the civil community.

(4) Religious bodies shall acquire legal capacity according to the general provisions of civil law.

(5) Religious bodies shall remain corporate bodies under public law in so far as they have been such heretofore. The other religious bodies shall be granted like rights upon application, where their constitution and the number of their members offer an assurance of their permanency. Where several such religious bodies under public law unite in one organization, such organization shall also be a corporate body under public law.

(6) Religious bodies that are corporate bodies under public

---

[104] See Art. 140 above.

law shall be entitled to levy taxes in accordance with Land law on the basis of the civil taxation lists.

(7) Associations whose purpose is the common cultivation of a philosophical persuasion shall have the same status as religious bodies.

(8) Such further regulation as may be required for the implementation of these provisions shall be a matter for Land legislation.

Article 138 (Weimar Constitution)

(1) State contributions to religious bodies, based on law or contract or special legal title, shall be redeemed by means of Land legislation. The principles for such redemption shall be established by the Reich.

(2) The right to own property and other rights of religious bodies or associations in respect of their institutions, foundations and other assets destined for purposes of worship, education or charity shall be guaranteed.

Article 139 (Weimar Constitution)

Sunday and the public holidays recognized by the state shall remain legally protected as days of rest from work and of spiritual edification.

Article 141 (Weimar Constitution)

To the extent that there exists a need for religious services and spiritual care in the army, in hospitals, prisons or other public institutions, the religious bodies shall be permitted to perform religious acts; in this connexion there shall be no compulsion of any kind.

6a

France: Declaration of the Rights of Man and the Citizen 1789

The representatives of the French people convened in National Assembly,

Considering that ignorance, forgetfulness, or contempt of human rights are the sole causes of public misfortune and government depravity,

Have resolved to set out in a solemn declaration the natural, inalienable and sacred human rights,

In order that this declaration, ever present to all members of the body social, may call constantly to mind their rights and duties,

So that the acts of the legislature and of the executive, measured at any moment against the final end of all political institutions, be rendered more respectful thereof,

And the claims of the citizenry, based henceforth on simple and incontestable principles, tend always to the support of the Constitution and the general weal.

Hence the National Assembly, in the presence and under the auspices of the Supreme Being, recognizes and declares the following Rights of Man and Citizen.

1 All men are born and remain free and equal in their rights. Social distinctions may be based only on public utility.

2 The final end of every political institution is the preservation of the natural and imprescriptible rights of man. Those rights are liberty, property, security, and resistance to oppression.

3 The source of all sovereignty lies essentially in the Nation. No corporation or individual may exercise any authority not expressly derived therefrom.

4 Liberty is the power to do anything which does not harm another; hence the only limits to the exercise of each man's

natural rights are those which secure to other members of society the enjoyment of the same rights. These limits may be fixed only by statute law.

5 Statute law is entitled to forbid only actions harmful to society. What is not forbidden by law may not be prohibited, and no one may be compelled to do that which it does not command.

6 Statute law is the expression of the general will. All citizens have the right to take part in person or through their representatives in its enactment. Whether it protects or punishes, it must be the same for all. Since all citizens are equal in its eyes, they are likewise eligible for all dignities, positions, and posts according to ability and without distinction other than that of their merits and abilities.

7 No one may be accused, arrested or detained save as prescribed by statute law and under the procedures therein laid down. Those who call for, further, carry out or procure the carrying out of arbitrary orders must be punished; but every citizen lawfully summoned or apprehended must comply forthwith; resistance renders them culpable.

8 The only punishments to be laid down by statute law are those strictly and clearly necessary, and no one may be punished save under a statute enacted and promulgated before the offence and lawfully applied.

9 Since everyone is presumed innocent until convicted, any unnecessary force used in making unavoidable arrests must be severely punished by the law.

10 No one may be persecuted for his opinions or creed, provided that their expression does not disturb the public order provided for by the law.

11 The free communication of thoughts and opinions is one of the most precious of human rights; hence every citizen may speak, write and publish freely, while, in cases determined by the law, being held to answer for any abuse of this freedom.

12 To safeguard the rights of man and citizen requires a police force; this force is thus established for the advantage of all, and not for the private benefit of those to whom it is entrusted.

13 The upkeep of the police force and the expenses of public administration necessitate a contribution from all; it must be borne by all citizens equally, according to their means.

14 All citizens have the right, directly or through their repre-

sentatives, to ascertain that this common contribution is necessary, to consent freely to its levy, to monitor its disbursement, and to determine its amount, basis of assessment, collection, and duration.

15 Society has the right to require of every public servant an account of his administration.

16 A society where rights are not secured or the separation of powers established has no constitution at all.

17 Property being an inviolable and sacred right, no one may be deprived of it save where public necessity, legally ascertained, clearly requires it; and then on condition of a just and previously determined compensation.

6b

Preamble to the Constitution of the Fourth French Republic 1946[1]

(1) On the morrow of the victory won by the free peoples over the régimes which sought to enslave and degrade the human person, the French people proclaim anew that all human beings without distinction of race, religion or belief possess inalienable and sacred rights. They solemnly reaffirm the rights and liberties of man and the citizen consecrated by the Declaration of Rights of 1789, and the fundamental principles recognized by the laws of the Republic.

(2) Furthermore, the people proclaim, as particularly necessary to our time, the following political, economic, and social principles.

(3) The law guarantees to women rights in every sphere equal to those of men.

(4) Anyone persecuted for the pursuit of freedom has the right of asylum within the territories of the Republic.

(5) Everyone has the duty to work and the right to employment. No one may be disadvantaged in work or employment because of their origins, opinions or beliefs.

(6) Everyone may defend their rights and interest by trade union activities and join the trade union of their choice.

(7) The right to strike is exercised within the framework of the laws which govern it.

(8) Through his representatives, every worker takes part in collective agreements on conditions of work, as well as in the management of the undertaking.

(9) Every resource or undertaking which is or acquires the character of a national public service or *de facto* monopoly must pass into public ownership.

---

[1] Para. nos. added by the translator.

(10) The nation shall ensure to both individuals and the family the conditions necessary for their development.

(11) It shall guarantee to all, and particularly to children, mothers, and elderly workers, health care, material security, rest, and leisure. Every human being who, by reason of age, mental or physical condition, or the economic situation, is incapable of working has the right to obtain from the community the appropriate means of subsistence.

(12) The nation proclaims the solidarity and equality of all the French, confronted by the burdens of a national calamity.

(13) The Nation shall guarantee, to child and adult, equal access to education, vocational training, and culture. The organization of free, secular, public instruction at all levels is a duty of the State.

(14) The French Republic, faithful to its traditions, shall conform to the rules of public international law. It will never engage in wars of conquest, nor use public force against the freedom of a people.

(15) Subject to reciprocity, France consents to limitations of sovereignty necessary for the realization and the defence of peace.

(16) France and the overseas people shall form a Union based on equality of rights and duties without distinction of race or religion.

(17) The French Union shall be composed of nations and peoples who pool or co-ordinate their resources and their efforts in order to develop their own cultures, increase their well-being, and ensure their security.

(18) Faithful to its traditional mission, France intends to lead the peoples under its care towards self-administration and the democratic management of their own affairs; rejecting any systems of colonization founded on arbitrary rule, France shall guarantee everyone equal access to public office, and the individual or collective exercise of the rights and freedoms proclaimed or confirmed above.

12 October 1946

6c

Constitution of the Fifth French Republic of 4 October 1958

The Government of the Republic, in accordance with the constitutional law of 3 June 1958, has proposed,
The French people have adopted,
The President of the Republic promulgates the constitutional law which follows:

PREAMBLE

The French people solemnly proclaim their commitment to the Rights of Man and the principles of human sovereignty as defined by the Declaration of 1789, reaffirmed and completed by the Preamble to the Constitution of 1946.

By virtue of these principles and that of the free self-determination of peoples, the Republic offers to those Overseas Territories which demonstrate the desire to join them, new institutions founded on the common ideal of liberty, equality and fraternity, and conceived with a view to their democratic evolution.

Article 1

The Republic and the peoples of the Overseas Territories who, by an act of free determination, adopt this Constitution, thereby institute a Community.

The Community is founded on the equality and solidarity of the peoples who compose it.

Article 2[1]

France is a Republic, indivisible, secular, democratic and social. It shall ensure the equality before the law of all citizens without distinction of origin, race or religion. It shall respect all beliefs.

The language of the Republic is French.

The national emblem is the tricolour flag, blue, white, and red.

The national anthem is the *Marseillaise*.

The motto of the Republic is 'Liberty, Equality, Fraternity'.

Its principle is government of the people, by the people, and for the people.

Article 3

National sovereignty belongs to the people, who exercise it through their representatives and by way of referendum.

No section of the people, nor any individual, may arrogate to themselves the exercise thereof.

The suffrage may be direct or indirect under the conditions laid down in the Constitution. It shall always be universal, equal, and secret.

All adult French citizens of either sex who enjoy civic and political rights are entitled to vote, under the conditions determined by legislation.

Article 4

Political parties and groups play a part in the exercise of the right to vote. They are formed, and function, freely. They must respect the principles of national sovereignty and of democracy.

TITLE II—THE PRESIDENT OF THE REPUBLIC

Article 5

The President of the Republic is the guardian of the Constitution. By the exercise of his judgement (*arbitrament*) he

[1] Amended by the constitutional law of 25 June 1992.

shall ensure the regular functioning of the public authorities, and the continuity of the State.

He is guarantor of national independence, territorial integrity, and of respect for Community agreements and for treaties.

Article 6[2]

The President of the Republic is elected for seven years by direct universal suffrage.

The method of implementing this article is laid down by an organic enactment.

Article 7[3]

The President of the Republic is elected by an absolute majority of the votes cast. If this is not obtained on the first ballot, there shall be a second ballot on the second Sunday following. The only candidates at this ballot are the two who received the highest number of votes at the first ballot, having, where necessary, taken account of the withdrawal of candidates who received more votes.

The ballot opens on formal instruction by the Government.

The election of the President shall take place not less than twenty and not more than thirty-five days before the expiry of the powers of the incumbent President.

Should the office of President fall vacant for any reason whatever, or should the Constitutional Council, on a reference by the Government and by an absolute majority of its members, decide that there is an impediment to the functioning of the Presidency, the functions of the office, save for those provided for by Articles 11 and 12 below, shall be temporarily carried on by the President of the Senate and, if the latter is in turn prevented from doing so, by the Government.

In the case of a vacancy, or where the Constitutional Council has declared the impediment to be permanent, voting for the election of a new President shall take place not less than twenty and not more than thirty-five days thereafter, unless the Constitutional Council certifies that this is prevented by some insuperable obstacle.

[2] As amended by constitutional law of 6 Nov. 1962.
[3] As amended by constitutional law of 6 Nov. 1962.

If, during the seven days before the latest date for the lodging of nominations, there occurs the death or disability of one of those who, in the thirty days before that date, publicly announced his candidature, the Constitutional Council may decide to postpone the election.

If, before the first ballot, one of the candidates dies or becomes unable to hold office, the Constitutional Council shall declare the election postponed.

If, before any withdrawals, one of the two candidates who received the greatest number of votes in the first ballot dies or becomes unable to hold office, the Constitutional Council shall call fresh elections. The same applies in the event of the death or inability to hold office of one of the two candidates eligible to stand for the second ballot.

All these cases shall be referred to the Constitutional Council under the conditions laid down by the second paragraph of Article 61 below, or under those for the presentation of candidates laid down by the organic enactment provided for by Article 6 above.

The Constitutional Council may extend the periods prescribed in the third and fifth paragraphs above, provided that polling takes place within thirty-five days of its decision. If the application of the provisions of this paragraph results in the postponement of the election beyond the expiry of the powers of the incumbent President, the latter shall remain in office until his successor is announced.

While the Presidency of the Republic is vacant, or between the declaration of permanent incapacity of the incumbent and the election of his successor, neither Articles 49 and 50 nor Article 89 of the Constitution may be applied.

Article 8

The President of the Republic appoints the Prime Minister. He terminates his functions when the latter tenders the resignation of the Government.

On the proposal of the Prime Minister, he appoints and dismisses the other members of the Government.

Article 9

The President of the Republic chairs the Council of Ministers.

Article 10

The President of the Republic shall promulgate enactments within fifteen days of the transmission to the Government of the enactment as finally adopted. Before the end of this period, he may ask Parliament to reconsider the enactment or certain of its provisions. Parliament may not refuse such reconsideration.

Article 11

On a proposal from the Government during the sessions of Parliament, or on a joint motion of its two Houses published in the *Official Journal*, the President of the Republic may put to a referendum any Government bill dealing with the organization of the public authorities, entailing approval of a Community agreement, or providing for authorization to ratify a treaty which, while not contrary to the Constitution, would affect the functioning of its institutions.

Should the referendum have approved the Government bill, the President of the Republic shall promulgate it within the time limit stipulated in the preceding Article.

Article 12

After consultation with the Prime Minister and the Presidents of the two Houses, the President of the Republic may declare the dissolution of the National Assembly.

General elections shall take place not less than twenty and not more than forty days after dissolution.

The National Assembly shall convene as of right on the second Thursday after its election. If this meeting takes place outside the periods provided for ordinary sessions, a session shall, as of right, be held for a fifteen-day period.

Within the year following these elections there may be no further dissolution.

Article 13

The President of the Republic signs ordinances and decrees decided upon in the Council of Ministers.

He makes appointments to the civil and military posts of the State.

Counsellors of State, the Grand Chancellor of the Legion of Honour, ambassadors and envoys-extraordinary, Master Councillors of the Court of Auditors, prefects, representatives of the Government in the Overseas Territories, general officers, rectors of academies, and heads of central government departments shall be appointed by the Council of Ministers.

An organic enactment shall determine the other posts to be filled by the Council of Ministers, and the conditions under which the President of the Republic may delegate his power to make appointments, to be exercised in his name.

Article 14

The President of the Republic accredits ambassadors and envoys-extraordinary to foreign powers; foreign ambassadors and envoys-extraordinary are accredited to the Presidency.

Article 15

The President of the Republic is commander-in-chief of the armed forces. He chairs the higher National Defence Councils and Committees.

Article 16

When the institutions of the Republic, the independence of the nation, the integrity of its territory or the fulfilment of its international commitments come under serious and immediate threat and the proper functioning of the constitutional public authorities is impaired, the President of the Republic shall, after official consultation of the Prime Minister, the Presidents of the two Houses, and the Constitutional Council, take the measures required by the circumstances.

He shall inform the Nation thereof.

These measures must be prompted by the intention to secure to the constitutional public authorities, within the shortest possible time, the means necessary to carry out their functions. The Constitutional Council shall be consulted thereon.

Parliament shall convene as of right.

During the exercise of emergency powers, the National Assembly shall not be dissolved.

Article 17

The President of the Republic has the right of pardon.

Article 18

The President of the Republic communicates with the two Houses by messages which he causes to be read before them and which may not form the subject-matter of debate.

If Parliament is not sitting, it is specially convened for this purpose.

Article 19

The acts of the President of the Republic, other than those provided for by Articles 8 (first paragraph), 11, 12, 16, 18, 54, 56, and 61 are counter-signed by the Prime Minister and, where appropriate, by the minister responsible.

TITLE III—THE GOVERNMENT

Article 20

The Government shall decide on and conduct national policy.

It shall have at its disposal the public service and the armed forces.

It shall be responsible to Parliament under the conditions and according to the procedures laid down by Articles 49 and 50.

Article 21

The Prime Minister shall direct the activities of the Government. He is responsible for national defence. He ensures the implementation of enactments. Subject to the provisions of Article 13, he has power to make regulations, and makes appointments to civil and military posts.

He may delegate certain of his powers to ministers.

If need be, he may deputize for the President of the Republic in chairing the councils and committees provided for under Article 15.

In exceptional cases, he may deputize for him as chair of the Council of Ministers, under an express delegation of authority and for a specific agenda.

Article 22

Where appropriate, the acts of the Prime Minister shall be counter-signed by the ministers entrusted with their implementation.

Article 23

The functions of members of the Government are incompatible with the exercise of any parliamentary mandate, with the holding of any office at national level in business, commercial or professional organizations, and with any public office or professional activity.

An organic enactment shall lay down the conditions providing for the replacement of the holders of such mandates, offices, or posts.

The replacement of members of Parliament shall take place in accordance with the provisions of Article 25.

TITLE IV—THE PARLIAMENT

Article 24

Parliament consists of the National Assembly and the Senate.

National Assembly deputies shall be elected by direct suffrage.

The Senate shall be elected by indirect suffrage and ensure the representation of the territorial units of the Republic. French people living outside France shall be represented in the Senate.

Article 25

An organic enactment shall lay down the term for which each House is elected, the number of its members, their emoluments, the conditions of eligibility, and the system of ineligibility or incompatibility.

Likewise it shall lay down the conditions under which, in the event of a seat falling vacant, persons are elected to replace deputies or senators until the holding of general or partial elections to the House to which they belong.

Article 26

No member of Parliament may be prosecuted, investigated, arrested, detained or tried as a result of opinions expressed or votes cast in the exercise of his functions.

During parliamentary sessions, no member of Parliament may be prosecuted or arrested for crimes or offences without the authorization of the House of which he is a member, save where he is apprehended in the commission of the offence.

When Parliament is not in session, no member of Parliament may be arrested without the authorization of the Bureau of the House of which he is a member, save when apprehended in the commission of an offence, or for authorized prosecution, or on final conviction.

At the request of the House of which he is a member, the detention or prosecution of a member of Parliament shall be suspended.

Article 27

All mandates purporting to bind a member are null and void.

A member's right to vote is personal to him.

An organic enactment may, for exceptional cases, authorize delegation of a vote. In that case no member may cast more than one proxy vote.

Article 28[4]

Parliament shall convene as of right in two ordinary sessions per year.

The first session shall open on 2 October and last eighty days.

The second session shall open on 2 April and may last no more than ninety days.

Should 2 October or 2 April be a public holiday, the session shall open on the first working day thereafter.

Article 29

At the request of the Prime Minister or of the majority of members of the National Assembly, Parliament shall convene in extraordinary session to consider a specific agenda.

Where a session is held at the request of members of the National Assembly, the decree ordering its closure shall issue as soon as Parliament has completed the agenda for which it was convened, and at the latest twelve days after it was convened.

Within a month of such closure, only the Prime Minister may call a further session.

Article 30

Save when Parliament convenes as of right, extraordinary sessions shall be opened and closed by decree of the President of the Republic.

Article 31

Members of the Government shall have access to the two Houses. They shall be heard on their request.

They may be assisted by Government commissioners.

Article 32

The President of the National Assembly shall be elected for the duration of the legislature. The President of the Senate shall be elected after each partial renewal of its membership.

[4] As amended by constitutional law of 30 Dec. 1963.

Article 33

The sittings of the two Houses shall be public. A verbatim report of the debates shall be published in the *Official Journal*.

At the request of the Prime Minister or of one-tenth of its members, either House may sit in closed committee.

TITLE V—RELATIONS BETWEEN PARLIAMENT AND GOVERNMENT

Article 34

Legislation is enacted by Parliament.

Legislation shall lay down the rules concerning:

—civic rights and the fundamental safeguards granted to citizens for the exercise of their public freedoms; the burdens imposed by national defence on both the persons and the property of citizens;

—the nationality, status, and capacity of persons, matrimonial property regimes, succession, and gifts;

—the definition of crimes and major offences and the punishments therefor; criminal procedure; amnesty; the creation of new types of court, and the status of the judiciary;

—the basis of assessment, rates, and modes of collecting of all types of tax; the currency system.

Legislation shall likewise lay down the rules concerning:

—the electoral systems for the Houses of Parliament and local councils;

—the creation of new categories of state enterprise;

—the basic guarantees conferred on the civil and military personnel of the State;

—the nationalization of undertakings and the transfer of their property from the public to the private sector.

Legislation shall lay down basic principles of:

—the general organization of national defence;

—the autonomy of local authorities, their powers and budgets;

—education;

—the law of property, real rights, and civil and commercial obligations;

—labour law, trade union law, and social security.

Finance legislation shall determine the resources and commitments of the State under the conditions and with the qualifications to be laid down by an organic enactment.

Policy legislation shall define the aims of the economic and social action of the State.

The provisions of this article may be clarified and complemented by an organic enactment.

Article 35

A declaration of war must be authorized by Parliament.

Article 36

A state of emergency may be declared by decree in the Council of Ministers. Only Parliament can authorize its prolongation beyond twelve days.

Article 37

Matters other than those which fall within the domain of legislation are regulatory in character.

Texts on such matters which take the form of legislation may be modified by decree issued after consultation with the Council of State. Those of such texts as take effect after this Constitution has come into force may be modified by decree only if the Constitutional Council confirms that, under the preceding paragraph, they are regulatory in character.

Article 38

In order to carry out its programme, the Government may ask Parliament to authorize it, for a limited period, to take by means of ordinances measures which fall normally within the domain of legislation.

The ordinances shall be adopted in the Council of Ministers after consultation with the Council of State. They come into force on publication, but lapse if a Government ratification bill is not laid before Parliament by the date specified in the enabling Act.

After the time limit referred to in the first paragraph of this

Article, ordinances in matters within the domain of legislation may be modified only by legislation.

Article 39

The Prime Minister and members of Parliament have the right to introduce legislation.

Government bills shall be discussed in the Council of Ministers after consultation with the Council of State and shall be filed with the Bureau of one of the two Houses. Finance bills shall be introduced in the National Assembly.

Article 40

Private members' bills and amendments are not admissible if their adoption would result in reducing public resources, or in creating or increasing a head of public expenditure.

Article 41

If, during the legislative process, it appears that a private member's bill or amendment does not fall within the domain of legislation, or is counter to a delegation of authority granted under Article 38, the Government may oppose it as inadmissible.

In case of disagreement between the Government and the President of the House concerned, at the request of one or other of them the Constitutional Council shall give a ruling within eight days.

Article 42

In the first of the two Houses in which a Government bill has been introduced, the Government's text shall be debated.

When sent a text passed by the other House, the House concerned shall debate the text transmitted.

Article 43

At the request of the Government or the House concerned, bills are sent for consideration to a committee set up especially for the purpose.

In the absence of such request they are sent to one of the standing committees, the number of which shall be limited to six in each House.

Article 44

Members of Parliament and the Government have the right of amendment.

Once the debate has opened, the Government may oppose the consideration of any amendment not already put before a committee.

If the Government so requests, the House concerned shall decide by a single vote on the whole or part of a text under debate with only those amendments proposed or accepted by the Government.

Article 45

Bills are considered successively by the two Houses with the aim of adopting an identical text.

Where disagreement prevents the adoption of a bill after two readings of each House (or, where the government has declared the matter urgent, after a single reading by each), the Prime Minister is entitled to call a meeting of a joint committee, with an equal number of members from each House, instructed to put forward a text on the provisions still under discussion.

The text drafted by the joint committee may be submitted by the Government for approval by the two Houses. Without Government consent, no amendment is admissible.

If the joint committee fails to arrive at a common text or if its text is not adopted under the preceding paragraph, there shall be a further reading in the National Assembly and the Senate, after which the Government may request the National Assembly to take the final decision. In this event, the National Assembly may reconsider either the text drafted by the joint committee or the text as last adopted by itself, modified, where appropriate, with one or more of the amendments adopted by the Senate.

Article 46

Legislation which this Constitution characterizes as organic enactments shall be passed and amended in the following way:

The bill shall be debated and voted on by the first House to which it is passed only at the end of a period of fifteen days from its introduction. The procedure of Article 45 shall apply. Nonetheless, in the absence of agreement between the two Houses, the National Assembly may adopt the text on final reading only by an absolute majority of its members.

Organic enactments concerning the Senate must be passed in the same terms by both Houses.

Organic enactments may not be promulgated until the Constitutional Council has confirmed their conformity with the Constitution.

Article 47

Parliament shall enact finance legislation under the conditions laid down by an organic enactment.

Should the National Assembly fail to reach a decision on first reading within forty days after the introduction of a finance bill, the Government refers it to the Senate which must reach a decision within fifteen days. Thereafter the procedure of Article 45 shall be followed.

Should Parliament fail to reach a decision within seventy days, the provisions of the bill may be brought into force by ordinance.

If a finance bill laying down revenue and expenditure for a fiscal year is not introduced in time to be promulgated before the commencement of that year, the Government shall request Parliament, as a matter of urgency, to authorize it to levy taxes, and shall make available by decree the funds needed to meet commitments already undertaken.

The periods laid down by this Article are suspended while Parliament is not in session.

The Court of Auditors assists the Parliament and the Government in supervising the implementation of finance Acts.

Article 48

The Houses' agenda shall include, as a matter of priority and in the order determined by the Government, debate on Government bills and on those of private members which have Government support.

At one sitting a week, priority shall be given to Parliamentary questions and Government answers thereto.

Article 49

After conferring with the Council of Ministers, the Prime Minister may make the Government's programme or general policy statement a matter of confidence in the Government.

By means of a censure motion, the National Assembly may call into question the issue of confidence in the Government. To be admissible, such a motion must be signed by at least a tenth of the members of the National Assembly. Voting may not take place until forty-eight hours after the motion was tabled. The only votes counted shall be those in favour of the censure motion, which may be adopted only by a majority of all members comprising the Assembly. If the motion is rejected, its signatories may not introduce another during the same session, save as provided by the following paragraph.

After conferring with the Council of Ministers, the Prime Minister may make the vote by the National Assembly on a text a matter of confidence in the Government. In this event the text is deemed adopted unless a motion of censure, tabled within forty-eight hours, is passed under the conditions laid down by the preceding paragraph.

The Prime Minister is entitled to seek the Senate's approval of a general policy statement.

Article 50

When the National Assembly passes a motion of censure or rejects the Government's programme or general policy statement, the Prime Minister must tender to the President of the Republic the resignation of the Government.

Article 51

Where necessary, the closure of extraordinary sessions is postponed as of right in order to permit recourse to the provisions of Article 49.

TITLE VI—TREATIES AND INTERNATIONAL AGREEMENTS

Article 52

The President of the Republic negotiates and ratifies treaties.

He shall be apprised of all negotiations on the conclusion of an international agreement not requiring ratification.

Article 53

Peace treaties, trade treaties, treaties or agreements concerning international organizations, those which commit national resources, those which modify provisions of a legislative character, those concerning personal status, and those involving the cession, exchange, or annexation of territory may be ratified or approved only under an enactment.

They take effect only after ratification or approval.

No cession, no exchange, no annexation of territory is valid without the consent of the population concerned.

Article 53–1[5]

The Republic may conclude with European states which, in the matter of asylum and the protection of human rights and fundamental liberties, are bound by undertakings identical with its own, agreements determining their respective competences in the scrutiny of requests for asylum made to them.

Nonetheless, even if the request does not fall within their competence under such agreements, the authorities of the Republic are always entitled to give asylum to any foreigner persecuted for actions in the cause of freedom or requesting asylum for some other reasons.

[5] Inserted by the constitutional law of 19 Nov. 1993.

Article 54[6]

If, on a reference by the President of the Republic, the Prime Minister, the President of either House, or sixty deputies or sixty senators, the Constitutional Council rules that an international agreement contains a clause contrary to the Constitution, its ratification or approval may be authorized only after amendment of the Constitution.

Article 55

Treaties or agreements duly ratified or approved shall, upon their publication, prevail over legislation, subject, for each agreement or treaty, to reciprocal application by the other party.

TITLE VII—THE CONSTITUTIONAL COUNCIL

Article 56

The Constitutional Council shall consist of nine members, whose term of office shall last nine years and shall not be renewable. One third of its membership shall be renewed every three years. Three of its members shall be appointed by the President of the Republic, three by the President of the National Assembly, and three by the President of the Senate.

In addition to the nine members provided for above, former Presidents of the Republic shall be life members as of right.

The President shall be appointed by the President of the Republic. He has the casting vote in case of a tie.

Article 57

The office of member of the Constitutional Council is incompatible with that of minister or member of Parliament. Other incompatibilities are determined by an organic enactment.

---

[6] Amended by the constitutional law of 25 June 1992.

Article 58

The Constitutional Council shall ensure the regularity of the election of the President of the Republic. It shall investigate complaints and announce the results of the vote.

Article 59

In case of dispute, the Constitutional Council rules on the regularity of the election of deputies and of senators.

Article 60

The Constitutional Council shall ensure the regularity of referendum procedures and announce the results thereof.

Article 61

Organic enactments before promulgation, and standing orders of the Houses of Parliament before they take effect, must be submitted to the Constitutional Council for a ruling on their conformity to the Constitution.

For the same purpose, before promulgation legislation may be referred to the Constitutional Council by the President of the Republic, the Prime Minister, the President of the National Assembly, the President of the Senate, or sixty deputies or sixty senators.[7]

In the cases provided for in the preceding two paragraphs, the Constitutional Council must give a ruling within a month. Nonetheless, at the request of the Government in case of urgency, this period is reduced to eight days.

In the above cases, a reference to the Constitutional Council suspends the period for promulgation.

Article 62

A provision held to be unconstitutional may be neither promulgated nor put into effect. Decisions of the Constitutional

[7] As amended by the constitutional law of 29 Oct. 1974.

Council are subject to no review. They bind the public powers and all administrative and judicial authorities.

Article 63

An organic enactment shall lay down the rules of organization and functioning of the Constitutional Council, the procedure before it, and in particular the time limits for referring disputes to it.

TITLE VIII—THE JUDICIARY

Article 64

The President of the Republic shall be the guardian of the independence of the judiciary.

He shall be assisted by the Higher Judiciary Council.

An organic enactment shall establish the status of judges.

Judges of the Bench shall be irremovable.

Article 65[8]

The Higher Judiciary Council is chaired by the President of the Republic. The Minister of Justice is *ex officio* vice-chairman. He may deputize for the President of the Republic.

The Higher Judiciary Council sits in two divisions, one with jurisdiction over the judiciary of the Bench, the other over the judiciary of the *parquet*.

The division with jurisdiction over the judiciary of the Bench consists, apart from the President of the Republic and the Keeper of the Seals, of five judges of the Bench and one of the *parquet*, one Counsellor of State nominated by the Council of State, and three persons belonging to neither Parliament nor the ordinary judiciary nominated respectively by the President of the Republic, the President of the National Assembly, and the President of the Senate.

The division with jurisdiction over the judiciary of the *parquet* consists, apart from the President of the Republic and the Keeper

---

[8] As amended by the constitutional law of 19 July 1993.

of the Seals, of five judges of the *parquet* and one of the Bench, and the Counsellor of State and three persons mentioned in the preceding paragraph.

The division of the Higher Judiciary Council with jurisdiction over the judiciary of the Bench puts forward proposals for appointments to the Bench on the Court of Cassation, for the posts of first President of a Court of Appeal, and for those of the President of a *Tribunal de Grande Instance*. The other judiciary of the Bench are appointed according to its advice.

It acts as disciplinary committee for the judiciary of the Bench and is then chaired by the first President of the Court of Cassation.

The division of the Higher Judiciary Council with jurisdiction over the judiciary of the *parquet* advises on appointments concerning the judiciary of the *parquet* save for those posts dealt with in the Council of Ministers.

It advises on disciplinary measures concerning the judiciary of the *parquet* and is then chaired by the Procurator-General at the Court of Cassation.

An organic enactment shall settle the conditions of application of this article.

Article 66

No one may be arbitrarily detained.

As the guardian of individual freedom, the judiciary shall enforce this principle within the conditions laid down by legislation.

TITLE IX—THE HIGH COURT OF JUSTICE

Article 67

A High Court of Justice shall be established.

It shall be composed of Members of Parliament elected from among themselves and in equal numbers by the National Assembly and the Senate after each general or partial renewal of those Houses.

An organic enactment shall lay down the composition of the High Court, its regulations, and procedure.

Article 68

Only in the case of high treason does the President of the Republic answer for acts carried out in the exercise of his office. He may be impeached only by an identical decision of both Houses taken in open ballot and by an absolute majority of their members. He shall be tried by the High Court of Justice.

TITLE X—CRIMINAL LIABILITY OF MEMBERS OF THE
GOVERNMENT

Article 68–1[9]

Members of the Government are criminally liable for acts carried out in the exercise of their office constituting crimes or major offences at the time they were committed.

They shall be tried by the Court of Justice of the Republic.

The Court of Justice of the Republic is bound by the definition of crimes and major offences, and by the sentences available, as laid down by enacted law.

Article 68–2

The Court of Justice of the Republic consists of fifteen judges: twelve members of parliament elected from among their members and an equal number by the National Assembly and the Senate after each general or partial renewal of those Houses, and three judges of the Bench at the Court of Cassation of whom one presides over the Court of Justice of the Republic.

Any person claiming to be injured by a crime or major offence committed by a member of the Government in the exercise of his functions may raise a complaint before an applications committee.

That committee directs either the discontinuance of the matter or its referral to the Procurator-General at the Court of Cassation for hearing by the Court of Justice of the Republic.

The Procurator-General at the Court of Cassation may also,

[9] Inserted by constitutional law of 19 July 1993.

ex officio, refer a matter to the Court of Justice of the Republic on the recommendation of the applications committee.

An organic enactment shall settle the conditions of application of this article.

TITLE XI—THE ECONOMIC AND SOCIAL COUNCIL

Article 69

The Economic and Social Council, at the request of the Government, shall give its opinion on Government bills, draft ordinances and decrees, and on the private members' bills submitted to it.

A member of the Economic and Social Council may be designated by it to present to the Houses of Parliament the Council's opinion on the bills submitted to it.

Article 70

The Economic and Social Council may likewise be consulted by the Government on any economic or social problem concerning the Republic or the Community. It shall be asked to advise on every plan or Government bill of an economic or social nature.

Article 71

The composition of the Economic and Social Council and its rules of procedure shall be laid down by an organic enactment.

TITLE XII—TERRITORIAL UNITS

Article 72

The territorial units of the Republic are the Communes, the Departments, and the Overseas Territories. Any other unit shall be created by legislation.

These units are free to govern themselves by elected councils

These units are free to govern themselves by elected councils and within the conditions provided for by legislation.

In the Departments and Territories, the Government delegate shall be responsible for national interests, administrative supervision, and respect for the law.

Article 73

The legislative structure and administrative organization of the Departments of the Overseas Territories may be adapted to their particular circumstances.

Article 74[10]

The special structure of the Overseas Territories of the Republic shall take into account their particular interests within the general interests of the Republic.

The status of an Overseas Territory is determined by organic enactment defining in particular the powers of its own institutions, and is modified in the same way after consultation of the territorial assembly concerned.

Other aspects of their particular structure are defined and modified by legislation after consultation with the territorial assembly concerned.

Article 75

Citizens of the Republic who lack the ordinary civil status referred to in Article 34 retain their personal status until they renounce it.

Article 76

The Overseas Territories may retain their status within the Republic.

If, by decision of their representative assembly within the period laid down by the first paragraph of Article 91, they express the wish to do so, they may become either overseas

---

[10] Amended by the constitutional law of 25 June 1992.

departments or, alone or with others, Member States of the Community.

Article 77

The Community established by this Constitution is composed of autonomous States which are self-governing and who manage their own affairs democratically and freely.

There is but one citizenship in the Community.

All its citizens are equal before the law, whatever their origin, race, and religion. They have the same duties.

Article 78

The Community's jurisdiction shall cover foreign policy, defence, currency, common economic and financial policy, and the control of strategic materials.

In the absence of particular agreement, it shall also cover the supervision of the administration of justice, higher education, the general organization of external and internal transport, and telecommunications.

New areas of common jurisdiction, or the transfer of jurisdiction from the Community to one of its members, may be established by special agreements.

Article 79

As soon as they have exercised the choice provided for by Article 76, Member States come within the provisions of Article 77.

Until the measures required for the implementation of the present Title enter into force, issues of common jurisdiction are resolved by the Republic.

[11] i.e. the French version of the British Commonwealth, not the European Community.

Article 80

The President of the Republic presides over and represents the Community.

Its organs are an executive Council, a Senate, and an Arbitration Court.

Article 81

The Member States of the Community shall participate in the election of the President under the conditions laid down in Article 6.

In his capacity as President of the Community, the President of the Republic is represented in each State of the Community.

Article 82

The executive Council of the Community is chaired by the President of the Community. It is composed of the Prime Minister of the Republic, the Heads of Government of each of the Member States of the Community, and the ministers responsible for common affairs on behalf of the Community.

The executive Council shall organize the co-operation of the members of the Community at governmental and administrative level.

The organization and procedure of the Executive Council shall be laid down by an organic enactment.

Article 83

The Senate of the Community is composed of delegates chosen from among their members by the Parliament of the Republic and the legislative assemblies of the other members. The number of delegates from each state shall reflect its population and its responsibilities within the Community.

The Senate of the Community shall hold two sessions a year, each opened and closed by the President of the Community and lasting no more than a month.

When called upon by the President of the Community, it considers common economic and financial policy before legislation thereon is enacted by the Parliament of the Republic and, where appropriate, the legislative assemblies of the other members of the Community.

The Senate of the Community scrutinizes the acts and the treaties and agreements referred to in Articles 35 and 53 which commit the Community.

In those fields where it has been delegated power by the legislative assemblies of the members of the Community, the Senate may make binding decisions. These decisions shall be promulgated in the same form as legislation in the territory of each state concerned.

An organic enactment shall lay down the composition of the Senate and its rules of procedure.

Article 84

A Community Arbitration Court shall rule on disputes arising among members of the Community. Its composition and jurisdiction are laid down by an organic enactment.

Article 85[12]

Notwithstanding the procedure provided for in Article 89, the provisions of this Title dealing with the functioning of the common institutions may be amended by legislation voted in the same terms by the Parliament of the Republic and the Senate of the Community.

The provisions of this Title may likewise be amended by agreements made between all the states of the Community; the new provisions shall be brought into force under the conditions specified by the constitution of each state.

Article 86[13]

A change of status of a Member State of the Community may be requested either by the Republic or by resolution of the legislative assembly of the state concerned, confirmed by local referendum held under the supervision of the Community institutions.

[12] Amended by the constitutional law of 4 June 1960.
[13] Amended by the constitutional law of 4 June 1960.

The procedures governing this change of status shall be laid down by an agreement approved by the Parliament of the Republic and the legislative assembly concerned.

In like manner, a Member State of the Community may become independent. It shall thereby cease to belong to the Community.

A Member State of the Community may likewise, by agreement, become independent without thereby ceasing to belong to the Community.

An independent state, not a member of the Community, may by agreement accede thereto without thereby losing independence.

The position of these states within the Community shall be determined by agreements concluded for that purpose, particularly those referred to in the preceding paragraphs and, where appropriate, those provided for in the second paragraph of Article 85.

Article 87

The particular agreements entered into for the application of this Title shall be approved by the Parliament of the Republic and the legislative assembly concerned.

TITLE XIV—ASSOCIATION AGREEMENTS

Article 88

The Republic or the Community may conclude agreements with states wishing to associate themselves with it in order to develop their cultures.

TITLE XV—THE EUROPEAN COMMUNITIES AND THE EUROPEAN UNION[14]

Article 88–1

The Republic is part of the European Communities and of the European Union, composed of states which, by the foundation

[14] Inserted by the constitutional law of 25 June 1992.

treaties, have freely chosen the common exercise of certain of their competences.

Article 88–2

On condition of reciprocity, and according to the terms laid down by the Treaty on European Union signed on 7 February 1992, France consents to the transfer of the competence necessary for creating economic and monetary union, and for laying down the rules on the crossing of the external borders of the Member States of the European Community.

Article 88–3

On condition of reciprocity, and according to the terms laid down in the Treaty on European Union signed on 7 February 1992, the right to vote and to stand in local elections may be granted to those citizens of the European Union who are resident in France. These citizens may not hold the office of mayor or deputy mayor, nor take part in the nomination of electors of the Senate or in elections to the Senate. An organic enactment passed in the same terms by the two Houses shall lay down the conditions of application of this article.

Article 88–4

On their transmission to the Council of the Communities, the Government shall lay before the National Assembly and the Senate all draft community acts containing provisions of a legislative nature. Both during and outside sessions of Parliament, resolutions may be voted in the context of this Article on terms laid down by the Standing Orders of each House.

TITLE XVI—AMENDMENT

Article 89

Constitutional amendments may be introduced both by the President of the Republic on the proposal of the Prime Minister, and by any member of Parliament.

Houses of Parliament in identical terms. The amendment becomes definitive on its approval by referendum.

Nevertheless, a Government amendment is not put to referendum when the President of the Republic decides to lay it before the two Houses of Parliament convened in Congress; in this event, the amendment may be approved only by three-fifths of the votes cast. The National Assembly Bureau acts as Congress Bureau.

No amendment process may be undertaken or maintained when the integrity of the territory is in jeopardy.

The republican form of government is not subject to amendment.

TITLE XVII—TRANSITIONAL PROVISIONS

Article 90

The ordinary session of Parliament is suspended. The term of office of members of the National Assembly shall expire on the day that the Assembly elected under this Constitution is convened.

Until then the Government alone has authority to convene Parliament.

The term of office of the members of the Assembly of the French Union shall expire at the same time as that of the members of the present National Assembly.

Article 91

The institutions of the Republic provided for by this Constitution shall be set up within four months of its promulgation.

The time limit is six months for the institutions of the Community.

The powers of the incumbent President of the Republic expire only on the announcement of the results of the election provided for by Articles 6 and 7 of this Constitution.

The Member States of the Community shall take part in this first election under the conditions following from their status at the date of promulgation of the Constitution.

Until the authorities provided for by their new structure are set up, the established authorities shall continue to exercise their functions in those states in accordance with the legislation and regulations in effect at the time this constitution comes into force.

Until it is finally constituted, the Senate shall consist of the present members of the Council of the Republic. The organic enactments on the final composition of the Senate must be enacted before 31 July 1959.

Until the Constitutional Council is set up, the powers conferred upon it by Articles 58 and 59 of the constitution shall be exercised by a committee composed of the Vice-President of the Council of State, as Chair, the First President of the Court of Cassation, and the First President of the Court of Auditors.

Until the entry into force of the measures needed for the application of Title XII, the peoples of the Member States of the Community shall continue to be represented in Parliament.

Article 92

The legislative measures needed to set up the institutions and, in the meantime, for the functioning of public authorities, shall be adopted in the Council of Ministers after consultation with the Council of State, by ordinances having the force of legislation.

During the period provided for in the first paragraph of Article 91, the government is authorized to lay down, by ordinances having the force of legislation and adopted according to the above procedure, the electoral system for the Assemblies provided for by the constitution.

During the same period and under the same conditions, the Government may likewise adopt in all fields those measures it deems necessary to the life of the Nation, the protection of citizens, or the preservation of liberties.

The present statute shall take effect as the constitution of the Republic and of the Community.

Article 93[15]

The provisions of Article 65 and of Title X in the version adopted by the constitutional enactment of 19 July 1993 shall come into force on the date of publication of the organic enactments on their application.

The provisions of Title X in the version adopted by the constitutional enactment of 19 July 1993 are applicable to acts committed before their entry into force.

Done at Paris, 4 October 1958.

[15] Added by the constitutional law of 19 July 1993.

7

Constitution of the Russian Federation

We, the multinational people of the Russian Federation,

united by a common destiny upon our land,
asserting human rights and freedoms and civil peace and concord,
preserving the unity of the state as formed by history,
proceeding from the generally recognized principles of the equality and self-determination of peoples,
revering the memory of our forebears who bequeathed us love and respect for the Fatherland and a faith in good and in justice,
restoring the sovereign statehood of Russia and asserting the immutability of its democratic foundation,
striving to ensure the well-being and the prosperity of Russia,
accepting responsibility for our homeland before present and future generations,
recognizing ourselves as part of the world community,
adopt the CONSTITUTION OF THE RUSSIAN FEDERATION.

SECTION ONE

Chapter 1. Foundations of the constitutional system

Article 1

(1) The Russian Federation–Russia is a democratic federative law-governed state with a republican form of government.

(2) The names Russian Federation and Russia are of equal validity.

Article 2

The individual and the individual's rights and freedoms shall be the supreme value. Recognition, observance and protection of human and civil rights and freedoms are the obligation of the state.

Article 3

(1) The holders of sovereignty and the sole sources of authority in the Russian Federation are its multinational people.

(2) The people shall exercise their authority directly and also through organs of state power and organs of local self-government.

(3) The supreme direct expression of the power of the people shall be the referendum and free elections.

(4) No-one may appropriate to themselves power in the Russian Federation. The seizure of power or the appropriation of its competences shall be prosecuted in accordance with federal law.

Article 4

(1) The sovereignty of the Russian Federation shall extend to the whole of its territory.

(2) The constitution of the Russian Federation and federal laws shall be paramount throughout the territory of the Russian Federation.

(3) The Russian Federation shall ensure the integrity and inviolability of its territory.

Article 5

(1) The Russian Federation consists of republics, areas, provinces, cities of federal significance, an autonomous province and autonomous districts which are equal components of the Russian Federation.

(2) A republic (state) has its own constitution and legislation. An area, province, city of federal significance, autonomous province or autonomous district has its own charter and legislation.

(3) The federal structure of the Russian Federation shall be based on its state integrity, on the unity of the system of state power, on the delimitation of areas of jurisdiction and powers between organs of state power of the Russian Federation and organs of state power of the components of the Russian Federation, and on the equality and self-determination of the peoples in the Russian Federation.

(4) All components of the Russian Federation shall be equal with each other in interrelationships with federal organs of state power.

Article 6

(1) Citizenship of the Russian Federation shall be acquired and terminated in accordance with federal law and shall be uniform and equal irrespective of the basis of its acquisition.

(2) Every citizen of the Russian Federation shall possess on its territory all rights and freedoms and bear equal obligations laid down by the constitution of the Russian Federation.

(3) A citizen of the Russian Federation may not be deprived of citizenship or of the right to change it.

Article 7

(1) The Russian Federation is a social state whose policy shall aim at creating conditions ensuring a worthy life and free development of the individual.

(2) In the Russian Federation people's labour and health shall be protected, a guaranteed minimum wage established, state support ensured for the family, motherhood, fatherhood and childhood, invalids and elderly citizens, the system of the social services developed, and state pensions, allowances and other guarantees of social protection established.

Article 8

(1) In the Russian Federation there shall be guaranteed the unity of the economic area, the free movement of goods, services and financial resources, support for competition and freedom of economic activity.

(2) In the Russian Federation private, state, municipal, and other forms of ownership shall enjoy equal recognition and protection.

Article 9

(1) The land and other natural resources shall be utilized and protected in the Russian Federation as the basis of the life and activity of the peoples inhabiting the corresponding territory.

(2) The land and other natural resources may be in private, state, municipal or other forms of ownership.

Article 10

State power in the Russian Federation shall be exercised on the basis of the separation of legislative, executive and judicial powers. The organs of legislative, executive and judicial power shall be independent.

Article 11

(1) State power in the Russian Federation shall be exercised by the president of the Russian Federation, the Federal Assembly (the Federation Council and the State Duma), the government of the Russian Federation and the courts of the Russian Federation.

(2) State power in the components of the Russian Federation shall be exercised by the organs of state power formed by them.

(3) The delimitation of areas of jurisdiction and competence between organs of state power of the Russian Federation and organs of state power of components of the Russian Federation shall be effected by the present constitution and the Federation Treaty and other treaties on the delimitation of areas of jurisdiction and competence.

Article 12

In the Russian Federation local self-government shall be recognized and guaranteed. Within the limits of its competences local self-government shall be independent. Organs of local self-government shall not form part of the system of organs of state power.

Article 13

(1) In the Russian Federation ideological diversity shall be recognized.

(2) No ideology may be established as that of the state or be made compulsory.

(3) In the Russian Federation political diversity and a multiparty system shall be recognized.

(4) Social associations shall be equal before the law.

(5) The creation and activity of social associations whose objectives and actions are directed towards the forcible alteration of the basic principles of the constitutional system and the violation of the integrity of the Russian Federation, the undermining of the security of the state, the creation of armed formations, or the kindling of social, racial, national or religious strife shall be prohibited.

Article 14

(1) The Russian Federation shall be a secular state. No religion may be established as that of the state or be made compulsory.

(2) Religious associations shall be separate from the state and are equal before the law.

Article 15

(1) The constitution of the Russian Federation shall have supreme legal force and direct effect and shall apply throughout the territory of the Russian Federation. Laws and other legal acts adopted in the Russian Federation must not contradict the constitution of the Russian Federation.

(2) Organs of state power, organs of local self-government, officials, citizens and associations thereof shall be obliged to observe the constitution of the Russian Federation and the laws.

(3) Laws are subject to official publication. Unpublished laws shall not be applied. Unless officially published for general information, normative legal acts affecting human and civil rights, freedoms and duties may not be applied.

(4) The generally recognized principles and norms of international law and the international treaties of the Russian Federa-

tion shall be a constituent part of its legal system. If an international treaty of the Russian Federation establishes rules other than those stipulated by the law, the rules of the international treaty shall apply.

Article 16

(1) The provisions of the present chapter of the constitution form the basic principles of the constitutional system of the Russian Federation and may not be altered save under the procedure laid down by the present constitution.

(2) No other provisions of the present constitution may contradict the basic principles of the constitutional system of the Russian Federation.

Chapter 2. Human and Civil Rights and Freedoms[1]

Article 17

(1) Human and civil rights and freedoms shall be recognized and guaranteed in the Russian Federation in accordance with the generally acknowledged principles and norms of international law and in conformity with the present constitution.

(2) Basic human rights and freedoms are inalienable and belong to each person from birth.

(3) The exercise of human and civil rights and freedoms must not violate the rights and freedoms of others.

Article 18

Human and civil rights and freedoms shall be directly effective. They determine the meaning, content and application of laws and the activity of the legislative and executive branches and of local self-government and are safeguarded by justice.

---

[1] Literally, 'rights and freedoms of man and citizen', thus echoing the 1789 French Declaration. In Russian, however, the word *chelovek* means both 'man' and 'human' (like the German *Mensch*).

Article 19

(1) All are equal before the law and the court.

(2) The state shall guarantee equality of human and civil rights and freedoms regardless of sex, race, nationality, language, origin, property and position, place of residence, attitude towards religion, convictions, membership of social associations, or other circumstances. Any forms of restriction of citizens' rights on the grounds of social, racial, national, linguistic or religious affiliation shall be prohibited.

(3) Men and women shall have equal rights and freedoms and equal opportunities for their exercise.

Article 20

(1) Everyone has the right to life.

(2) Until its abolition the death penalty may be prescribed by federal law as the supreme penalty for particularly grave crimes against life, the accused being granted the right to trial by jury.

Article 21

(1) The dignity of the individual shall be protected by the state. Nothing may be grounds for belittling it.

(2) No one may be subjected to torture, violence or other cruel or humiliating treatment or punishment. No one may be subjected to medical, scientific or other experiments without having freely consented thereto.

Article 22

(1) Everyone has the right to freedom and inviolability of the person.

(2) Arrest, detention and custody shall be permitted only by authority of judicial order. An individual cannot be detained for a period of more than forty-eight hours without a judicial decision.

Article 23

(1) Everyone has the right to inviolability of their private life, personal and family privacy, and defence of their honour and good name.

(2) Everyone has the right to privacy of correspondence, telephone conversations and postal, telegraph and other communications. Curtailment of this right is permitted only on the basis of a judicial decision.

Article 24

(1) The collection, storage, utilization and dissemination of information about a person's private life without his consent shall not be permitted.

(2) Unless otherwise provided for by law, organs of state power and organs of local self-government and their officials are obliged to ensure that everyone has the opportunity to consult documents and materials directly affecting their rights and freedoms.

Article 25

Dwellings shall be inviolable. No one shall be entitled to enter a dwelling against the wishes of its residents save in cases prescribed by federal law or on the basis of a judicial decision.

Article 26

(1) Everyone shall be entitled to determine and indicate their own national affiliation. No one may be compelled to determine and indicate their own national affiliation.

(2) Everyone shall have the right to use their native language and to the free choice of language of communication, education, instruction and creativity.

Article 27

(1) Everyone legally present on the territory of the Russian Federation shall have the right to travel freely and choose their place of stay and residence.

(2) Everyone may freely travel outside the Russian Federation. A citizen of the Russian Federation has the right without impediment to return to the Russian Federation.

Article 28

Everyone shall be guaranteed freedom of conscience and freedom of religion, including the right to profess any religion individually or together with others or not to profess any, and freely to choose, hold and disseminate religious and other convictions and to act in accordance with them.

Article 29

(1) Everyone shall be guaranteed freedom of thought and speech.

(2) Propaganda or agitation arousing social, racial, national or religious hatred and enmity shall not be permitted. Propaganda of social, racial, national, religious or linguistic supremacy shall be prohibited.

(3) No one may be compelled to express his opinions and convictions or to renounce them.

(4) Everyone shall have the right freely to seek, receive, pass on, produce and disseminate information by any lawful means. The list of information constituting a state secret is determined by federal law.

(5) The freedom of mass information shall be guaranteed. Censorship shall be prohibited.

Article 30

(1) Everyone shall have the right of association, including the right to form trade unions to protect their interests. The freedom of the activity of social associations shall be guaranteed.

(2) No one may be compelled to join or to remain in any association.

Article 31

Citizens of the Russian Federation shall have the right to assemble peacefully without weapons and to hold meetings, rallies and demonstrations, processions and pickets.

Article 32

(1) Citizens of the Russian Federation shall have the right to participate in the administration of the state's affairs both directly and via their representatives.

(2) Citizens of the Russian Federation shall have the right to elect and to be elected to organs of state power and organs of local self-government, and also to take part in a referendum.

(3) Citizens found by a court to be incompetent and those detained by sentence of a court in places of imprisonment shall not have the right to elect and to be elected.

(4) Citizens of the Russian Federation shall have equal access to state service.

(5) Citizens of the Russian Federation shall have the right to take part in the administration of justice.

Article 33

Citizens of the Russian Federation shall have the right to appeal personally and also to address individual and collective appeals to state organs and organs of local self-government.

Article 34

(1) Everyone shall have the right to make free use of their abilities and property for entrepreneurial and other economic activity not prohibited by law.

(2) Economic activity directed towards monopolization and unfair competition shall not be permitted.

Article 35

(1) The right of private ownership shall be protected by law.

(2) Everyone shall be entitled to own property and to possess,

utilize and dispose of it both individually and together with others.

(3) No one may be deprived of their property save by court decision. The compulsory expropriation of property for state requirements may be carried out only with full compensation determined in advance.

(4) The right of inheritance shall be guaranteed.

Article 36

(1) Citizens and their associations shall be entitled to hold land in private ownership.

(2) Owners shall freely possess, utilize and dispose of land and other natural resources provided that this does not damage the environment and does not violate the rights and lawful interests of others.

(3) The conditions and procedure for the use of land shall be defined on the basis of federal law.

Article 37

(1) Labour shall be free. Everyone has the right freely to dispose of their abilities for labour and to choose their type of activity and occupation.

(2) Forced labour shall be prohibited.

(3) Everyone shall have the right to work in conditions meeting the requirements of safety and hygiene, to be paid for their work without any sort of discrimination and at not less than the minimum rate prescribed by federal law, and also the right to protection from unemployment.

(4) The right to individual and collective labour disputes utilizing the methods of resolving them prescribed by federal law, including the right to strike, shall be recognized.

(5) Everyone shall have the right to leisure. A person working on the basis of a contract of employment shall be guaranteed the working hours, days off and holidays prescribed by federal law and paid annual leave.

Article 38

(1) Maternity and childhood and the family shall be under the state's protection.

(2) Concern for children and their upbringing are the equal right and duty of the parents.

(3) Able-bodied children who have reached the age of 18 years must take care of disabled parents.

Article 39

(1) Everyone shall be guaranteed social security in old age, in the event of sickness, disability or loss of breadwinner, for the raising of children, and in other cases prescribed by law.

(2) State pensions and social allowances shall be prescribed by law.

(3) Voluntary social insurance, and the creation of additional forms of social security and charity are encouraged.

Article 40

(1) Everyone shall have the right to housing. No one may be arbitrarily deprived of housing.

(2) Organs of state power and organs of local self-government shall encourage housing construction and create the conditions for exercise of the right to housing.

(3) In accordance with the norms prescribed by law, housing shall be provided free or at affordable cost from state, municipal and other housing stocks to low-income and other citizens referred to in the law who are in need of housing.

Article 41

(1) Everyone shall have the right to health care and medical assistance. Medical assistance in state and municipal health care establishments is provided free to citizens by means of funds from the relevant budget, insurance contributions and other revenue.

(2) In the Russian Federation federal programmes to protect and improve the population's health shall be financed, measures to develop state, municipal and private health care systems shall

be taken, and activities conducive to the improvement of people's health, the development of physical culture and sport, and ecological and sanitary and epidemiological well-being shall be encouraged.

(3) The concealment by officials of facts and circumstances creating a threat to people's lives and health shall entail responsibility in accordance with federal law.

Article 42

Everyone shall have the right to a decent environment, reliable information about the state of the environment and compensation for injury caused to their health or property by ecological offences.

Article 43

(1) Everyone shall have the right to education.

(2) General access to free pre-school, basic general and secondary vocational education in state or municipal educational establishments and in enterprises shall be guaranteed.

(3) Everyone shall be entitled on a competitive basis to receive free higher education in a state or municipal educational establishment or in an enterprise.

(4) Basic general education is compulsory. Parents or persons *in loco parentis* shall ensure that children receive basic general education.

(5) The Russian Federation shall establish federal state educational standards and support various forms of education and self-education.

Article 44

(1) Everyone shall be guaranteed freedom of literary, artistic, scientific, technical and other types of creation and instruction. Intellectual property shall be protected by law.

(2) Everyone shall have the right to participate in cultural life and use cultural institutions and to have access to cultural treasures.

(3) Everyone must look to preserve the historical and cultural heritage and look after historical and cultural monuments.

Article 45

(1) State protection of human and civil rights and freedoms in the Russian Federation shall be guaranteed.

(2) Everyone shall be entitled to protect their rights and freedoms by any means not prohibited by law.

Article 46

(1) Everyone shall be guaranteed judicial protection of their rights and freedoms.

(2) The decisions and actions (or inaction) of organs of state power, organs of local self-government, public associations and officials may be appealed in court.

(3) Everyone shall be entitled, in accordance with the Russian Federation's international treaties, to appeal to interstate organs for the protection of human rights and freedoms if all available means of legal protection inside the state have been exhausted.

Article 47

(1) No one may be deprived of the right to have their case heard by the court and the judges to whose jurisdiction it is assigned by law.

(2) In the situations provided for by federal law, a person charged with having committed a crime shall have the right to have the case heard by a court with a jury.

Article 48

(1) Everyone shall be guaranteed the right to receive qualified legal assistance. In the situations provided for by law, legal assistance shall be rendered free of charge.

(2) Everyone detained in custody and charged with having committed a crime shall have the right to make use of the assistance of a lawyer (defence attorney) from the moment of detention, placing in custody, or indictment respectively.

Article 49

(1) Everyone charged with having committed a crime shall be presumed innocent until their guilt is proved as provided by federal law and established by means of a court verdict which has entered into legal effect.

(2) The accused shall not be obliged to prove innocence.

(3) Any undispelled doubts regarding a person's guilt shall be interpreted in the accused's favour.

Article 50

(1) No one may be tried a second time for the same crime.

(2) Evidence acquired in breach of federal law may not be utilized in the administration of justice.

(3) Everyone sentenced for a crime shall have the right to have their sentence reviewed by a superior court as provided by federal law, as well as the right to appeal for pardon or a lighter punishment.

Article 51

(1) No one shall be obliged to testify against themselves, their spouse or close relatives, the range of the latter being defined by federal law.

(2) Federal law may lay down other instances of freedom from the obligation to testify.

Article 52

The rights of the victims of crimes or of abuses of power shall be protected by law. The state secures the victims' access to justice and to compensation for injury caused.

Article 53

Everyone shall have the right to compensation from the state for injury caused by the unlawful action (or inaction) of organs of state power or their officials.

Article 54

(1) No law establishing or increasing liability may be retroactive.

(2) No one may be held liable for an act which, at the time it was committed, was not declared to be a breach of the law. If, after a breach of the law has been committed, liability therefor is abolished or mitigated the new law shall be applied.

Article 55

(1) The listing of basic rights and freedoms in the constitution of the Russian Federation must not be interpreted as denying or diminishing other universally recognized human and civil rights and freedoms.

(2) Laws abolishing or diminishing human and civil rights and freedoms must not be promulgated in the Russian Federation.

(3) Human and civil rights and freedoms may be curtailed by federal law only to the extent to which it may be necessary for the purpose of protecting the foundations of the constitutional system, morality, and the health, rights and lawful interests of other individuals, or of ensuring the country's defence and the state's security.

Article 56

(1) In accordance with federal constitutional law, particular restrictions of rights and freedoms may be introduced, with an indication of their extent and duration, in a state of emergency in order to ensure the safety of citizens and the protection of the constitutional system.

(2) A state of emergency may be introduced throughout the territory of the Russian Federation or in individual localities thereof in the circumstances and according to the procedure provided by federal constitutional law.

(3) The rights and freedoms contains in Articles 20, 21, 23(1), 24, 28, 34(1), 40(1), and 46–54 of the constitution of the Russian Federation may not be restricted.

Article 57

Everyone shall be obliged to pay lawfully levied taxes and duties. Laws introducing new taxes or detrimental to the taxpayers' situation cannot be retroactive.

Article 58

Everyone shall be obliged to protect nature and the environment and to show solicitude for the riches of nature.

Article 59

(1) The protection of the fatherland shall be the duty and obligation of citizens of the Russian Federation.

(2) Citizens of the Russian Federation shall perform military service as provided for by the federal law.

(3) Where the convictions or religious beliefs of a citizen of the Russian Federation are in conflict with the performance of military service, as well as in other instances as provided by federal law, the citizen shall have the right to perform alternative civil service as a substitute.

Article 60

A citizen of the Russian Federation may independently exercise all rights and obligations in full from the age of 18 years.

Article 61

(1) A citizen of the Russian Federation cannot be expelled from the Russian Federation or extradited to another state.

(2) The Russian Federation shall guarantee the safeguarding and protection of its citizens outside its borders.

Article 62

(1) A citizen of the Russian Federation may hold the citizenship of a foreign state (dual citizenship) in accordance with federal law or an international treaty of the Russian Federation.

(2) Unless otherwise provided by federal law or an international treaty of the Russian Federation, the fact that a citizen of the Russian Federation holds citizenship of a foreign state shall not diminish his rights and freedoms or exempt him from obligations stemming from Russian citizenship.

(3) Save as otherwise provided for by federal law or an international treaty of the Russian Federation, foreign citizens and stateless persons in the Russian Federation shall enjoy equal rights and bear equal obligations with citizens of the Russian Federation.

Article 63

(1) The Russian Federation shall offer political asylum to foreign citizens and stateless persons in accordance with generally accepted norms of international law.

(2) The Russian Federation shall not permit the extradition to other states of persons persecuted for their political beliefs or for actions (or inaction) which are not considered a crime in the Russian Federation. The extradition to other states of persons accused of having committed crimes, or the transfer of those who have been convicted to serve their sentence in other states, shall be carried out on the basis of federal law or an international treaty of the Russian Federation.

Article 64

The provisions of this chapter shall comprise the foundations of the individual's legal status in the Russian Federation and cannot be amended save by the procedure laid down in this constitution.

Chapter 3. Federative Structure

Article 65

(1) The composition of the Russian Federation comprises the following components of the Russian Federation:

the Republic of Adygea (Adygea), the Republic of Altay, the Republic of Bashkortostan, the Republic of Buryatia, the

Republic of Dagestan, the Ingush Republic, the Kabardino-Balkar Republic, the Republic of Kalmykia–Khalmg Tangch, the Karachay–Cherkess Republic, the Republic of Karelia, the Republic of Komi, the Republic of Mari El, the Republic of Mordovia, the Republic of Sakha (Yakutia), the Republic of North Ossetia, the Republic of Tatarstan (Tatarstan), the Republic of Tuva, the Udmurt Republic, the Republic of Khakassia, the Chechen Republic, the Chuvash Republic—Chavash Respubliki;

Altay Area, Krasnodar Area, Krasnoyarsk Area, Primorskii Area, Stavropol Area, Khabarovsk Area.

Amur Province, Arkhangelsk Province, Astrakhan Province, Belgorod Province, Bryansk Province, Vladimir Province, Volgograd Province, Vologda Province, Voronezh Province, Ivanovo Province, Irkutsk Province, Kaliningrad Province, Kaluga Province, Kamchatka Province, Kurgan Province, Kursk Province, Leningrad Province, Lipetsk Province, Magadan Province, Moscow Province, Murmansk Province, Nizhniy Novgorod Province, Novgorod Province, Novosibirsk Province, Omsk Province, Orenburg Province, Orel Province, Penza Province, Perm Province, Pskov Province, Rostov Province, Ryazan Province, Samara Province, Saratov Province, Sakhalin Province, Sverdlovsk Province, Smolensk Province, Tambov Province, Tver Province, Tomsk Province, Tula Province, Tyumen Province, Ulyanovsk Province, Chelyabinsk Province, Chita Province, Yaroslavl Province;

Moscow, St Petersburg—cities of federal significance;

the Jewish Autonomous Province;

the Aga Buryat Autonomous District, the Komi–Permyak Autonomous District, the Koryak Autonomous District, the Nenetsk Autonomous District, the Taymyr (Dolgano–Nenets) Autonomous District, the Ust–Orda Buryat Autonomous District, the Khant–Mansiysk Autonomous District, the Chukotsk Autonomous District, the Evenk Autonomous District, the Yamalo–Nenetsk Autonomous District.

(2) The admission to the Russian Federation and the formation as part of the Russian Federation of a new component shall be carried out in accordance with the procedure laid down by federal constitutional law.

Article 66

(1) The status of a republic shall be determined by the constitution of the Russian Federation and by the constitution of the republic.

(2) The status of an area, province, city of federal significance, autonomous province and autonomous district shall be determined by the constitution of the Russian Federation and the charter of the area, province, city of federal significance, autonomous province and autonomous district adopted by the legislative (representative) body of the relevant component of the Russian Federation.

(3) A federal law on the autonomous province or an autonomous district may be adopted upon submission by the legislative and executive organs of the autonomous province or autonomous district.

(4) The relations of autonomous districts forming part of an area or province may be regulated by federal law and by treaty between the organs of state power of an autonomous district and the organs of state power of the appropriate area or province.

(5) The status of a component of the Russian Federation may be changed by the mutual consent of the Russian Federation and the component of the Russian Federation in accordance with federal constitutional law.

Article 67

(1) The territory of the Russian Federation includes the territories of its components, inland stretches of water and territorial waters and the airspace over these.

(2) The Russian Federation possesses sovereign rights and exercises jurisdiction over the continental shelf and within the exclusive economic zone of the Russian Federation in accordance with the procedures defined by federal law and the norms of international law.

(3) The borders between components of the Russian Federation may be altered with their mutual consent.

Article 68

(1) The Russian language shall be the state language of the Russian Federation throughout its territory.

(2) Republics shall be entitled to establish their own state languages. They shall be used alongside the state language of the Russian Federation in the organs of state power, organs of local self-government and state institutions of the republics.

(3) The Russian Federation shall guarantee all its peoples the right to retain their mother tongues and to create conditions for their study and development.

Article 69

The Russian Federation shall guarantee the rights of numerically small indigenous peoples in accordance with generally accepted principles and norms of international law and the international treaties of the Russian Federation.

Article 70

(1) The state flag, emblem and anthem of the Russian Federation, the description of these, and the procedure for their official use shall be laid down by federal constitutional law.

(2) The capital of the Russian Federation shall be the city of Moscow. The status of the capital is laid down by federal law.

Article 71

The following fall within the jurisdiction of the Russian Federation:

- (a) the adoption and amendment of the constitution of the Russian Federation and federal laws, and the monitoring of compliance with them;
- (b) the federative structure and territory of the Russian Federation;
- (c) the regulation and protection of human and civil rights and freedoms; citizenship of the Russian Federation; the regulation and protection of the rights of national minorities;

(d)   the establishment of a system of federal organs of legislative, executive and judicial power, the procedure for
their organization and activity; the formation of federal
organs of state power;

(e)   federal state property and the administration thereof;

(f)   the establishment of the fundamentals of federal policy
and the federal programmes in the sphere of state, economic, ecological, social, cultural and national development of the Russian Federation;

(g)   the establishment of the legal foundations of the single
market; financial, currency, credit and customs regulation; the issue of currency, and the foundations of pric-
ing policy; federal economic services, including federal
banks;

(h)   the federal budget; federal taxes and duties; federal
regional development funds;

(i)   federal energy systems, nuclear power generation, fissile
materials; federal transport, means of communication,
information and connections; activity in space;

(j)   the Russian Federation's foreign policy and international relations and the Russian Federation's international treaties; issues of war and peace;

(k)   the Russian Federation's foreign economic relations;

(l)   defence and security; defence production; the determination of the procedure for the sale and purchase of
weapons, ammunition, military hardware and other military property; the production of toxic substances, nar-
cotic substances and the procedure for their use;

(m)   the determination of the status and protection of the
state border, territorial seas, airspace, the exclusive economic zone and the continental shelf of the Russian
Federation;

(n)   the judicial system; the procuracy; legislation in the field
of criminal law, criminal procedure and criminal executive
law; amnesty and pardon; legislation in the field of civil
law, the law of civil procedure and the law of arbitral procedure; the legal regulation of intellectual property;

(o)   federal law relating to the conflict of laws;

(p)   the meteorological service, standards and standard
weights and measurements, the metric system and mea-

surement of time; geodesy and cartography; geographic names; official statistical records and accounting;

(q) state awards and honorary titles of the Russian Federation;

(r) the federal civil service.

Article 72

(1) The following fall within the joint jurisdiction of the Russian Federation and the components of the Russian Federation:

(a) ensuring compatibility with the constitution of the Russian Federation and federal laws of the constitutions and laws of republics, and the charters, laws and other normative legal acts of areas, provinces, cities of federal significance, the autonomous province and autonomous districts;

(b) the protection of human and civil rights and freedoms; the protection of the rights of national minorities; the ensuring of legality, law and order and public safety; the arrangements relating to border zones;

(c) issues relating to the ownership, use and disposal of land, mineral resources, water and other natural resources;

(d) the delimitation of state property;

(e) the use of the natural environment; environmental protection and the ensuring of ecological safety; natural sites under special protection; the protection of historical and cultural monuments;

(f) general issues of training, education, science, culture, physical fitness and sport;

(g) the co-ordination of pubic health issues; the protection of the family, motherhood, fatherhood, and childhood; social protection, including social security;

(h) the implementation of measures for combating catastrophes, natural disasters and epidemics and the elimination of their consequences;

(i) the establishment of general principles of taxation and levying of duties in the Russian Federation;

(j) administrative, administrative–procedural, employment, family, housing, land, water and forestry legislation,

and legislation on mineral resources and on environmental protection;

(k)   personnel of judicial and law enforcement organs; attor-
neys and notaries;

(l)   the protection of the indigenous habitat and traditional
way of life of numerically small ethnic communities;

(m)   the establishment of the general principles for the organization of a system of organs of state power and
local self-government;

(n)   the co-ordination of the international and foreign economic relations of components of the Russian Federation, and the fulfilment of the Russian Federation's
international treaties.

(2) The provisions of this article extend in equal measure to
the republics, areas, provinces, cities of federal significance, the
autonomous province and autonomous districts.

Article 73

Outside the limits of the Russian Federation's jurisdiction and
the powers of the Russian Federation over the objects of joint
jurisdiction of the Russian Federation and the components of the
Russian Federation, the components of the Russian Federation
shall enjoy state power in its entirety.

Article 74

(1) The establishment of customs borders, duties, charges, and
any other hindrances to the free movement of goods, services,
and financial assets shall not be permitted on the territory of the
Russian Federation.

(2) Restrictions on the movement of goods and services may
be introduced in accordance with federal law if this is necessary
to ensure safety, the protection of the life and health of people,
and the protection of nature and cultural assets.

Article 75

(1) The monetary unit in the Russian Federation shall be the
rouble. Monetary issue shall be carried out exclusively by the

Central Bank of the Russian Federation. The introduction and issue of other currencies shall not be permitted in the Russian Federation.

(2) The protection and the guaranteeing of the stability of the rouble shall be the basic function of the Central Bank of the Russian Federation which it carries out independently of the other organs of state power.

(3) The system of taxes levied for the federal budget and the general principles of taxation and levies in the Russian Federation shall be established by federal law.

(4) State loans are issued in accordance with a procedure determined by federal law and are raised on a voluntary basis.

Article 76

(1) The Russian Federation's areas of jurisdiction shall be governed by federal constitutional laws and federal laws which are directly effective throughout the territory of the Russian Federation.

(2) The areas of joint jurisdiction of the Russian Federation and components of the Russian Federation shall be governed by federal laws, and by laws and other normative legal acts of the components of the Russian Federation adopted in accordance therewith.

(3) Federal laws may not conflict with federal constitutional laws.

(4) Outside the limits of the Russian Federation's jurisdiction and the joint jurisdiction of the Russian Federation and the components of the Russian Federation, the republics, areas, provinces, cities of federal significance, the autonomous province and the autonomous districts shall exercise their own legal regulation, including the adoption of laws and other normative legal acts.

(5) The laws and other normative legal acts of the components of the Russian Federation cannot conflict with federal laws adopted in accordance with the first and second parts of this article. In the event of conflict between the federal law and another act issued in the Russian Federation, the federal law shall take effect.

(6) In the event of conflict between the federal law and a normative legal act of a component of the Russian Federation pro-

mulgated in accordance with the fourth part of this article, the normative legal enactment of the component of the Russian Federation is to take effect.

Article 77

(1) The system of organs of state power of the republics, areas, provinces, cities of federal significance, the autonomous province and autonomous districts shall be established by the components of the Russian Federation independently in accordance with the fundamentals of the constitutional structure of the Russian Federation and the general principles of the organization of representative and executive organs of state power laid down by federal law.

(2) Within the limits of the Russian Federation's jurisdiction and the powers of the Russian Federation over the objects of joint jurisdiction of the Russian Federation and the components of the Russian Federation, the federal organs of executive power and the organs of executive power of the components of the Russian Federation shall form a unified system of executive power in the Russian Federation.

Article 78

(1) In order to exercise their powers, the federal organs of executive power may create their own territorial organs and appoint the appropriate officials.

(2) The federal organs of executive power, by agreement with the organs of executive power of the components of the Russian Federation may transfer to them the implementation of some of their powers provided that this does not conflict with the constitution of the Russian Federation and federal laws.

(3) By agreement with the federal organs of executive power the organs of executive power of the components of the Russian Federation may transfer to them the implementation of some of their powers.

(4) The president of the Russian Federation and the government of the Russian Federation shall ensure, in accordance with the constitution of the Russian Federation, the exercise of the powers of federal state authority throughout the territory of the Russian Federation.

Article 79

The Russian Federation may participate in interstate unions and transfer to them part of its powers in accordance with international treaties provided this does not entail restriction of human and civil rights and freedoms nor conflict with the fundamentals of the constitutional structure of the Russian Federation.

Chapter 4. President of the Russian Federation

Article 80

(1) The President of the Russian Federation shall be the head of state.

(2) The President of the Russian Federation shall be the guarantor of the constitution of the Russian Federation and of human and civil rights and freedoms. Within the procedure established by the constitution of the Russian Federation, he shall take measures to safeguard the sovereignty of the Russian Federation and its independence and state integrity, and ensure the co-ordinated functioning and collaboration of organs of state power.

(3) The President of the Russian Federation, in accordance with the constitution of the Russian Federation and with federal laws, shall determine the basic guidelines of the state's domestic and foreign policy.

(4) The President of the Russian Federation, in his capacity as head of state, shall represent the Russian Federation within the country and in international relations.

Article 81

(1) The President of the Russian Federation shall be elected for four years by citizens of the Russian Federation on the basis of universal, equal and direct suffrage in a secret ballot.

(2) A citizen of the Russian Federation who is at least 35 years of age and has been permanently resident in the Russian Federation for at least 10 years may be elected President of the Russian Federation.

(3) The same person may not hold the office of President of the Russian Federation for more than two consecutive terms.

(4) The procedure of elections for President of the Russian Federation shall be determined by a federal law.

Article 82

(1) At his inauguration the President of the Russian Federation shall swear the following oath to the people:

In exercising the powers of President of the Russian Federation I swear to respect and protect human and civil rights and freedoms, to observe and defend the constitution of the Russian Federation, to defend the state's sovereignty and independence and its security and integrity, and faithfully to serve the people.

(2) The oath shall be administered in a ceremonial atmosphere in the presence of members of the Federation Council, deputies of the State Duma and judges of the Constitutional Court of the Russian Federation.

Article 83

The President of the Russian Federation:

- (a) appoints with the consent of the State Duma the chair of the Government of the Russian Federation;
- (b) has the right to chair sessions of the Government of the Russian Federation;
- (c) takes a decision on the dismissal [*otstavka*] of the Government of the Russian Federation;
- (d) submits to the State Duma the candidate for appointment to the office of chair of the Central Bank of the Russian Federation; raises before the State Duma the question of removing from office the chair of the Central Bank of the Russian Federation;
- (e) on the proposal of the chair of the Government of the Russian Federation appoints and removes from office the deputy chairs of the Government of the Russian Federation and federal ministers;
- (f) submits to the Federation Council candidates for appointment to the office of judges of the Constitutional Court of the Russian Federation, the Supreme Court of the Russian Federation and the Higher Court of Arbitration

of the Russian Federation, and also the candidate for procurator-general of the Russian Federation; submits to the Federation Council the proposal on removing from office the procurator-general of the Russian Federation; appoints the judges of other federal courts;

(g) forms and heads the Security Council of the Russian Federation, whose status is defined by federal law;

(h) approves the military doctrine of the Russian Federation;

(i) forms the administration of the President of the Russian Federation;

(j) appoints and removes plenipotentiary representatives of the President of the Russian Federation;

(k) appoints and removes the high command of the Armed Forces of the Russian Federation;

(l) appoints and recalls, following consultations with the relevant committees or commissions of the chambers of the Federal Assembly, diplomatic representatives of the Russian Federation in foreign states and international organizations.

Article 84

The President of the Russian Federation:

(a) calls elections to the State Duma in accordance with the constitution of the Russian Federation and federal law;

(b) dissolves the State Duma in instances and according to the procedure laid down by the constitution of the Russian Federation;

(c) calls referendums according to the procedure prescribed by federal constitutional law;

(d) submits bills to the State Duma;

(e) signs and promulgates federal laws;

(f) delivers to the Federal Assembly annual messages on the situation in the country and on the basic guidelines of the state's domestic and foreign policy.

Article 85

(1) The President of the Russian Federation may use conciliation procedures to resolve disagreements between organs of state power of the Russian Federation and organs of state power of components of the Russian Federation, and also between organs of state power of components of the Russian Federation. In the event of failure to reach an agreed solution he may refer the resolution of the dispute for examination by the appropriate court.

(2) Pending a decision on the matter by the appropriate court, the President of the Russian Federation shall be entitled to suspend the operation of acts of the organs of executive power of components of the Russian Federation if these acts contravene the constitution of the Russian Federation and federal laws, or the Russian Federation's international obligations or violate human and civil rights and freedoms.

Article 86

The President of the Russian Federation:

  (a) exercises leadership of the foreign policy of the Russian Federation;
  (b) conducts negotiations and signs international treaties of the Russian Federation;
  (c) signs instruments of ratification;
  (d) accepts the credentials and letters of recall of accredited diplomatic representatives.

Article 87

(1) The President of the Russian Federation shall be supreme commander-in-chief of the Armed Forces of the Russian Federation.

(2) In the event of aggression against the Russian Federation or an immediate threat of aggression the President of the Russian Federation shall introduce martial law on the territory of the Russian Federation or in individual localities of that territory and shall immediately notify the Federation Council and State Duma of this.

(3) The regime of martial law shall be defined by federal constitutional law.

Article 88

In the circumstances and in accordance with the procedure laid down by federal constitutional law, the President of the Russian Federation shall introduce on the territory of the Russian Federation or in particular localities of that territory a state of emergency and shall immediately inform the Federation Council and State Duma thereof.

Article 89

The President of the Russian Federation:
- (a) decides questions of citizenship of the Russian Federation and of granting political asylum;
- (b) confers state awards of the Russian Federation and awards honorary titles of the Russian Federation and higher military and higher special ranks;
- (c) grants pardons.

Article 90

(1) The President of the Russian Federation issues edicts and decrees.

(2) Implementation of the edicts and decrees of the President of the Russian Federation shall be mandatory throughout the territory of the Russian Federation.

(3) The decrees and directives of the President of the Russian Federation must not contravene the constitution of the Russian Federation and federal laws.

Article 91

The President of the Russian Federation shall enjoy immunity.

Article 92

(1) The President of the Russian Federation shall take up his powers from the moment he swears the oath and, on the expiry of his term of office, shall cease to hold them from the moment that the newly elected President of the Russian Federation takes the oath.

(2) The President of the Russian Federation shall cease to exercise his powers prematurely in the event of his resignation, persistent inability to exercise his powers for health reasons, or removal from office. In such event, elections for President of the Russian Federation must take place within three months of the premature cessation of the exercise of powers.

(3) In all instances where the President of the Russian Federation is unable to perform his duties, they shall be temporarily carried out by the chair of the Government of the Russian Federation. The acting President of the Russian Federation has no right to dissolve the State Duma, call a referendum, or submit proposals on amendments to and revision of provisions of the constitution of the Russian Federation.

Article 93

(1) The President of the Russian Federation may be removed from office by the Federation Council only on the grounds of treason or the commission of some other grave crime on a charge laid by the State Duma and confirmed by a ruling of the Supreme Court of the Russian Federation that the actions of the President of the Russian Federation contain the elements of such crime, and a ruling by the Constitutional Court of the Russian Federation that the established procedure for laying the charge has been observed.

(2) The decision by the State Duma on laying the charge and the decision by the Federation Council on removing the President from office must be adopted by a vote of two-thirds of the total number in each chamber on the initiative of at least one-third of the deputies of the State Duma, and accompanied by a ruling by a special commission formed by the State Duma.

(3) The decision by the Federation Council on removing the President of the Russian Federation from office must be taken

within three months of the laying of the charge against the President by the State Duma. If the decision by the Federation Council is not taken within this period of time, the charge against the President shall be deemed rejected.

Chapter 5. Federal Assembly

Article 94

The Federal Assembly—Parliament—of the Russian Federation shall be the representative and legislative organ of the Russian Federation.

Article 95

(1) The Federal Assembly shall consist of two chambers—the Federation Council and the State Duma.

(2) The Federation Council shall consist of two representatives from each component of the Russian Federation; one each from the representative and executive organs of state power.

(3) The State Duma shall consist of 450 deputies.

Article 96

(1) The State Duma shall be elected for a term of four years.

(2) The procedure for forming the Federation Council and the procedure for electing deputies of the State Duma shall be laid down by federal laws.

Article 97

(1) A citizen of the Russian Federation who has attained the age of 21 years and has the right to participate in elections may be elected deputy of the State Duma.

(2) One and the same person cannot simultaneously be a member of the Federation Council and a deputy of the State Duma. A deputy of the State Duma may not be a deputy of any other representative organs of state power or organs of local self-government.

(3) Deputies of the State Duma shall work on a full-time pro-

fessional basis. Deputies of the State Duma cannot be in state service or engage in any other paid activity, apart from teaching, scientific or other creative activity.

Article 98

(1) Members of the Federation Council and deputies of the State Duma shall enjoy immunity for the duration of their term of office. They cannot be detained, arrested or searched unless detained at the scene of a crime, nor can they be subjected to a body search except as provided by federal law in order to secure the safety of others.

(2) The issue of lifting immunity shall be decided by the appropriate chamber of the Federal Assembly upon submission by the Procurator-General of the Russian Federation.

Article 99

(1) The Federal Assembly shall be a permanently functioning body.

(2) The State Duma shall meet for its first session on the thirtieth day after its election. The President of the Russian Federation may convene a session of the State Duma prior to this date.

(3) The first session of the State Duma shall be opened by the oldest deputy.

(4) From the moment that the work of a newly elected State Duma begins, the powers of the previously-elected State Duma shall cease.

Article 100

(1) The Federation Council and the State Duma shall sit separately.

(2) Sessions of the Federation Council and the State Duma are open. In instances provided for by the standing orders of a chamber it shall be entitled to conduct closed sessions.

(3) Chambers may convene jointly to hear messages from the President of the Russian Federation, messages from the Constitutional Court of the Russian Federation, and addresses by the leaders of foreign states.

Article 101

(1) The Federation Council shall elect from its membership the chair of the Federation Council and his deputies. The State Duma shall elect from its members the chair of the State Duma and his deputies.

(2) The chair of the Federation Council and his deputies, and the chair of the State Duma and his deputies, shall chair sessions and conduct the internal procedures of the chamber.

(3) The Federation Council and the State Duma shall form committees and commissions and conduct parliamentary hearings into matters under their jurisdiction.

(4) Each of the chambers shall adopt its own standing orders and decide matters relating to the internal procedure governing its activity.

(5) In order to monitor the implementation of the federal budget the Federation Council and the State Duma shall form a comptroller's office whose composition and working procedure shall be determined by federal law.

Article 102

(1) The jurisdiction of the Federation Council shall include:

    (a) confirming alterations to borders between components of the Russian Federation;

    (b) confirming an edict of the President of the Russian Federation on the introduction of martial law;

    (c) confirming an edict of the President of the Russian Federation on the introduction of a state of emergency;

    (d) deciding the question of the possibility of the use of the Russian Federation Armed Forces outside the borders of the territory of the Russian Federation;

    (e) calling elections for the President of the Russian Federation;

    (f) removing the President of the Russian Federation from office;

    (g) appointing judges of the Constitutional Court of the Russian Federation, the Supreme Court of the Russian Federation and the Higher Court of Arbitration of the Russian Federation;

(h) appointing and removing from office the Procurator-General of the Russian Federation;

(i) appointing and removing from office the deputy chair of the comptroller's office and half of its staff of auditors.

(2) The Federation Council shall adopt decrees on matters allotted to its jurisdiction by the constitution of the Russian Federation.

(3) Decrees of the Federation Council shall be adopted by a majority of the votes of the total number of Federation Council members unless some other procedure for adopting a decision is provided for by the constitution of the Russian Federation.

Article 103

(1) Within the jurisdiction of the State Duma shall fall:

(a) giving consent to the President of the Russian Federation for the appointment of the chair of the Government of the Russian Federation;

(b) deciding a motion of confidence in the Government of the Russian Federation;

(c) appointing and removing from office the chair of the Central Bank of the Russian Federation;

(d) appointing and removing from office the chair of the comptroller's office and half of its staff of auditors;

(e) appointing and removing from office the commissioner for human rights, who shall operate in accordance with federal constitutional law;

(f) declaring an amnesty;

(g) laying a charge against the President of the Russian Federation to remove him from office.

(2) The State Duma shall adopt decrees on matters allotted to its jurisdiction by the constitution of the Russian Federation.

(3) Decrees of the State Duma shall be adopted by a majority of the votes of the total number of deputies of the State Duma unless some other procedure for adopting a decision is stipulated by the constitution of the Russian Federation.

Article 104

(1) The right of legislative initiative shall vest in the President of the Russian Federation, the Federation Council, members of the Federation Council, deputies of the State Duma, the Government of the Russian Federation and legislative (representative) organs of components of the Russian Federation. In matters within their jurisdiction, the right of legislative initiative shall also be vested in the Constitutional Court of the Russian Federation, the Supreme Court of the Russian Federation, and the Higher Court of Arbitration of the Russian Federation.

(2) Bills shall be introduced into the State Duma.

(3) Bills on the introduction or abolition of taxes, exemption from the payment of taxes, the floating of state loans, the alteration of the financial obligations of the state and other draft laws envisaging expenditure funded out of the state budget may be introduced only on a conclusion formulated by the Government of the Russian Federation.

Article 105

(1) Federal laws shall be adopted by the State Duma.

(2) Federal laws shall be adopted by a majority of the votes of the total number of deputies of the State Duma unless otherwise provided by the constitution of the Russian Federation.

(3) Federal laws adopted by the State Duma shall within five days be passed to the Federation Council for examination.

(4) A federal law shall be deemed approved by the Federation Council if more than half of the total number of members of this chamber have voted for it or if it has not been examined by the Federation Council within fourteen days. In the event of the rejection of a federal law by the Federation Council the chambers may form a conciliation commission to overcome differences which have arisen, after which the federal law shall be subject to a second examination by the State Duma.

(5) In the event of disagreement by the State Duma with a decision of the Federation Council, a federal law shall be deemed adopted if at least two-thirds of the total number of deputies of the State Duma vote for it in a second vote.

Article 106

Federal laws adopted by the State Duma must be examined by the Federation Council when they concern questions of:
- (a) the federal budget;
- (b) federal taxes and charges;
- (c) financial, foreign currency, credit and customs regulation and money issue;
- (d) the ratification and denunciation of international treaties of the Russian Federation;
- (e) the status and protection of the state border of the Russian Federation;
- (f) war and peace.

Article 107

(1) A federal law that has been adopted shall, within five days, be submitted to the President of the Russian Federation for signature and promulgation.

(2) The President of the Russian Federation signs and promulgates the federal law within fourteen days.

(3) If, within fourteen days of the federal law's submission, the President of the Russian Federation rejects it, the State Duma and the Federation Council shall re-examine the said law in accordance with the procedure laid down by the constitution of the Russian Federation. If, after a second examination, the federal law in the version previously adopted is approved by the votes of a majority of at least two-thirds of the total number of members of the Federation Council and deputies of the State Duma it is to be signed by the President of the Russian Federation within seven days and promulgated.

Article 108

(1) Federal constitutional laws shall be adopted on matters stipulated by the constitution of the Russian Federation.

(2) A federal constitutional law shall be deemed adopted if approved by the votes of a majority of at least three-quarters of the total number of members of the Federation Council and at least two-thirds of the total number of deputies of the State

Duma. A federal constitutional law that has been adopted is to be signed by the President of the Russian Federation and promulgated within fourteen days.

Article 109

(1) The State Duma may be dissolved by the President of the Russian Federation in the circumstances provided for in Articles 111 and 117 of the constitution of the Russian Federation.

(2) On dissolution of the State Duma, the President of the Russian Federation shall set the date of elections so as to ensure that the newly elected State Duma is convened within four months of the date of dissolution.

(3) For one year following its election, the State Duma may not be dissolved on the grounds laid down in Article 117 of the constitution of the Russian Federation.

(4) The State Duma may not be dissolved from the moment it lays a charge against the President of the Russian Federation, until the adoption of the appropriate decision by the Federation Council.

(5) The State Duma may not be dissolved during the period of operation of martial law or state of emergency on the whole territory of the Russian Federation, or within the six months preceding the expiry of the term of office of the President of the Russian Federation.

Chapter 6. Government of the Russian Federation

Article 110

(1) Executive power in the Russian Federation shall be exercised by the government of the Russian Federation.

(2) The government of the Russian Federation shall consist of the chair of the government of the Russian Federation, the deputy chairs of the government of the Russian Federation and the Federal ministers.

Article 111

(1) The chair of the government of the Russian Federation shall be appointed by the President of the Russian Federation with the consent of the State Duma.

(2) A nomination for the chairmanship of the government of the Russian Federation shall be submitted within two weeks of the entry into office of a newly-elected President of the Russian Federation or the resignation of the government of the Russian Federation or within a week of the rejection of a candidacy by the State Duma.

(3) The State Duma shall examine the candidacy for the chairmanship of the government of the Russian Federation put forward by the President of the Russian Federation within a week of the day the candidacy proposal is submitted.

(4) Following three rejections by the State Duma of candidacies put forward for the chair of the government of the Russian Federation, the President of the Russian Federation shall appoint a chair of the government of the Russian Federation, dissolve the State Duma and call new elections.

Article 112

(1) Within one week following his appointment, the chair of the government of the Russian Federation shall submit to the President of the Russian Federation proposals on the structure of the federal organs of executive power.

(2) The chair of the government of the Russian Federation shall propose to the President of the Russian Federation candidacies for the posts of deputy chairs of the government of the Russian Federation and federal ministers.

Article 113

The chair of the government of the Russian Federation, in accordance with the constitution of the Russian Federation, federal laws and decrees of the President of the Russian Federation shall define the basic guidelines for the activity of the government of the Russian Federation and organize its work.

Article 114

(1) The government of the Russian Federation shall:

(a) draft the federal budget, submit it to the State Duma and ensure its implementation; submit to the State Duma a report on the implementation of the federal budget;

(b) ensure the carrying out of a single fiscal, credit and monetary policy in the Russian Federation;

(c) ensure the carrying out of a single state policy in the Russian Federation in the sphere of culture, science, education, health, social security and ecology;

(d) administer federal property;

(e) adopt measures to ensure the defence of the country, state security and the realization of the foreign policy of the Russian Federation;

(f) adopt measures to ensure the rule of law, civil rights and freedoms, the protection of property and public order, and the struggle against crime;

(g) exercise other powers vested in it by the constitution of the Russian Federation, federal laws and decrees of the President of the Russian Federation.

(2) The procedure for the activity of the Government of the Russian Federation shall be defined by federal constitutional law.

Article 115

(1) On the basis of and in implementation of the constitution of the Russian Federation, federal laws and normative edicts of the President of the Russian Federation, the Government of the Russian Federation shall issue decrees and directives and ensure their implementation.

(2) Implementation of decrees and directives of the Government of the Russian Federation shall be mandatory in the Russian Federation.

(3) In the event of conflict with the constitution of the Russian Federation, with federal laws, or with edicts of the President of the Russian Federation, decrees and directives of the Government of the Russian Federation may be abrogated by the President of the Russian Federation.

Article 116

The government of the Russian Federation shall surrender its powers to a newly elected President of the Russian Federation.

Article 117

(1) The government of the Russian Federation may offer its resignation, which shall be accepted or rejected by the President of the Russian Federation.

(2) The President of the Russian Federation may adopt a decision on the dismissal of the government of the Russian Federation.

(3) The State Duma may express no confidence in the Government of the Russian Federation. A motion of no confidence in the government of the Russian Federation shall be adopted by a majority of votes of the total number of deputies of the State Duma. Following an expression of no confidence by the State Duma in the government of the Russian Federation, the President of the Russian Federation shall be entitled to announce the dismissal of the government of the Russian Federation or to disagree with the decision of the State Duma. If, for a second time within three months, the State Duma expresses no confidence in the government of the Russian Federation, the President of the Russian Federation shall announce the dismissal of the government or dissolve the State Duma.

(4) The chair of the government of the Russian Federation may put before the State Duma a motion of confidence in the government of the Russian Federation. If the State Duma refuses its confidence, the President shall adopt a decision within seven days on the dismissal of the government of the Russian Federation or on the dissolution of the State Duma and the holding of new elections.

(5) On resignation or surrender of its powers, the government of the Russian Federation, on the instructions of the President of the Russian Federation, shall continue to act until the formation of the new government of the Russian Federation.

Chapter 7. The Judicial Power

Article 118

(1) Justice in the Russian Federation shall be administered only by the court.

(2) Judicial power shall be exercised by means of constitutional, civil, administrative and criminal court proceedings.

(3) The judicial system of the Russian Federation shall be laid down by the constitution of the Russian Federation and by federal constitutional law. The creation of emergency courts is not permitted.

Article 119

Citizens of the Russian Federation who have attained the age of 25 and have higher legal education and at least five years' experience in the legal profession may be judges. Additional requirements for judges in the courts of the Russian Federation may be laid down by federal law.

Article 120

(1) Judges shall be independent and subordinate only to the constitution of the Russian Federation and to federal law.

(2) The courts, having determined in the course of examining a case that an act of a state organ or other organ is not in accordance with the law, shall take a decision in accordance with the law.

Article 121

(1) Judges may not be removed.

(2) A judge's powers may not be terminated or suspended save under the procedure and on the grounds laid down by federal law.

Article 122

(1) Judges shall enjoy immunity.

(2) A judge may not be subjected to criminal proceedings save under the procedure defined by federal law.

Article 123

(1) The examination of cases in all courts shall be open. Hearing a case in closed session shall be permitted in circumstances stipulated in federal law.

(2) The examination of criminal cases in the courts in the absence of the accused shall not be permitted, save in circumstances provided for by federal law.

(3) Court proceedings shall be conducted by the adversarial system, and with equal rights of the parties.

(4) In circumstances provided for by federal law, court proceedings shall be conducted with the participation of jurors.

Article 124

The financing of courts shall be effected solely from the federal budget and must ensure the possibility of the full and independent administration of justice in accordance with federal law.

Article 125

(1) The Constitutional Court of the Russian Federation shall consist of nineteen judges.

(2) At the request of the President of the Russian Federation, the Federation Council, the State Duma, one-fifth of the members of the Federation Council or deputies of the State Duma, the Government of the Russian Federation, the Supreme Court of the Russian Federation, the Higher Court of Arbitration of the Russian Federation, or the organs of legislative and executive power of the components of the Russian Federation, the Constitutional Court of the Russian Federation, shall resolve cases relating to the conformity with the constitution of the Russian Federation of:

(a) federal laws and normative acts of the President of the Russian Federation, the Federation Council, the State Duma or the government of the Russian Federation;
(b) the constitutions of republics and the charters of components of the Russian Federation and laws and other normative acts issued by them on matters falling within the jurisdiction of organs of state power of the Russian Federation or within the joint jurisdiction of organs of state power of the Russian Federation and organs of state power of components of the Russian Federation;
(c) treaties between organs of state power of the Russian Federation and organs of state power of components of the Russian Federation and treaties between organs of state power of components of the Russian Federation;
(d) international treaties of the Russian Federation that have not entered into force.

(3) The Constitutional Court of the Russian Federation shall resolve disputes over their respective competences arising:

(a) between federal organs of state power;
(b) between organs of state power of the Russian Federation and organs of state power of components of the Russian Federation;
(c) between the highest state organs of components of the Russian Federation.

(4) The Constitutional Court of the Russian Federation, on the basis of complaints regarding the violation of citizens' constitutional rights and freedoms and at the request of courts, shall examine the constitutionality of the law applied or applicable in the specific case, in accordance with the procedure laid down by federal law.

(5) At the request of the President of the Russian Federation, the Federation Council, the State Duma, the government of the Russian Federation or the organs of legislative power of components of the Russian Federation, the Constitutional Court of the Russian Federation shall provide an interpretation of the constitution of the Russian Federation.

(6) Acts or particular provisions thereof that are found to be unconstitutional shall lose their force; international treaties of the Russian Federation that are incompatible with the constitution of the Russian Federation may neither take effect nor be applied.

(7) At the request of the Federation Council, the Constitutional Court of the Russian Federation shall issue a ruling on whether due procedure has been observed in the laying of a charge of treason or the commission of some other grave crime against the President of the Russian Federation.

Article 126

The Supreme Court of the Russian Federation shall be the highest judicial organ for civil, criminal, administrative or other cases subject to the courts of general jurisdiction. Within the procedural forms laid down by federal law it shall exercise judicial supervision over their activity and provide clarification on questions of judicial practice.

Article 127

The Higher Court of Arbitration of the Russian Federation shall be the highest judicial organ for the resolution of economic disputes and other cases examined by the courts of arbitration. Within the procedural forms laid down by federal law it shall exercise judicial supervision over their activity and provide clarification on questions of judicial practice.

Article 128

(1) Judges of the Constitutional Court of the Russian Federation, the Supreme Court of the Russian Federation, and the Higher Court of Arbitration of the Russian Federation shall be appointed by the Federation Council on the proposal of the President of the Russian Federation.

(2) Judges of other federal courts shall be appointed by the President of the Russian Federation in accordance with the procedure laid down by federal law.

(3) The powers, procedure for formation, and the activity of the Constitutional Court of the Russian Federation, the Supreme Court of the Russian Federation, the Higher Court of Arbitration of the Russian Federation and other federal courts shall be laid down by federal constitutional law.

Article 129

(1) The Russian Federation Procuracy is a single centralized system in which lower-level procurators are subordinate to higher-level procurators and to the Procurator-General of the Russian Federation.

(2) The Procurator-General of the Russian Federation shall be appointed and released from office by the Federation Council on the proposal of the President of the Russian Federation.

(3) The procurators of components of the Russian Federation shall be appointed by the Russian Federation Procurator-General by agreement with the Federation components.

(4) Other procurators shall be appointed by the Procurator-General of the Russian Federation.

(5) The powers, organization, and procedure of activity of the Russian Federation Procuracy shall be defined by federal law.

Chapter 8. Local self-government

Article 130

(1) Local self-government in the Russian Federation shall ensure that the population autonomously resolves questions of local importance and the possession, utilization, and disposal of municipal property.

(2) Local self-government shall be exercised by citizens by means of referendums, elections and other forms of direct expression of will and through elected and other organs of local self-government.

Article 131

(1) Local self-government in urban and rural settlements and other territories shall be exercised with due consideration for historical and other local traditions. The structure of local self-government organs shall be autonomously determined by the population.

(2) Changes to the borders of territories where local self-government is exercised shall be permitted after taking into account the opinion of the population of the relevant territories.

Article 132

(1) Organs of local self-government shall autonomously administer municipal property, formulate, approve and implement the local budget, levy local taxes and charges, implement the protection of public order and also resolve other questions of local importance.

(2) Particular state powers may by law be vested in organs of local self-government, with the transfer of the material and financial resources necessary to exercise them. The exercise of delegated powers shall fall under supervision by the state.

Article 133

Local self-government in the Russian Federation shall be guaranteed by the right to judicial protection, compensation for additional expenditure arising as a result of decisions taken by organs of state power, and the prohibition of the restriction of the rights of local self-government established by the constitution of the Russian Federation and federal laws.

Chapter 9. Constitutional amendments and revision of the constitution

Article 134

Proposals to amend or revise provisions of the constitution of the Russian Federation may be submitted by the President of the Russian Federation, the Federation Council, the State Duma, the government of the Russian Federation, legislative (representative) organs of components of the Russian Federation, and also by a group numbering at least one-fifth of members of the Federation Council or of deputies of the State Duma.

Article 135

(1) The provisions of Chapters 1, 2 and 9 of the constitution of the Russian Federation may not be revised by the Federal Assembly.

(2) If a proposal to revise the provisions of Chapters 1, 2 and 9 of the constitution of the Russian Federation is supported by a

vote of three-fifths of the total number of members of the Federation Council and deputies of the State Duma then, in accordance with federal constitutional law, a Constitutional Assembly shall be convened.

(3) The Constitutional Assembly shall either confirm the immutability of the constitution of the Russian Federation or draw up a draft of a new constitution of the Russian Federation which shall be adopted by the Constitutional Assembly by a vote of two-thirds of the total number of its members or submitted to nationwide vote. If a nationwide vote is held, the constitution of the Russian Federation shall be considered adopted if votes for it are cast by more than one-half of the electors taking part in the vote, provided that more than one-half of the electorate has taken part in the vote.

Article 136

Amendments to Chapters 3–8 of the constitution of the Russian Federation shall be adopted by the procedure provided for the adoption of federal constitutional law and shall come into force after they have been approved by the organs of legislative power of at least two-thirds of the components of the Russian Federation.

Article 137

(1) Amendments to Article 65 of the constitution of the Russian Federation, which defines the composition of the Russian Federation, shall be submitted on the basis of federal constitutional law relating to admission to the Russian Federation and the formation within it of a new component of the Russian Federation and to alteration of the constitutional– legal status of a component of the Russian Federation.

(2) In the event of changes to the name of a republic, area, province, city of federal significance, autonomous province or autonomous district, the new name of the component of the Russian Federation shall be incorporated in Article 65 of the constitution of the Russian Federation.

Concluding and transitional provisions

(1) The constitution of the Russian Federation shall come into force on the day of its official publication following the results of the nationwide vote.

The day of the nationwide vote—12 December 1993—shall be deemed the day of the adoption of the constitution of the Russian Federation.

The constitution (basic law) of the Russian Federation—Russia, adopted on 12 April 1978 with its subsequent amendments and additions, shall simultaneously cease to take effect.

In the event of non-conformity of the provisions of the constitution of the Russian Federation with provisions of the Federation Treaty—the treaty on the delimitation of areas of jurisdiction and powers between federal organs of state power of the Russian Federation and organs of state power of sovereign republics within the Russian Federation, the treaty on the delimitation of areas of jurisdiction and powers between federal organs of state power of the Russian Federation and organs of state power of areas, provinces and the cities of Moscow and St. Petersburg in the Russian Federation, the treaty on the delimitation of areas of jurisdiction and powers between federal organs of state power of the Russian Federation and organs of state power of the autonomous provinces and autonomous districts of the Russian Federation, as well as other treaties between organs of state power of components of the Russian Federation—the provisions of the constitution of the Russian Federation shall take effect.

(2) Laws and other legal acts in force on the territory of the Russian Federation prior to the entry into force of the present constitution shall be applied to the extent to which they do not contravene the constitution of the Russian Federation.

(3) From the day the present constitution comes into force, the President of the Russian Federation, elected in accordance with the constitution (Basic Law) of the Russian Federation—Russia, shall exercise the powers thereby conferred on him until the expiry of the term for which he was elected.

(4) From the day the present constitution comes into force, the Council of Ministers—government—of the Russian Federation shall acquire the rights, obligations and responsibility of the government of the Russian Federation established by the Constitution of the Russian Federation and shall thenceforth be known as the government of the Russian Federation.

(5) Courts in the Russian Federation shall administer justice in accordance with their powers as laid down by the present Constitution.

After the Constitution has come into force, the judges of all courts in the Russian Federation shall retain their powers until the expiry of the term for which they were elected. Vacancies shall be filled according to the procedure laid down by the present Constitution.

(6) Pending the entry into force of the federal law laying down the procedure for the examination of cases by a court with the participation of jurors, the former procedure for judicial examination of such cases shall be retained.

The former procedures for the arrest, holding in custody and detention of persons suspected of having committed a crime shall be retained until such time as the criminal procedure legislation of the Russian Federation is brought into line with the provisions of the present Constitution.

(7) The first Federation Council and the first State Duma shall be elected for a two-year term.

(8) The Federation Council shall convene for its first session on the thirtieth day following its election. The first session of the Federation Council shall be opened by the President of the Russian Federation.

(9) A deputy of the first State Duma may simultaneously be a member of the government of the Russian Federation. To the extent that they concern responsibility for actions (or inaction) associated with the performance of official duties, the provisions of the present Constitution on the immunity of deputies do not extend to deputies of the State Duma who are members of the government of the Russian Federation.

Deputies of the Federation Council shall fulfil their functions on a part-time basis.

8

European Convention on Human Rights of 4 November 1950 [Extracts[1]]

The Governments signatory hereto, being Members of the Council of Europe,

CONSIDERING the Universal Declaration of Human Rights proclaimed by the General Assembly of the United Nations on 10 December 1948;

CONSIDERING that this Declaration aims at securing the universal and effective recognition and observance of the Rights therein declared;

CONSIDERING that the aim of the Council of Europe is the achievement of greater unity between its Members and that one of the methods by which the aim is to be pursued is the maintenance and further realization of Human Rights and Fundamental Freedoms;

REAFFIRMING their profound belief in those Fundamental Freedoms which are the foundation of justice and peace in the world and are best maintained on the one hand by an effective political democracy and on the other by a common understanding and observance of the Human Rights upon which they depend;

BEING RESOLVED, as the Governments of European countries which are like-minded and have a common heritage of political traditions, ideals, freedom and the rule of law to take the first steps for the collective enforcement of certain of the Rights stated in the Universal Declaration;

HAVE agreed as follows:

---

[1] For the full text and protocols see Ian Brownlie, *Basic Documents on Human Rights* (3rd edn., Oxford University Press, 1992), 325 ff.

Article 1

The High Contracting Parties shall secure to everyone within their jurisdiction the rights and freedoms defined in Section I of this Convention.

SECTION I

Article 2

1. Everyone's right to life shall be protected by law. No one shall be deprived of his life intentionally save in the execution of a sentence of a court following his conviction of a crime for which this penalty is provided by law.
2. Deprivation of life shall not be regarded as inflicted in contravention of this Article when it results from the use of force which is no more than absolutely necessary:

   (a) in defence of any person from unlawful violence;
   (b) in order to effect a lawful arrest or to prevent the escape of a person lawfully detained;
   (c) in action lawfully taken for the purpose of quelling a riot or insurrection.

Article 3

No one shall be subjected to torture or to inhuman or degrading treatment or punishment.

Article 4

1. No one shall be held in slavery or servitude.
2. No one shall be required to perform forced or compulsory labour.
3. For the purpose of this Article the term 'forced or compulsory labour' shall not include:

   (a) any work required to be done in the ordinary course of detention imposed according to the provisions of Article 5 of this Convention or during conditional release from such detention;

    (b) any service of a military character or, in case of consci-
entious objectors in countries where they are recognized,
service exacted instead of compulsory military service;

    (c) any service exacted in case of an emergency or calamity
threatening the life or well-being of the community;

    (d) any work or service which forms part of normal civic
obligations.

Article 5

1. Everyone has the right to liberty and security of person. No
one shall be deprived of his liberty save in the following cases
and in accordance with a procedure prescribed by law:

    (a) the lawful detention of a person after conviction by a
competent court;

    (b) the lawful arrest or detention of a person for non-
compliance with the lawful order of a court or in order
to secure the fulfilment of any obligation prescribed by
law;

    (c) the lawful arrest or detention of a person effected for the
purpose of bringing him before the competent legal
authority on reasonable suspicion of having committed
an offence or when it is reasonably considered necessary
to prevent his committing an offence or fleeing after
having done so;

    (d) the detention of a minor by lawful order for the purpose
of educational supervision or his lawful detention for the
purpose of bringing him before the competent legal
authority;

    (e) the lawful detention of persons for the prevention of the
spreading of infectious diseases, of persons of unsound
mind, alcoholics or drug addicts, or vagrants;

    (f) the lawful arrest or detention of a person to prevent his
effecting an unauthorized entry into the country or of a
person against whom action is being taken with a view
to deportation or extradition.

2. Everyone who is arrested shall be informed promptly, in a
language which he understands, of the reasons for his arrest and
of any charge against him.

3. Everyone arrested or detained in accordance with the provisions of paragraph 1(c) of this Article shall be brought promptly before a judge or other officer authorized by law to exercise judicial power and shall be entitled to trial within a reasonable time or to release pending trial. Release may be conditioned by guarantees to appear for trial.

4. Everyone who is deprived of his liberty by arrest or detention shall be entitled to take proceedings by which the lawfulness of his detention shall be decided speedily by a court and his release ordered if the detention is not lawful.

5. Everyone who has been the victim of arrest or detention in contravention of the provisions of this article shall have an enforceable right to compensation.

Article 6

1. In the determination of his civil rights and obligations or of any criminal charge against him, everyone is entitled to a fair and public hearing within a reasonable time by an independent and impartial tribunal established by law. Judgment shall be pronounced publicly but the press and public may be excluded from all or part of the trial in the interest of morals, public order or national security in a democratic society, where the interests of juveniles or the protection of the private life of the parties so require, or to the extent strictly necessary in the opinion of the court in special circumstances where publicity would prejudice the interests of justice.

2. Everyone charged with a criminal offence shall be presumed innocent until proved guilty according to law.

3. Everyone charged with a criminal offence has the following minimum rights:

    (a) to be informed promptly, in a language which he understands and in detail, of the nature and cause of the accusation against him;

    (b) to have adequate time and facilities for the preparation of his defence;

    (c) to defend himself in person or through legal assistance of his own choosing or, if he has not sufficient means to pay for legal assistance, to be given it free when the interests of justice so require;

    (d) to examine or have examined witnesses against him and to obtain the attendance and examination of witnesses on his behalf under the same conditions as witnesses against him;

    (e) to have the free assistance of an interpreter if he cannot understand or speak the language used in court.

Article 7

1. No one shall be held guilty of any criminal offence on account of any act or omission which did not constitute a criminal offence under national or international law at the time when it was committed. Nor shall a heavier penalty be imposed than the one that was applicable at the time the criminal offence was committed.

2. This article shall not prejudice the trial and punishment of any person for any act or omission which, at the time when it was committed, was criminal according to the general principles of law recognized by civilized nations.

Article 8

1. Everyone has the right to respect for his private and family life, his home and his correspondence.

2. There shall be no interference by a public authority with the exercise of this right except such as is in accordance with the law and is necessary in a democratic society in the interests of national security, public safety or the economic well-being of the country, for the prevention of disorder or crime, for the protection of health or morals, or for the protection of the rights and freedoms of others.

Article 9

1. Everyone has the right to freedom of thought, conscience and religion; this right includes freedom to change his religion or belief, and freedom, either alone or in community with others and in public or private, to manifest his religion or belief, in worship, teaching, practice and observance.

2. Freedom to manifest one's religion or beliefs shall be subject only to such limitations as are prescribed by law and are necessary in a democratic society in the interests of public safety,

for the protection of public order, health or morals, or for the protection of the rights and freedoms of others.

Article 10

1. Everyone has the right to freedom of expression. This right shall include freedom to hold opinions and to receive and impart information and ideas without interference by public authority and regardless of frontiers. This article shall not prevent States from requiring the licensing of broadcasting, television or cinema enterprises.

2. The exercise of these freedoms, since it carries with it duties and responsibilities, may be subject to such formalities, conditions, restrictions or penalties as are prescribed by law and are necessary in a democratic society, in the interests of national security, territorial integrity or public safety, for the prevention of disorder or crime, for the protection of health or morals, for the protection of the reputation or rights of others, for preventing the disclosure of information received in confidence, or for maintaining the authority and impartiality of the judiciary.

Article 11

1. Everyone has the right to freedom of peaceful assembly and to freedom of association with others, including the right to form and to join trade unions for the protection of his interests.

2. No restrictions shall be placed on the exercise of these rights other than such as are prescribed by law and are necessary in a democratic society in the interests of national security or public safety, for the prevention of disorder or crime, for the protection of health or morals or for the protection of the rights and freedoms of others. This Article shall not prevent the imposition of lawful restrictions on the exercise of these rights by members of the armed forces, of the police or of the administration of the State.

Article 12

Men and women of marriageable age have the right to marry and to found a family, according to the national laws governing the exercise of this right.

Article 13

Everyone whose rights and freedoms as set forth in this Convention are violated shall have an effective remedy before a national authority notwithstanding that the violation has been committed by persons acting in an official capacity.

Article 14

The enjoyment of the rights and freedoms set forth in this Convention shall be secured without discrimination on any ground such as sex, race, colour, language, religion, political or other opinion, national or social origin, association with a national minority, property, birth or other status.

Article 15

1. In time of war or other public emergency threatening the life of the nation any High Contracting Party may take measures derogating from its obligations under this Convention to the extent strictly required by the exigencies of the situation, provided that such measures are not inconsistent with its other obligations under international law.

2. No derogation from Article 2, except in respect of deaths resulting from lawful acts of war, or from Articles 3, 4 (paragraph 1) and 7 shall be made under this provision.

3. Any High Contracting Party availing itself of this right of derogation shall keep the Secretary-General of the Council of Europe fully informed of the measures which it has taken and the reasons therefor. It shall also inform the Secretary-General of the Council of Europe when such measures have ceased to operate and the provisions of the Convention are again being fully executed.

Article 16

Nothing in Articles 10, 11 and 14 shall be regarded as preventing the High Contracting Parties from imposing restrictions on the political activity of aliens.

Article 17

Nothing in this Convention may be interpreted as implying for any State, group or person any right to engage in any activity or perform any act aimed at the destruction of any of the rights and freedoms set forth herein or at their limitation to a greater extent than is provided for in the Convention.

Article 18

The restrictions permitted under this Convention to the said rights and freedoms shall not be applied for any purpose other than those for which they have been prescribed.

SECTION II

Article 19[2]

To ensure the observance of the engagements undertaken by the High Contracting Parties in the present Convention, there shall be set up:

1. A European Commission of Human Rights hereinafter referred to as 'the Commission';
2. A European Court of Human Rights, hereinafter referred to as 'the Court'.

---

[2] On 11 May 1994 Protocol No. 11 to the ECHR was signed by many members (including the UK). Under it a new permanent Court will replace the present Commission and Court. Art. 19 will then read:

'To ensure the observance of the engagements undertaken by the High Contracting Parties in the Convention and the protocols thereto, there shall be set up a European Court of Human Rights, hereinafter referred to as "the Court". It shall function on a permanent basis.'

European Community, European Union

NOTE ON THE FOLLOWING

The texts which follow attempt to select the main institutional, if not constitutional, provisions of the Treaties. They give the initial articles which spell out the general aims and activities, but omit most of the very important economic and monetary provisions required to ensure that the European Community is a single area in which goods, people, corporations, services, and capital can move and settle freely. The EC Treaty's structural and jurisdictional provisions on the Parliament, Commission, Council, and Court, and on the legislative and budgetary procedures are given in full, as are its final general provisions.

9

Treaty Establishing the European Economic Community as Amended by Subsequent Treaties. Rome, 25 March, 1957 [Extracts[1]]

His Majesty The King of the Belgians, the President of the Federal Republic of Germany, the President of the French Republic, the President of the Italian Republic, Her Royal Highness The Grand Duchess of Luxembourg, Her Majesty The Queen of the Netherlands,

DETERMINED to lay the foundations of an ever closer union among the peoples of Europe,

RESOLVED to ensure the economic and social progress of their countries by common action to eliminate the barriers which divide Europe,

AFFIRMING as the essential objective of their efforts the constant improvement of the living and working conditions of their peoples,

RECOGNIZING that the removal of existing obstacles calls for concerted action in order to guarantee steady expansion, balanced trade and fair competition,

ANXIOUS to strengthen the unity of their economies and to ensure their harmonious development by reducing the differences existing between the various regions and the backwardness of the less favoured regions,

DESIRING to contribute, by means of a common commercial policy, to the progressive abolition of restrictions on international trade,

---

[1] For the full text with protocols etc., see Bernard Rudden and Derrick Wyatt (eds.), *Basic Community Laws* (5th edn., Oxford University Press, 1994).

INTENDING to confirm the solidarity which binds Europe and the overseas countries and desiring to ensure the development of their prosperity, in accordance with the principles of the Charter of the United Nations,

RESOLVED by thus pooling their resources to preserve and strengthen peace and liberty, and calling upon the other peoples of Europe who share their ideal to join in their efforts,

HAVE decided to create a European Economic Community and to this end have designated as their Plenipotentiaries: [names omitted]

WHO, having exchanged their full powers, found in good and due form,

HAVE agreed as follows:

PART ONE. PRINCIPLES

Article 1

By this Treaty, the High Contracting Parties establish among themselves a European Community.

Article 2

The Community shall have as its task, by establishing a common market and an economic and monetary union and by implementing the common policies or activities referred to in Articles 3 and 3a, to promote throughout the Community a harmonious and balanced development of economic activities, sustainable and non-inflationary growth respecting the environment, a high degree of convergence of economic performance, a high level of employment and of social protection, the raising of the standard of living and quality of life, and economic and social cohesion and solidarity among Member States.

Article 3

For the purposes set out in Article 2, the activities of the Community shall include, as provided in this Treaty and in accordance with the timetable set out therein:

(a) the elimination, as between Member States, of customs duties and quantitative restrictions on the import and export of goods, and of all other measures having equivalent effect;

(b) a common commercial policy;

(c) an internal market characterized by the abolition, as between Member States of obstacles to the free movement of goods, persons, services and capital;

(d) measures concerning the entry and movement of persons in the internal market as provided for in Article 100c;

(e) a common policy in the sphere of agriculture and fisheries;

(f) a common policy in the sphere of transport;

(g) a system ensuring that competition in the internal market is not distorted;

(h) the approximation of the laws of Member States to the extent required for the functioning of the common market;

(i) a policy in the social sphere comprising a European Social Fund;

(j) the strengthening of economic and social cohesion;

(k) a policy in the sphere of the environment;

(l) the strengthening of the competitiveness of Community industry;

(m) the promotion of research and technological development;

(n) encouragement for the establishment and development of trans-European networks;

(o) a contribution to the attainment of a high level of health protection;

(p) a contribution to education and training of quality and to the flowering of the cultures of the Member States;

(q) a policy in the sphere of development co-operation;

(r) the association of the overseas countries and territories in order to increase trade and promote jointly economic and social development;

(s) a contribution to the strengthening of consumer protection;

(t) measures in the spheres of energy, civil protection and tourism.

Article 3a

1. For the purposes set out in Article 2, the activities of the Member States and the Community shall include, as provided in this Treaty and in accordance with the timetable set out therein, the adoption of an economic policy which is based on the close co-ordination of Member States' economic policies, on the internal market and on the definition of common objectives, and conducted in accordance with the principle of an open market economy with free competition.

2. Concurrently with the foregoing, and as provided in this Treaty and in accordance with the timetable and the procedures set out therein, these activities shall include the irrevocable fixing of exchange rates leading to the introduction of a single currency, the ECU, and the definition and conduct of a single monetary policy and exchange rate policy the primary objective of both of which shall be to maintain price stability and, without prejudice to this objective, to support the general economic policies in the Community, in accordance with the principle of an open market economy with free competition.

3. These activities of the Member States and the Community shall entail compliance with the following guiding principles: stable prices, sound public finances and monetary conditions and a sustainable balance of payments.

Article 3b

The Community shall act within the limit of the powers conferred upon it by this Treaty and of the objectives assigned to it therein.

In areas which do not fall within its exclusive competence, the Community shall take action, in accordance with the principle of subsidiarity, only if and in so far as the objectives of the proposed action cannot be sufficiently achieved by the Member States and can therefore, by reason of the scale or effects of the proposed action, be better achieved by the Community.

Any action by the Community shall not go beyond what is necessary to achieve the objectives of this Treaty.

Article 4

1. The tasks entrusted to the Community shall be carried out by the following institutions:

—a European Parliament,
—a Council,
—a Commission,
—a Court of Justice,
—a Court of Auditors.

Each institution shall act within the limits of the powers conferred upon it by this Treaty.

2. The Council and the Commission shall be assisted by an Economic and Social Committee and a Committee of the Regions acting in an advisory capacity.

Article 4a

A European System of Central Banks (hereinafter referred to as 'ESCB') and a European Central Bank (hereinafter referred to as 'ECB') shall be established in accordance with the procedures laid down in this Treaty; they shall act within the limits of the powers conferred upon them by this Treaty and by the Statute of the ESCB and of the ECB (hereinafter referred to as 'Statute of the ESCB') annexed thereto.

Article 4b

A European Investment Bank is hereby established, which shall act within the limit of the powers conferred upon it by this Treaty and the Statute annexed thereto.

Article 5

Member States shall take all appropriate measures, whether general or particular, to ensure fulfilment of the obligations arising out of this Treaty or resulting from action taken by the institutions of the Community. They shall facilitate the achievement of the Community's tasks.

They shall abstain from any measure which could jeopardize the attainment of the objectives of this Treaty.

Article 6

Within the scope of application of this Treaty, and without prejudice to any special provisions contained therein, any discrimination on the grounds of nationality shall be prohibited.

The Council, on a proposal from the Commission and in co-operation with the European Parliament may adopt by a qualified majority rules designed to prohibit such discrimination.

Article 7a

The Community shall adopt measures with the aim of progressively establishing the internal market over a period expiring on 31 December 1992, in accordance with the provisions of this Article and of Articles 8b, 8c, 28, 57(2), 59, 70(1), 84, 99, 100a and 100b and without prejudice to the other provisions of this Treaty.

The internal market shall comprise an area without internal frontiers in which the free movement of goods, persons, services and capital is ensured in accordance with the provisions of this Treaty.

PART TWO.   CITIZENSHIP OF THE UNION

Article 8

1. Citizenship of the Union is hereby established. Every person holding the nationality of a Member State shall be a citizen of the Union.

2. Citizens of the Union shall enjoy the rights conferred by this Treaty and shall be subject to the duties imposed thereby.

Article 8a

1. Every citizen of the Union shall have the right to move and reside freely within the territory of the Member States, subject to the limitations and conditions laid down in this Treaty and by the measures adopted to give it effect.

2. The Council may adopt provisions with a view to facilitating the exercise of the rights referred to in paragraph 1; save as otherwise provided in this Treaty, the Council shall act unanimously on a proposal from the Commission after obtaining the assent of the European Parliament.

Article 8b

1. Every citizen of the Union residing in a Member State of which he is not a national shall have the right to vote and to stand as a candidate at municipal elections in the Member State in which he resides, under the same conditions as nationals of that State. This right shall be exercised subject to detailed arrangements to be adopted before 31 December 1994 by the Council, acting unanimously, on a proposal from the Commission and after consulting the European Parliament; these arrangements may provide for derogations where warranted by problems specific to a Member State.

2. Without prejudice to Article 138(3) and to the provisions adopted for its implementation, every citizen of the Union residing in a Member State of which he is not a national shall have the right to vote and to stand as a candidate in elections to the European Parliament in the Member State in which he resides, under the same conditions as nationals of that State. This right shall be exercised subject to detailed arrangements to be adopted before 31 December 1993 by the Council, acting unanimously on a proposal from the Commission and after consulting the European Parliament; these arrangements may provide for derogations where warranted by problems specific to a Member State.

Article 8c

Every citizen of the Union shall, in the territory of a third country in which the Member State of which he is a national is not represented, be entitled to protection by the diplomatic or consular authorities of any Member State, on the same conditions as the nationals of that State. Before 31 December 1993, Member States shall establish the necessary rules among themselves and start the international negotiations required to secure this protection.

Article 8d

Every citizen of the Union shall have the right to petition the European Parliament in accordance with Article 138d.

Every citizen of the Union may apply to the Ombudsman established in accordance with Article 138e.

Article 8e

The Commission shall report to the European Parliament, to the Council and to the Economic and Social Committee before 31 December 1993 and then every three years on the application of the provisions of this Part. This report shall take account of the development of the Union.

On this basis, and without prejudice to the other provisions of this Treaty, the Council, acting unanimously on a proposal from the Commission and after consulting the European Parliament, may adopt provisions to strengthen or to add to the rights laid down in this Part, which it shall recommend to the Member States for adoption in accordance with their respective constitutional requirements.

Article 100c

1. The Council, acting unanimously on a proposal from the Commission and after consulting the European Parliament, shall determine the third countries whose nationals must be in possession of a visa when crossing the external borders of the Member States.

2. However, in the event of an emergency situation in a third country posing a threat of a sudden inflow of nationals from that country into the Community, the Council, acting by a qualified majority on a recommendation from the Commission, may introduce, for a period not exceeding six months, a visa requirement for nationals from the country in question. The visa requirement established under this paragraph may be extended in accordance with the procedure referred to in paragraph 1.

3. From 1 January 1996, the Council shall adopt the decisions referred to in paragraph 1 by a qualified majority. The Council shall, before that date, acting by a qualified majority on a pro-

posal from the Commission and after consulting the European Parliament, adopt measures relating to a uniform format for visas.

4. In the areas referred to in this Article, the Commission shall examine any request made by a Member State that it submit a proposal to the Council.

5. This Article shall be without prejudice to the exercise of the responsibilities incumbent upon the Member States with regard to the maintenance of law and order and the safeguarding of internal security.

6. This Article shall apply to other areas if so decided pursuant to Article K.9 of the provisions of the Treaty on European Union which relate to co-operation in the fields of justice and home affairs, subject to the voting conditions determined at the same time.

7. The provisions of the conventions in force between the Member States governing areas covered by this Article shall remain in force until their content has been replaced by directives or measures adopted pursuant to this Article.

PART FIVE.   INSTITUTIONS OF THE COMMUNITY

Title 1.   Provisions governing the Institutions

Section 1.   The European Parliament

Article 137

The European Parliament, which shall consist of representatives of the peoples of the States brought together in the Community, shall exercise the powers conferred upon it by this Treaty.

Article 138

[Sections 1 and 2 provided for delegates designated by the Member States' Parliaments from among their members. They lapsed on 17 July 1979.]

3. The European Parliament shall draw up proposals for elec-

tions by direct universal suffrage in accordance with a uniform procedure in all Member States. The Council shall, acting unanimously after obtaining the assent of the European Parliament, which shall act by a majority of its component members, lay down the appropriate provision, which it shall recommend to Member States for adoption in accordance with their respective constitutional requirements.

Council Decision and Act of 20 September 1976 on Direct Elections (as amended)

Article 1

The representatives in the European Parliament of the peoples of the States brought together in the Community shall be elected by direct universal suffrage.

Article 2

The number of representatives elected in each Member State Shall be as follows:

Belgium	25
Denmark	16
Germany	99
Greece	25
Spain	64
France	87
Ireland	15
Italy	87
Luxembourg	6
Netherlands	31
Austria	21
Portugal	25
Finland	16
Sweden	22
United Kingdom	87

Article 138a

Political parties at European level are important as a factor for integration within the Union. They contribute to forming a European awareness and to expressing the political will of the citizens of the Union.

Article 138b

In so far as provided in this Treaty, the European Parliament shall participate in the process leading up to the adoption of Community acts by exercising its powers under the procedures laid down in Articles 189b and 189c and by giving its assent or delivering advisory opinions.

The European Parliament may, acting by a majority of its members, request the Commission to submit any appropriate proposal on matters on which it considers that a Community act is required for the purpose of implementing this Treaty.

Article 138c

In the course of its duties, the European Parliament may, at the request of a quarter of its members, set up a temporary Committee of Inquiry to investigate, without prejudice to the powers conferred by this Treaty on other institutions or bodies, alleged contraventions or maladministration in the implementation of Community law, except where the alleged facts are being examined before a court and while the case is still subject to legal proceedings.

The temporary Committee of Inquiry shall cease to exist on the submission of its report.

The detailed provisions governing the exercise of the right of inquiry shall be determined by common accord of the European Parliament, the Council and the Commission.

Article 138d

Any citizen of the Union, and any natural or legal person residing or having his registered office in a Member State, shall have the right to address, individually or in association with other citizens or persons, a petition to the European Parliament on a matter which comes within the Community's fields of activity and which affects him, her or it directly.

Article 138e

1. The European Parliament shall appoint an Ombudsman empowered to receive complaints from any citizen of the Union or any natural or legal person residing or having its registered office in a Member State concerning instances of maladministration in the activities of the Community institutions or bodies, with the exception of the Court of Justice and the Court of First Instance acting in their judicial role.

In accordance with his duties, the Ombudsman shall conduct inquiries for which he finds grounds, either on his own initiative or on the basis of complaints submitted to him direct or through a member of the European Parliament, except where the alleged facts are or have been the subject of legal proceedings. Where the Ombudsman establishes an instance of maladministration, he shall refer the matter to the institution concerned, which shall have a period of three months in which to inform him of its views. The Ombudsman shall then forward a report to the European Parliament and the institution concerned. The person lodging the complaint shall be informed of the outcome of such inquiries.

The Ombudsman shall submit an annual report to the European Parliament on the outcome of his inquiries.

2. The Ombudsman shall be appointed after each election of the European Parliament for the duration of its term of office. The Ombudsman shall be eligible for reappointment.

The Ombudsman may be dismissed by the Court of Justice at the request of the European Parliament if he no longer fulfils the conditions required for the performance of his duties or if he is guilty of serious misconduct.

3. The Ombudsman shall be completely independent in the performance of his duties. In the performance of those duties he shall neither seek nor take instructions from any body. The Ombudsman may not, during his term of office, engage in any other occupation, whether gainful or not.

4. The European Parliament shall, after seeking an opinion from the Commission and with the approval of the Council acting by a qualified majority, lay down the regulations and general conditions governing the Ombudsman's duties.

Article 139

The European Parliament shall hold an annual session. It shall meet, without requiring to be convened, on the second Tuesday in March.

The European Parliament may meet in extraordinary session at the request of a majority of its members or at the request of the Council or of the Commission.

Article 140

The European Parliament shall elect its President and its officers from among its members.

Members of the Commission may attend all meetings and shall, at their request, be heard on behalf of the Commission.

The Commission shall reply orally or in writing to questions put to it by the European Parliament or by its members.

The Council shall be heard by the European Parliament in accordance with the conditions laid down by the Council in its rules of procedure.

Article 141

Save as otherwise provided in this Treaty, the European Parliament shall act by an absolute majority of the votes cast.

The rules of procedure shall determine the quorum.

Article 142

The European Parliament shall adopt its rules of procedure, acting by a majority of its members.

The proceedings of the European Parliament shall be published in the manner laid down in its rules of procedure.

Article 143

The European Parliament shall discuss in open session the annual general report submitted to it by the Commission.

Article 144

If a motion of censure on the activities of the Commission is tabled before it, the European Parliament shall not vote thereon until at least three days after the motion has been tabled and only by open vote.

If the motion of censure is carried by a two-thirds majority of the votes cast, representing a majority of the members of the European Parliament, the members of the Commission shall resign as a body. They shall continue to deal with current business until they are replaced in accordance with Article 158.

In this case, the term of office of the members of the Commission appointed to replace them shall expire on the date which the term of office of the members of the Commission obliged to resign as a body would have expired.

Section 2.   The Council

Article 145

To ensure that the objectives set out in this Treaty are attained, the Council shall, in accordance with the provisions of this Treaty:

- ensure co-ordination of the general economic policies of the Member States;
- have power to take decisions;
- confer on the Commission, in the acts which the Council adopts, powers for the implementation of the rules which the Council lays down. The Council may impose certain requirements in respect of the exercise of these powers. The Council may also reserve the right, in specific cases, to exercise directly implementing powers itself. The procedures referred to above must be consonant with principles and rules to be laid down in advance by the Council, acting unanimously on a proposal from the Commission and after obtaining the opinion of the European Parliament.

Article 146

The Council shall consist of a representative of each Member State at ministerial level, authorized to commit the government of that Member State.

The office of President shall be held in turn by each Member State in the Council for a term of six months, in the order decided by the Council acting unanimously.

Article 147

The Council shall meet when convened by its President on his initiative or at the request of one of its members or of the Commission.

Article 148

1. Save as otherwise provided in this Treaty, the Council shall act by a majority of its members.

2. Where the Council is required to act by a qualified majority, the votes of its members shall be weighted as follows:

Belgium	5
Denmark	3
Germany	10
Greece	5
Spain	8
France	10
Ireland	3
Italy	10
Luxembourg	2
Netherlands	5
Austria	4
Portugal	5
Finland	3
Sweden	4
United Kingdom	10

For their adoption, acts of the Council shall require at least:

62 votes in favour where this Treaty requires them to be adopted on a proposal from the commission.

62 votes in favour, cast by at least ten members, in other cases.

3. Abstentions by members present in person or represented shall not prevent the adoption by the Council of acts which require unanimity.

Article 149 (repealed)

Article 150

Where a vote is taken, any member of the Council may also act on behalf of not more than one other member.

Article 151

1. A committee consisting of the Permanent Representatives of the Member States shall be responsible for preparing the work of the Council and for carrying out the tasks assigned to it by the Council.

2. The Council shall be assisted by a General Secretariat, under the direction of a Secretary-General. The Secretary-General shall be appointed by the Council acting unanimously. The Council shall decide on the organization of the General Secretariat.

3. The Council shall adopt its rules of procedure.

Article 154

The Council shall, acting by a qualified majority, determine the salaries, allowances and pensions of the President and members of the Commission, and of the president, Judges, Advocates-General and Registrar of the Court of Justice. It shall also, again by a qualified majority, determine any payment to be made instead of remuneration.

Section 3. The Commission

Article 155

In order to ensure the proper functioning and development of the common market, the Commission shall:

- ensure that the provisions of this Treaty and the measures taken by the institutions pursuant thereto are applied;
- formulate recommendations or deliver opinions on matters dealt with in this Treaty, if it expressly so provides or if the Commission considers it necessary;
- have its power of decision and participate in the shaping of measures taken by the Council and by the European Parliament in the manner provided for in this Treaty;
- exercise the powers conferred on it by the Council for the implementation of the rules laid down by the latter.

Article 156

The Commission shall publish annually, not later than one month before the opening of the session of the European Parliament, a general report on the activities of the Community.

Article 157

1. The Commission shall consist of twenty members, who shall be chosen on the grounds of their general competence and whose independence is beyond doubt.

The number of members of the Commission may be altered by the Council, acting unanimously.

Only nationals of Member States may be members of the Commission.

The Commission must include at least one national of each of the Member States, but may not include more than two members having the nationality of the same State.

2. The members of the Commission shall, in the general interest of the Community, be completely independent in the performance of their duties.

In the performance of these duties, they shall neither seek nor take instructions from any government or from any other body. They shall refrain from any action incompatible with their duties. Each Member State undertakes to respect this principle and not to seek to influence the members of the Commission in the performance of their tasks.

The members of the Commission may not, during their term of office, engage in any other occupation, whether gainful or not. When entering upon their duties they shall give a solemn undertaking that, both during and after their term of office, they will respect the obligations arising therefrom and in particular their duty to behave with integrity and discretion as regards the acceptance, after they have ceased to hold office, of certain appointments or benefits. In the event of any breach of these obligations, the Court of Justice may, on application by the Council or the Commission, rule that the member concerned be, according to the circumstances, either compulsorily retired in accordance with Article 160 or deprived of his right to a pension or other benefits in its stead.

Article 158

1. The members of the Commission shall be appointed, in accordance with the procedure referred to in paragraph 2, for a period of five years, subject, if need be, to Article 144.

Their term of office shall be renewable.

2. The governments of the Member States shall nominate by common accord, after consulting the European Parliament, the person they intend to appoint as President of the Commission.

The governments of the Member States shall, in consultation with the nominee for President, nominate the other persons whom they intend to appoint as members of the Commission.

The President and the other members of the Commission thus nominated shall be subject as a body to a vote of approval by the European Parliament. After approval by the European Parliament, the President and the other members of the Commission shall be appointed by common accord of the governments of the Member States.

3. Paragraphs 1 and 2 shall be applied for the first time to the President and the other members of the Commission whose term of office begins on 7 January 1995.

The President and the other members of the Commission whose term of office begins on 7 January 1993 shall be appointed by common accord of the governments of the Member States. Their term of office shall expire on 6 January 1995.

Article 159

Apart from normal replacement, or death, the duties of a member of the Commission shall end when he resigns or is compulsorily retired.

The vacancy thus caused shall be filled for the remainder of the member's term of office by a new member appointed by common accord of the governments of the Member States. The Council may, acting unanimously, decide that such a vacancy need not be filled.

In the event of resignation, compulsory retirement or death, the President shall be replaced for the remainder of his term of office. The procedure laid down in Article 158(2) shall be applicable for the replacement of the President.

Save in the case of compulsory retirement under Article 160, members of the Commission shall remain in office until they have been replaced.

Article 163

The Commission shall act by a majority of the number of members provided for in Article 157.

A meeting of the Commission shall be valid only if the number of members laid down in its rules of procedure is present.

Section 4. The Court of Justice

Article 164

The Court of Justice shall ensure that in the interpretation and application of this Treaty the law is observed.

Article 165

The Court of Justice shall consist of fifteen judges.

The Court of Justice shall sit in plenary session. It may, however, form chambers each consisting of three of five judges, either to undertake certain preparatory inquiries or to adjudicate on particular categories of cases in accordance with rules laid down for these purposes.

The Court of Justice shall sit in plenary session when a Member State or a Community institution that is a party to the proceedings so requests.

Should the Court of Justice so request, the Council may, acting unanimously, increase the number of judges and make necessary adjustments to the second and third paragraphs of this Article and to the second of Article 167.

Article 166

The Court of Justice shall be assisted by eight Advocates-General.

It shall be the duty of the Advocate-General, acting with complete impartiality and independence, to make, in open court, reasoned submissions on cases brought before the Court of Justice, in order to assist the Court in the performance of the task assigned to it in Article 164.

Should the Court of Justice so request, the Council may, acting unanimously, increase the number of Advocates-General and make the necessary adjustments to the third paragraph of Article 167.

Article 167

The Judges and Advocates-General shall be chosen from persons whose independence is beyond doubt and who possess the qualifications required for appointment to the highest judicial offices in their respective countries or who are jurisconsults of recognised competence; they shall be appointed by common accord of the Governments of the Member States for a term of six years.

Every three years there shall be a partial replacement of the judges. Eight and seven Judges shall be replaced alternately.

Every three years there shall be a partial replacement of the Advocates-General. Four Advocates-General shall be replaced on each occasion. Retiring Judges and Advocates-General shall be eligible for reappointment.

The Judges shall elect the President of the Court of Justice from among their number for a term of three years. He may be re-elected.

Article 168

The Court of Justice shall appoint its Registrar and lay down the rules governing his service.

Article 168a

1. A Court of First Instance shall be attached to the Court of Justice with jurisdiction to hear and determine at first instance, subject to a right of appeal to the Court of Justice on points of law only and in accordance with the conditions laid down by Statute, certain classes of action or proceeding defined in accordance with the conditions laid down in paragraph 2. The Court of First Instance shall not be competent to hear and determine questions referred for a preliminary ruling under Article 177.

2. At the request of the Court of Justice and after consulting the European Parliament and the Commission, the Council, acting unanimously, shall determine the classes of action or proceeding referred to in paragraph 1 and the composition of the Court of First Instance and shall adopt the necessary adjustments and additional provisions to the Statute of the Court of Justice. Unless the Council decides otherwise, the provisions of this Treaty relating to the Court of Justice, in particular the provisions of the Protocol on the Statute of the Court of Justice, shall apply to the Court of First Instance.

3. The members of the Court of First Instance shall be chosen from persons whose independence is beyond doubt and who possess the ability required for appointment to judicial office; they shall be appointed by common accord of the governments of the Member States for a term of six years. The membership shall be partially renewed every three years. Retiring members shall be eligible for reappointment.

4. The Court of First Instance shall establish its rules of procedure in agreement with the Court of Justice. Those rules shall require the unanimous approval of the Council.

Article 169

If the Commission considers that a Member State has failed to fulfil an obligation under this Treaty, it shall deliver a reasoned opinion on the matter after giving the State concerned the opportunity to submit its observations.

If the State concerned does not comply with the opinion within the period laid down by the Commission the latter may bring the matter before the Court of Justice.

Article 170

A Member State which considers that another Member State has failed to fulfil an obligation under this Treaty may bring the matter before the Court of Justice.

Before a Member State brings an action against another Member State for an alleged infringement of an obligation under this Treaty, it shall bring the matter before the Commission.

The Commission shall deliver a reasoned opinion after each of the States concerned has been given the opportunity to submit its own case and its observations on the other party's case both orally and in writing.

If the Commission has not delivered an opinion within three months of the date on which the matter was brought before it, the absence of such opinion shall not prevent the matter from being brought before the Court of Justice.

Article 171

1. If the Court of Justice finds that a Member State has failed to fulfil an obligation under this Treaty, the State shall be required to take the necessary measures to comply with the judgment of the Court of Justice.

2. If the Commission considers that the Member State concerned has not taken such measures it shall, after giving that State the opportunity to submit its observations, issue a reasoned opinion specifying the points on which the Member State concerned has not complied with the judgment of the Court of Justice.

If the Member State concerned fails to take the necessary measures to comply with the Court's judgment within the time-limit laid down by the Commission, the latter may bring the case before the Court of Justice. In so doing it shall specify the amount of lump sum or penalty payment to be paid by the Member State concerned which it considers appropriate in the circumstances.

If the Court of Justice finds that the Member State concerned has not complied with its judgment it may impose a lump sum or penalty payment on it.

This procedure shall be without prejudice to Article 170.

Article 172

Regulations adopted jointly by the European Parliament and the Council, and by the Council, pursuant to the provisions of this Treaty, may give the Court of Justice unlimited jurisdiction with regard to the penalties provided for in such regulations.

Article 173

The Court of Justice shall review the legality of acts adopted jointly by the European Parliament and the Council, of acts of the Council, of the Commission and of the ECB, other than recommendations and opinions, and of acts of the European Parliament intended to produce legal effects *vis-à-vis* third parties.

It shall for this purpose have jurisdiction in actions brought by a Member State, the Council or the Commission on grounds of lack of competence, infringement of an essential procedural requirement, infringement of this Treaty or of any rule of law relating to its application, or misuse of powers.

The Court shall have jurisdiction under the same conditions, in actions brought by the European Parliament and by the ECB for the purpose of protecting their prerogatives.

Any natural or legal person may, under the same conditions, institute proceedings against a decision addressed to that person or against a decision which, although in the form of a regulation or a decision addressed to another person, is of direct and individual concern to the former.

The proceedings provided for in this Article shall be instituted within two months of the publication of the measure, or of its notification to the plaintiff, or, in the absence thereof, of the day on which it came to the knowledge of the latter, as the case may be.

Article 174

If the action is well founded, the Court of Justice shall declare the act concerned to be void.

In the case of a regulation, however, the Court of Justice shall, if it considers this necessary, state which of the effects of the regulation which it has declared void shall be considered as definitive.

Article 175

Should the European Parliament, the Council or the Commission, in infringement of this Treaty, fail to act, the Member States and the other institutions of the Community may bring an action before the Court of Justice to have the infringement established.

The action shall be admissible only if the institution concerned has first been called upon to act. If, within two months of being so called upon, the institution concerned has not defined its position, the action may be brought within a further period of two months.

Any natural or legal person may, under the conditions laid down in the preceding paragraphs, complain to the Court of Justice that an institution of the Community has failed to address to that person any act other than a recommendation or an opinion.

The Court of Justice shall have jurisdiction, under the same conditions, in actions or proceedings brought by the ECB in the areas falling within the latter's field of competence and in actions or proceedings brought against the latter.

Article 176

The institution or institutions whose act has been declared void or whose failure to act has been declared contrary to this Treaty shall be required to take the necessary measures to comply with the judgment of the Court of Justice.

This obligation shall not affect any obligation which may result from the application of the second paragraph of Article 215.

This Article shall also apply to the ECB.

Article 177

The Court of Justice shall have jurisdiction to give preliminary rulings concerning:

(a) the interpretation of the Treaty;
(b) the validity and interpretation of acts of the institutions of the Community and of the ECB;
(c) the interpretation of the statutes of bodies established by an act of the Council, where those statutes so provide.

Where such a question is raised before any court or tribunal of a Member State, that court or tribunal may, if it considers that a decision on the question is necessary to enable it to give judgment, request the Court of Justice to give a ruling thereon.

Where any such question is raised in a case pending before a court or tribunal of a Member State against whose decisions there is no judicial remedy under national law, the court or tribunal shall bring the matter before the Court of Justice.

Article 178

The Court of Justice shall have jurisdiction in disputes relating to the compensation for damage provided for in the second paragraph of Article 215.

Article 180

The Court of Justice shall, within the limits hereinafter laid down, have jurisdiction in disputes concerning:

(a) the fulfilment by Member States of obligations under the Statute of the European Investment Bank. In this connection, the Board of Directors of the Bank shall enjoy the powers conferred upon the Commission by Article 169;
(b) measures adopted by the Board of Governors of the European Investment Bank. In this connection, any Member State, the Commission or the Board of

Directors of the Bank may institute proceedings under the conditions laid down in Article 173;

(c) measures adopted by the Board of Directors of the European Investment Bank. Proceedings against such measures may be instituted only by Member States or by the Commission, under the conditions laid down in Article 173, and solely on the grounds of non-compliance with the procedure provided for in Article 21(2), (5), (6) and (7) of the Statute of the Bank;

(d) the fulfilment by the national central banks of obligations under this Treaty and the Statute of the ESCB. In this connection the powers of the Council of the ECB in respect of national central banks shall be the same as those conferred upon the commission in respect of Member States by Article 169. If the Court of Justice finds that a national central bank has failed to fulfil an obligation under this Treaty, that bank shall be required to take the necessary measures to comply with the judgment of the Court of Justice.

Article 181

The Court of Justice shall have jurisdiction to give judgment pursuant to any arbitration clause contained in a contract concluded by or on behalf of the Community, whether that contract be governed by public or private law.

Article 182

The Court of Justice shall have jurisdiction in any dispute between Member States which relates to the subject matter of this Treaty if the dispute is submitted to it under a special agreement between the parties.

Article 183

Save where jurisdiction is conferred on the Court by this treaty, disputes to which the Community is a party shall not on that ground be excluded from the jurisdiction of the courts or tribunals of the Member States.

Article 184

Notwithstanding the expiry of the period laid down in the fifth paragraph of Article 173, any party may, in proceedings in which a regulation adopted jointly by the European Parliament and the Council, or a regulation of the Council, of the Commission, or of the ECB is at issue, plead the grounds specified in the second paragraph of Article 173 in order to invoke before the Court of Justice the inapplicability of that regulation.

Section 5.   The Court of Auditors

Article 188a

The Court of Auditors shall carry out the audit.

Article 189

In order to carry out their task and in accordance with the provisions of the Treaty, the European Parliament acting jointly with the Council, the Council and the Commission shall make regulations and issue directives, take decisions, make recommendations or deliver opinions.

A regulation shall have general application. It shall be binding in its entirety and directly applicable in all Member States.

A directive shall be binding, as to the result to be achieved, upon each Member State to which it is addressed, but shall leave to the national authorities the choice of form and methods.

A decision shall be binding in its entirety upon those to whom it is addressed.

Recommendations and opinions shall have no binding force.

Article 189a

1. Where, in pursuance of the Treaty, the Council acts on a proposal from the Commission, unanimity shall be required for an act constituting an amendment to that proposal, subject to Article 189b(4) and (5).

2. As long as the Council has not acted, the Commission may

alter its proposal at any time during the procedures leading to the adoption of a Community act.

Article 189b

1. Where reference is made in the Treaty to this Article for the adoption of an act, the following procedures shall apply.
2. The Commission shall submit a proposal to the European Parliament and the Council.

The Council, acting by a qualified majority after obtaining the opinion of the European Parliament, shall adopt a common position. The common position shall be communicated to the European Parliament. The Council shall inform the European Parliament fully of the reasons which led it to adopt its common position. The Commission shall inform the European Parliament fully of its position.

If, within three months of such communication, the European Parliament:

(a) approves the common position, the Council shall definitively adopt the act in question in accordance with that common position;

(b) has not taken a decision, the Council shall adopt the act in question in accordance with its common position;

(c) indicates, by an absolute majority of its component members, that it intends to reject the common position, it shall immediately inform the Council. The Council may convene a meeting of the Conciliation Committee referred to in paragraph 4 to explain further its position. The European Parliament shall thereafter either confirm, by an absolute majority of its component members, its rejection of the common position, in which event the proposed act shall be deemed not to have been adopted, or propose amendments in accordance with subparagraph (d) of this paragraph;

(d) proposes amendments to the common position by an absolute majority of its component members, the amended text shall be forwarded to the Council and to the Commission which shall deliver an opinion on those amendments.

3. If, within three months of the matter being referred to it, the Council, acting by a qualified majority, approves all the amendments of the European Parliament, it shall amend its common position accordingly and adopt the act in question; however, the Council shall act unanimously on the amendments on which the Commission has delivered a negative opinion. If the Council does not approve the act in question, the President of the Council, in agreement with the President of the European Parliament, shall forthwith convene a meeting of the Conciliation Committee.

4. The Conciliation Committee, which shall be composed of the members of the Council or their representatives and an equal number of representatives of the European Parliament, shall have the task of reaching agreement on a joint text, by a qualified majority of the members of the Council or their representatives and by a majority of the representatives of the European Parliament. The Commission shall take part in the Conciliation Committee's proceedings and shall take all the necessary initiatives with a view to reconciling the positions of the European Parliament and the Council.

5. If within six weeks of its being convened, the Conciliation Committee approves a joint text, the European Parliament, acting by an absolute majority of the votes cast, and the Council, acting by a qualified majority, shall have a period of six weeks from that approval in which to adopt the act in question in accordance with the joint text. If one of the two institutions fails to approve the proposed act, it shall be deemed not to have been adopted.

6. Where the Conciliation Committee does not approve a joint text, the proposed act shall be deemed not to have been adopted unless the Council, acting by a qualified majority within six weeks of expiry of the period granted to the Conciliation Committee, confirms the common position to which it agreed before the conciliation procedure was initiated, possibly with the amendments proposed by the European Parliament. In this case, the act in question shall be finally adopted unless the European Parliament, within six weeks of the date of confirmation by the Council, rejects the text by an absolute majority of its component members, in which case the proposed act shall be deemed not to have been adopted.

7. The periods of three months and six weeks referred to in

this Article may be extended by a maximum of one month and two weeks respectively by common accord of the European Parliament and the Council. The period of three months referred to in paragraph 2 shall be automatically extended by two months where paragraph 2(c) applies.

8. The scope of the procedure under this Article may be widened, in accordance with the procedure provided for in Article N(2) of the Treaty on European Union, on the basis of a report to be submitted to the Council by the Commission by 1996 at the latest.

Article 189c

Where reference is made in this Treaty to this Article for the adoption of an act, the following procedure shall apply:

(a) The Council, acting by a qualified majority on a proposal from the Commission and after obtaining the opinion of the European Parliament, shall adopt a common position.

(b) The Council's common position shall be communicated to the European Parliament. The Council and the Commission shall inform the European Parliament fully of the reasons which led the Council to adopt its common position and also of the Commission's position.

If, within three months of such communication, the European Parliament approves this common position or has not taken a decision within that period, the Council shall definitively adopt the act in question in accordance with the common position.

(c) The European Parliament may, within the period of three months referred to in point (b), by an absolute majority of its component members, propose amendments to the Council's common position. The European Parliament may also, by the same majority, reject the Council's common position. The result of the proceedings shall be transmitted to the Council and the Commission.

If the European Parliament has rejected the Council's common position, unanimity shall be required for the Council to act on a second reading.

(d) The Commission shall, within a period of one month, re-examine the proposal on the basis of which the Council adopted its common position, by taking into account the amendments proposed by the European Parliament.

The Commission shall forward to the Council, at the same time as its re-examined proposal, the amendments of the European Parliament which it has not accepted, and shall express its opinion on them. The Council may adopt these amendments unanimously.

(e) The Council, acting by a qualified majority, shall adopt the proposal as re-examined by the Commission.

Unanimity shall be required for the Council to amend the proposal as re-examined by the Commission.

(f) In the cases referred to in points (c), (d) and (e), the Council shall be required to act within a period of three months. If no decision is taken within this period, the commission proposal shall be deemed not to have been adopted.

(g) The periods referred to in points (b) and (f) may be extended by a maximum of one month by common accord between the Council and the European Parliament.

Article 190

Regulations, directives and decisions adopted jointly by the European Parliament and the Council, and such acts adopted by the Council or the Commission, shall state the reasons on which they are based and shall refer to any proposals or opinions which were required to be obtained pursuant to this Treaty.

Article 191

1. Regulations, directives and decisions adopted in accordance with the procedures referred to in Article 189b shall be signed by the President of the European Parliament and by the President of the Council and published in the *Official Journal* of the Community. They shall enter into force on the date specified in them or, in the absence thereof, on the twentieth day following that of their publication.

2. Regulations of the Council and of the Commission, as well

as directives of those institutions which are addressed to all Member States, shall be published in the *Official Journal* of the Community. They shall enter into force on the date specified in them or, in the absence thereof, on the twentieth day following that of their publication.

3. Other directives, and decisions, shall be notified to those to whom they are addressed and shall take effect upon such notification.

Article 192

Decisions of the Council or of the Commission which impose a pecuniary obligation on persons other than States shall be enforceable.

Enforcement shall be governed by the rules of civil procedure in force in the State in the territory of which it is carried out. The order for its enforcement shall be appended to the decision, without other formality than verification of the authenticity of the decision, by the national authority which the Government of each Member State shall designate for this purpose and shall make known to the Commission and to the Court of Justice.

When these formalities have been completed on application by the party concerned, the latter may proceed to enforcement in accordance with the national law, by bringing the matter directly before the competent authority.

Enforcement may be suspended only by a decision of the Court of Justice. However, the courts of the country concerned shall have jurisdiction over complaints that enforcement is being carried out in an irregular manner.

Article 198a

A Committee consisting of representatives of regional and local bodies, hereinafter referred to as 'the Committee of the Regions', is hereby established with advisory status.

The number of members of the Committee of the Regions shall be as follows:

Belgium   12
Denmark   9

Germany	24
Greece	12
Spain	21
France	24
Ireland	9
Italy	24
Luxembourg	6
Netherlands	12
Austria	12
Portugal	12
Finland	9
Sweden	12
United Kingdom	24

The members of the Committee and an equal number of alternate members shall be appointed for four years by the Council acting unanimously on proposals from the respective Member States. Their term of office shall be renewable.

The members of the Committee may not be bound by any mandatory instructions. They shall be completely independent in the performance of their duties, in the general interest of the Community.

Article 198b

The Committee of the Regions shall elect its chairman and officers from among its members for a term of two years.

It shall adopt its rules of procedure and shall submit them for approval to the Council, acting unanimously.

The Committee shall be convened by its chairman at the request of the Council or of the Commission. It may also meet on its own initiative.

Article 198c

The Committee of the Regions shall be consulted by the Council or by the Commission where this Treaty so provides and in all other cases in which one of these two institutions considers it appropriate.

The Council or the Commission shall, if it considers it necessary, set the Committee, for the submission of its opinion, a time-limit which may not be less than one month from the date on which the chairman receives notification to this effect. Upon expiry of the time-limit the absence of an opinion shall not prevent further action.

Where the Economic and Social Committee is consulted pursuant to Article 198, the Committee of the Regions shall be informed by the Council or the Commission of the request for an opinion. Where it considers that specific regional interests are involved, the Committee of the Regions may issue an opinion on the matter.

It may issue an opinion on its own initiative in cases in which it considers such action appropriate.

The opinion of the Committee, together with a record of the proceedings, shall be forwarded to the Council and to the Commission.

Article 201

Without prejudice to other revenue, the budget shall be financed wholly from own resources.

The Council, acting unanimously on a proposal from the Commission and after consulting the European Parliament, shall lay down provisions relating to the system of own resources of the Community, which it shall recommend to the Member States for adoption in accordance with their respective constitutional requirements.

Article 201a

With a view to maintaining budgetary discipline, the Commission shall not make any proposal for a Community act, or alter its proposals, or adopt any implementing measure which is likely to have appreciable implications for the budget without providing the assurance that the proposal or that measure is capable of being financed within the limit of the Community's own resources arising under provisions laid down by the Council pursuant to Article 201.

Article 203

1. The financial year shall run from 1 January to 31 December.

2. Each institution of the Community shall, before 1 July, draw up estimates of its expenditure. The Commission shall consolidate these estimates in a preliminary draft budget. It shall attach thereto an opinion which may contain different estimates.

The preliminary draft budget shall contain an estimate of revenue and an estimate of expenditure.

3. The Commission shall place the preliminary draft budget before the Council not later than 1 September of the year preceding that in which the budget is to be implemented.

The Council shall consult the Commission and, where appropriate, the other institutions concerned whenever it intends to depart from the preliminary draft budget.

The Council acting by a qualified majority, shall establish the draft budget and forward it to the European Parliament.

4. The draft budget shall be placed before the European Parliament not later than 5 October of the year preceding that in which the budget is to be implemented.

The European Parliament shall have the right to amend the draft budget, acting by a majority of its members, and to propose to the Council, acting by an absolute majority of the votes cast, modifications to the draft budget relating to expenditure necessarily resulting from this Treaty or from acts adopted in accordance therewith.

If, within forty-five days of the draft budget being placed before it, the European Parliament has given its approval, the budget shall stand as finally adopted. If within this period the European Parliament has not amended the draft budget nor proposed any modifications thereto, the budget shall be deemed to be finally adopted.

If within this period the European Parliament has adopted amendments or proposed modifications, the draft budget together with the amendments or proposed modifications shall be forwarded to the Council.

5. After discussing the draft budget with the Commission and, where appropriate, with the other institutions concerned, the Council shall act under the following conditions:

(a) The Council may, acting by a qualified majority, modify any of the amendments adopted by the European Parliament;

(b) With regard to the proposed modifications:

where a modification proposed by the European Parliament does not have the effect of increasing the total amount of the expenditure of an institution, owing in particular to the fact that the increase in expenditure which it would involve would be expressly compensated by one or more proposed modifications correspondingly reducing expenditure, the Council may, acting by a qualified majority, reject the proposed modification. In the absence of a decision to reject it, the proposed modification shall stand as accepted;

where a modification proposed by the European Parliament has the effect of increasing the total amount of the expenditure of an institution, the Council may, acting by a qualified majority, accept this proposed modification. In the absence of a decision to accept it, the proposed modification shall stand as rejected; where in pursuance of one of the two preceding sub-paragraphs, the Council has rejected a proposed modification, it may, acting by a qualified majority, either retain the amount shown in the draft budget or fix another amount.

The draft budget shall be modified on the basis of the proposed modifications accepted by the Council.

If, within fifteen days of the draft budget being placed before it, the Council has not modified any of the amendments adopted by the European Parliament and if the modifications proposed by the latter have been accepted, the budget shall be deemed to be finally adopted. The Council shall inform the European Parliament that it has not modified any of the amendments and that the proposed modifications have been accepted.

If, within this period the Council has modified one or more of the amendments adopted by the European Parliament or if the modifications proposed by the latter have been rejected or modified, the modified draft budget shall again be forwarded to the European Parliament. The Council shall inform the European Parliament of the results of its deliberations.

6. Within fifteen days of the draft budget being placed before it, the European Parliament, which shall have been notified of the action taken on its proposed modifications, may, acting by a majority of its members and three-fifths of the votes cast, amend or reject the modifications to its amendments made by the

Council and shall adopt the budget accordingly. If, within this period the European Parliament has not acted, the budget shall be deemed to be finally adopted.

7. When the procedure provided for in this Article has been completed, the President of the European Parliament shall declare that the budget has been finally adopted.

8. However, the European Parliament, acting by a majority of its members and two-thirds of the votes cast, may if there are important reasons reject the draft budget and ask for a new draft to be submitted to it.

9. A maximum rate of increase in relation to the expenditure of the same type to be incurred during the current year shall be fixed annually for the total expenditure other than that necessarily resulting from this Treaty or from acts adopted in accordance therewith.

The Commission shall, after consulting the Economic Policy Committee, declare what this maximum rate is as it results from:

- the trend, in terms of volume, of the gross national products within the Community;
- the average variation in the budgets of the Member States; and
- the trend of the cost of living during the preceding financial year.

The maximum rate shall be communicated, before 1 May, to all the institutions of the Community. The latter shall be required to conform to this during the budgetary procedure, subject to the provisions of the fourth and fifth subparagraphs of this paragraph.

If, in respect of expenditure other than that necessarily resulting from this Treaty or from acts adopted in accordance therewith, the actual rate of increase in the draft budget established by the Council is over half the maximum rate, the European Parliament may, exercising its right of amendment, further increase the total amount of that expenditure to a limit not exceeding half the maximum rate.

Where the European Parliament, the Council or the Commission consider that the activities of the Communities require that the rate determined according to the procedure laid down in this paragraph should be exceeded, another rate may be fixed by agreement between the Council, acting by a qualified majority, and the European Parliament, acting by a majority of its members and three-fifths of the votes cast.

10. Each institution shall exercise the powers conferred upon it by this Article, with due regard for the provisions of the Treaty and for acts adopted in accordance therewith, in particular those relating to the Communities' own resources and to the balance between revenue and expenditure.

Article 204

If, at the beginning of a financial year, the budget has not yet been voted, a sum equivalent to not more than one-twelfth of the budget appropriations for the preceding financial year may be spent each month in respect of any chapter or other subdivision of the budget in accordance with the provisions of the regulations made pursuant to Art. 209; this arrangement shall not, however, have the effect of placing at the disposal of the Commission appropriations in excess of one-twelfth of those provided for in the draft budget in course of preparation.

The Council may, acting by a qualified majority, provided that the other conditions laid down in the first subparagraph are observed, authorize expenditure in excess of one-twelfth.

If the decision relates to expenditure which does not necessarily result from this Treaty or from acts adopted in accordance therewith, the Council shall forward it immediately to the European Parliament; within thirty days the European Parliament, acting by a majority of its members and three-fifths of the votes cast, may adopt a different decision on the expenditure in excess of the one-twelfth referred to in the first subparagraph. This part of the decision of the Council shall be suspended until the European Parliament has taken its decision. If within the period the European Parliament has not taken a decision which differs from the decision of the Council, the latter shall be deemed to be finally adopted.

The decisions referred to in the second and third subparagraphs shall lay down the necessary measures relating to resources to ensure application of this Article.

Article 205

The Commission shall implement the budget, in accordance with the provisions of the regulations made pursuant to Article 209, on its own responsibility and within the limits of the appropriations, having regard to the principles of sound financial management.

The regulations shall lay down detailed rules for each institution concerning its part in effecting its own expenditure.

Within the budget, the Commission may, subject to the limits and conditions laid down in the regulations made pursuant to Article 209, transfer appropriations from one chapter to another or from one subdivision to another.

Article 205a

The Commission shall submit annually to the Council and to the European Parliament the accounts of the preceding financial year relating to the implementation of the budget. The Commission shall also forward to them a financial statement of the assets and liabilities of the Community.

Article 206

1. The European Parliament, acting on a recommendation from the Council which shall act by qualified majority, shall give a discharge to the Commission in respect of the implementation of the budget. To this end, the Council and the European Parliament in turn shall examine the accounts and the financial statement referred to in Article 205a, the annual report by the Court of Auditors together with the replies of the institutions under audit to the observations of the Court of Auditors and any relevant special reports by the Court of Auditors.

2. Before giving a discharge to the Commission, or for any other purpose in connection with the exercise of its power over the implementation of the budget, the European Parliament may ask to hear the Commission give evidence with regard to the execution of expenditure or the operation of financial control systems. The Commission shall submit any necessary information to the European Parliament at the latter's request.

3. The Commission shall take all appropriate steps to act on the observations in the decisions giving discharge and on other observations by the European Parliament relating to the execution of expenditure, as well as on comments accompanying the recommendations on discharge adopted by the Council. At the request of the European Parliament or the Council, the Commission shall report on the measures taken in the light of these observations and comments and in particular on the instructions given to the departments which are responsible for the implementation of the budget. These reports shall also be forwarded to the Court of Auditors.

PART SIX.　GENERAL AND FINAL PROVISIONS

Article 210

The Community shall have legal personality.

Article 211

In each of the Member States, the Community shall enjoy the most extensive legal capacity accorded to legal persons under their laws; it may, in particular, acquire or dispose of movable and immovable property and may be a party to legal proceedings. To this end, the Community shall be represented by the Commission.

Article 214

The members of the institutions of the Community, the members of committees and the officials and other servants of the Community shall be required, even after their duties have ceased, not to disclose information of the kind covered by the obligation of professional secrecy, in particular information about undertakings, their business relations or their cost components.

Article 215

The contractual liability of the Community shall be governed by the law applicable to the contract in question.

In the case of non-contractual liability, the Community shall, in accordance with the general principles common to the law of the Member States, make good any damage caused by its institutions or by its servants in the performance of their duties.

The preceding paragraph shall apply under the same conditions to damage caused by the ECB or by its servants in the performance of their duties.

The personal liability of its servants towards the Community shall be governed by the provisions laid down in their Staff Regulations or in the Conditions of Employment applicable to them.

Article 216

The seat of the institutions of the Community shall be determined by common accord of the Governments of the Member States.

Article 217

The rules governing the languages of the institutions of the Community shall, without prejudice to the provisions contained in the rules of procedure of the Court of Justice, be determined by the Council, acting unanimously.

Article 218

The European Communities shall enjoy in the territories of the Member States such privileges and immunities as are necessary for the performance of their tasks, under the conditions laid down in the Protocol annexed to this treaty. The same shall apply to the European Investment Bank.

Article 219

Member States undertake not to submit a dispute concerning the interpretation or application of this Treaty to any method of settlement other than those provided for therein.

Article 222

This Treaty shall in no way prejudice the rules in Member States governing the system of property ownership.

Article 223

1. The provisions of this Treaty shall not preclude the application of the following rules:

   (a) No Member State shall be obliged to supply information the disclosure of which it considers contrary to the essential interests of its security;

   (b) Any Member State may take such measures as it considers necessary for the protection of the essential interests of its security which are connected with the production of or trade in arms, munitions and war material; such measures shall not, however, adversely affect the conditions of competition in the common market regarding products which are not intended for specifically military purposes.

2. During the first year after the entry into force of this Treaty, the Council shall, acting unanimously, draw up a list of products to which the provisions of paragraph 1(b) shall apply.

3. The Council may, acting unanimously on a proposal from the Commission, make changes in this list.

Article 224

Member States shall consult each other with a view to taking together the steps needed to prevent the functioning of the common market being affected by measures which a Member State may be called upon to take in the event of serious internal disturbance affecting the maintenance of law and order, in the event of war or serious international tension constituting a threat of war, or in order to carry out obligations it has accepted for the purpose of maintaining peace and international security.

Article 225

If measures taken in the circumstances referred to in Articles 223 and 224 have the effect of distorting the conditions of competition in the common market, the Commission shall, together with the State concerned, examine how these measures can be adjusted to the rules laid down in this Treaty.

By way of derogation from the procedure laid down in Articles 169 and 170, the Commission or any Member State may bring the matter directly before the Court of Justice if it considers that another Member State is making improper use of the powers provided for in Articles 223 and 224. The Court of Justice shall give its ruling in camera.

Article 227

1. This Treaty shall apply to the Kingdom of Belgium, the Kingdom of Denmark, the Federal Republic of Germany, the Hellenic Republic, the Kingdom of Spain, the French Republic, Ireland, the Italian Republic, the Grand Duchy of Luxembourg, the Kingdom of the Netherlands, the Republic of Austria, the Portuguese Republic, the Republic of Finland, the Kingdom of Sweden and the United Kingdom of Great Britain and Northern Ireland

[there follow provisions for overseas territories].

Article 228

1. Where this Treaty provides for the conclusion of agreements between the Community and one or more States or international organizations, the Commission shall make recommendations to the Council, which shall authorize the Commission to open the necessary negotiations. The Commission shall conduct these negotiations in consultation with special committees appointed by the Council to assist it in this task and within the framework of such directives as the Council may issue to it.

In exercising the powers conferred upon it by this paragraph, the Council shall act by a qualified majority, except in the cases provided for in the second sentence of paragraph 2, for which it shall act unanimously.

2. Subject to the powers vested in the Commission in this field, the agreements shall be concluded by the Council, acting by a qualified majority on a proposal from the Commission. The Council shall act unanimously when the agreement covers a field for which unanimity is required for the adoption of internal rules, and for the agreements referred to in Article 238.

3. The Council shall conclude agreements after consulting the European Parliament, except for the agreements referred to in Article 113(3), including cases where the agreement covers a field for which the procedure referred to in Article 189b or that referred to in Article 189c is required for the adoption of internal rules. The European Parliament shall deliver its opinion within a time limit which the Council may lay down according to the urgency of the matter. In the absence of an opinion within that time limit, the Council may act.

By way of derogation from the previous subparagraph, agreements referred to in Article 238, other agreements establishing a specific institutional framework by organizing co-operation procedures, agreements having important budgetary implications for the Community and agreements entailing amendment of an act adopted under the procedure referred to in Article 189b shall be concluded after the assent of the European Parliament has been obtained.

The Council and the European Parliament may, in an urgent situation, agree upon a time limit for the assent.

4. When concluding an agreement, the Council may, by way of derogation from paragraph 2, authorize the Commission to approve modifications on behalf of the Community where the agreement provides for them to be adopted by a simplified procedure or by a body set up by the agreement; it may attach specific conditions to such authorization.

5. When the Council envisages concluding an agreement which calls for amendments to this Treaty, the amendments must first be adopted in accordance with the procedure laid down in Article N of the Treaty on European Union.

6. The Council, the Commission or a Member State may obtain the opinion of the Court of Justice as to whether an agreement envisaged is compatible with the provisions of this Treaty. Where the opinion of the Court of Justice is adverse, the agreement may enter into force only in accordance with Article N of the Treaty on European Union.

7. Agreements concluded under the conditions set out in this Article shall be binding on the institutions of the Community and on Member States.

Article 228a

Where it is provided, in a common position or in a joint action adopted according to the provisions of the Treaty on European Union relating to the common foreign and security policy, for an action by the Community to interrupt or to reduce, in part or completely, economic relations with one or more third countries, the Council shall take the necessary urgent measures. The Council shall act by a qualified majority on a proposal from the Commission.

Article 229

It shall be for the Commission to ensure the maintenance of all appropriate relations with the organs of the United Nations, of its specialized agencies and of the General Agreement on Tariffs and Trade. The Commission shall also maintain such relations as are appropriate with all international organizations.

Article 230

The Community shall establish all appropriate forms of co-operation with the Council of Europe.

Article 231

The Community shall establish close co-operation with the Organization for European Economic Co-operation, the details to be determined by common accord.

Article 235

If action by the Community should prove necessary to attain, in the course of the operation of the common market, one of the objectives of the Community and this Treaty has not provided the necessary powers, the Council shall, acting unanimously on a proposal from the Commission and after consulting the European Parliament, take the appropriate measures.

Article 238

The Community may conclude with one or more states or international organizations agreements establishing an association involving reciprocal rights and obligations, common action and special procedures.

Article 239

The Protocols annexed to this Treaty by common accord of the Member States shall form an integral part thereof.

Article 240

This Treaty is concluded for an unlimited period.

Article 247

This Treaty shall be ratified by the High Contracting Parties in accordance with their respective constitutional requirements. The instruments of ratification shall be deposited with the Government of the Italian Republic.

This Treaty shall enter into force on the first day of the month following the deposit of the instrument of ratification by the last signatory State to take this step. If, however, such deposit is made less than fifteen days before the beginning of the following month, this Treaty shall not enter into force until the first day of the second month after the date of such deposit.

Article 248

This Treaty, drawn up in a single original in the Dutch, French, German and Italian languages, all four texts being equally authentic, shall be deposited in the archives of the Government of the Italian Republic, which shall transmit a certified copy to each of the Governments of the other signatory States.

In witness whereof, the undersigned Plenipotentiaries have signed this Treaty.

Done at Rome this twenty-fifth day of March in the year one thousand nine hundred and fifty-seven.

[Here follow the signatures.]

10

Treaty on European Union
Maastricht, 7 February 1992

[*N.B. Extracts only; formal provisions abbreviated*]

[The Heads of State of the Kingdom of Belgium, the Kingdom of Denmark, the Federal Republic of Germany, the Hellenic Republic, the Kingdom of Spain, the French Republic, Ireland, the Italian Republic, the Grand Duchy of Luxembourg, the Kingdom of the Netherlands, the Portuguese Republic, the United Kingdom of Great Britain and Northern Ireland]

RESOLVED to mark a new stage in the process of European integration undertaken with the establishment of the European Communities,

RECALLING the historic importance of the ending of the division of the European continent and the need to create firm bases for the construction of the future Europe,

CONFIRMING their attachment to the principles of liberty, democracy and respect for human rights and fundamental freedoms and of the rule of law,

DESIRING to deepen the solidarity between their peoples while respecting their history, their culture and their traditions,

DESIRING to enhance further the democratic and efficient functioning of the institutions so as to enable them better to carry out, within a single institutional framework, the tasks entrusted to them,

RESOLVED to achieve the strengthening and the convergence of their economies and to establish an economic and monetary union including, in accordance with the provisions of this Treaty, a single and stable currency,

DETERMINED to promote economic and social progress for their peoples, within the context of the accomplishment of the internal market and of reinforced cohesion and environmental protection, and to implement policies ensuring that advances in economic integration are accompanied by parallel progress in other fields,

RESOLVED to establish a citizenship common to the nationals of their countries,

RESOLVED to implement a common foreign and security policy including the eventual framing of a common defence policy, which might in time lead to a common defence, thereby reinforcing the European identity and its independence in order to promote peace, security and progress in Europe and in the world,

REAFFIRMING their objective to facilitate the free movement of persons while ensuring the safety and security of their peoples, by including provisions on justice and home affairs in this Treaty,

RESOLVED to continue the process of creating an ever closer union among the peoples of Europe, in which decisions are taken as closely as possible to the citizen in accordance with the principle of subsidiarity,

IN VIEW of further steps to be taken in order to advance European integration,

HAVE DECIDED to establish a European Union and to this end have designated as their plenipotentiaries [names omitted],

WHO, having exchanged their full powers, found in good and due form,

HAVE agreed as follows:

TITLE I. COMMON PROVISIONS

Article A

By this Treaty, the High Contracting Parties establish among themselves a European Union, hereinafter called 'the Union'. This Treaty marks a new stage in the process of creating an ever closer union among the peoples of Europe, in which decisions are taken as closely as possible to the citizen.

The Union shall be founded on the European Communities, supplemented by the policies and forms of co-operation established by this Treaty. Its task shall be to organize, in a manner demonstrating consistency and solidarity, relations between the Member States and between their peoples.

Article B

The Union shall set itself the following objectives:

— to promote economic and social progress which is balanced and sustainable, in particular through the creation of an area without internal frontiers, through the strengthening of economic and social cohesion and through the establishment of economic and monetary union, ultimately including a single currency in accordance with the provisions of this Treaty;

— to assert its identity on the international scene, in particular through the implementation of a common foreign and security policy including the eventual framing of a common defence policy, which might in time lead to a common defence;

— to strengthen the protection of the rights and interests of the nationals of its Member States through the introduction of a citizenship of the Union;

— to develop close co-operation on justice and home affairs;

— to maintain in full the '*acquis communautaire*' and build on it with a view to considering, through the procedure referred to in Article N(2), to what extent the policies and forms of co-operation introduced by this Treaty may need to be revised with the aim of ensuring the effectiveness of the mechanisms and the institutions of the Community.

The objectives of the Union shall be achieved as provided in this Treaty and in accordance with the conditions and the timetable set out therein while respecting the principle of subsidiarity as defined in Article 3b of the Treaty establishing the European Community.

Article C

The Union shall be served by a single institutional framework which shall ensure the consistency and the continuity of the activities carried out in order to attain its objectives while respecting and building upon the '*acquis communautaire*'.

The Union shall in particular ensure the consistency of its external activities as a whole in the context of its external relations, security, economic and development policies. The Council and the Commission shall be responsible for ensuring such consistency. They shall ensure the implementation of these policies, each in accordance with its respective powers.

Article D

The European Council shall provide the Union with the necessary impetus for its development and shall define the general political guidelines thereof.

The European Council shall bring together the Heads of State or of Government of the Member States and the President of the Commission. They shall be assisted by the Ministers for Foreign Affairs of the Member States and by a Member of the Commission. The European Council shall meet at least twice a year, under the chairmanship of the Head of State or of Government of the Member State which holds the Presidency of the Council.

The European Council shall submit to the European Parliament a report after each of its meetings and a yearly written report on the progress achieved by the Union.

Article E

The European Parliament, the Council, the Commission and the Court of Justice shall exercise their powers under the conditions and for the purposes provided for, on the one hand, by the provisions of the Treaties establishing the European Communities and of the subsequent Treaties and Acts modifying and supplementing them and, on the other hand, by the other provisions of this Treaty.

Article F

1. The Union shall respect the national identities of its Member States, whose systems of government are founded on the principles of democracy.

2. The Union shall respect fundamental rights, as guaranteed by the European Convention for the Protection of Human Rights and Fundamental Freedoms signed in Rome on 4 November 1950

and as they result from the constitutional traditions common to the Member States, as general principles of Community law.

3. The Union shall provide itself with the means necessary to attain its objectives and carry through its policies.

TITLE V. PROVISIONS ON A COMMON FOREIGN AND SECURITY POLICY

Article J

A common foreign and security policy is hereby established which shall be governed by the following provisions.

Article J.1

1. The Union and its Member States shall define and implement a common foreign and security policy, governed by the provisions of the Title and covering all areas of foreign and security policy.

2. The objectives of the common foreign and security policy shall be:

— to safeguard the common values, fundamental interests and independence of the Union;

— to strengthen the security of the Union and its Member States in all ways;

— to preserve peace and strengthen international security, in accordance with the principles of the United Nations Charter as well as the principles of the Helsinki Final Act and the objectives of the Paris Charter;

— to promote international co-operation;

— to develop and consolidate democracy and the rule of law, and respect for human rights and fundamental freedoms.

3. The Union shall pursue these objectives:

— by establishing systematic co-operation between Member States in the conduct of policy, in accordance with Article J.2;

— by gradually implementing, in accordance with Article J.3, joint action in the areas in which the Member States have important interests in common.

4. The Member States shall support the Union's external and security policy actively and unreservedly in a spirit of loyalty and mutual solidarity. They shall refrain from any action which is contrary to the interests of the Union or likely to impair its effectiveness as a cohesive force in international relations. The Council shall ensure that these principles are complied with.

Article J.2

1. Member States shall inform and consult one another within the Council on any matter of foreign and security policy of general interest in order to ensure that their combined influence is exerted as effectively as possible by means of concerted and convergent action.

2. Whenever it deems it necessary, the Council shall define a common position.

Member States shall ensure that their national policies conform on the common positions.

3. Member States shall co-ordinate their action in international organizations and at international conferences. They shall uphold the common positions in such fora.

In international organizations and at international conferences where not all the Member States participate, those which do take part shall uphold the common positions.

Article J.3

The procedure for adopting joint action in matters covered by foreign and security policy shall be the following:

1. The Council shall decide, on the basis of general guidelines from the European Council, that a matter should be the subject of joint action.

Whenever the Council decides on the principle of joint action, it shall lay down the specific scope, the Union's general and specific objectives in carrying out such action, if necessary its duration, and the means, procedures and conditions for its implementation.

2. The Council shall, when adopting the joint action and at any stage during its development, define those matters on which decisions are to be taken by a qualified majority.

Where the Council is required to act by a qualified majority pursuant to the preceding subparagraph, the votes of its members shall be weighted in accordance with Article 148(2) of the Treaty establishing the European Community, and for their adoption, acts of the Council shall require at least fifty-four [sixty-four] votes in favour, cast by at least eight [eleven] members.

3. If there is a change in circumstances having a substantial effect on a question subject to joint action, the Council shall review the principles and objectives of that action and take the necessary decisions. As long as the Council has not acted, the joint action shall stand.

4. Joint actions shall commit the Member States in the positions they adopt and in the conduct of their activity.

5. Whenever there is any plan to adopt a national position or take national action pursuant to a joint action, information shall be provided in time to allow, if necessary, for prior consultations within the Council. The obligation to provide prior information shall not apply to measures which are merely a national transposition of Council decisions.

6. In cases of imperative need arising from changes in the situation and failing a Council decision, Member States may take the necessary measures as a matter of urgency having regard to the general objectives of the joint action. The Member State concerned shall inform the Council immediately of any such measures.

7. Should there be any major difficulties in implementing a joint action, a Member State shall refer them to the Council which shall discuss them and seek appropriate solutions. Such solutions shall not run counter to the objectives of the joint action or impair its effectiveness.

Article J.4

1. The common foreign and security policy shall include all questions related to the security of the Union, including the eventual framing of a common defence policy, which might in time lead to a common defence.

2. The Union requests the Western European Union (WEU), which is an integral part of the development of the Union, to elaborate and implement decisions and actions of the Union

which have defence implications. The Council shall, in agreement with the institutions of the WEU, adopt the necessary practical arrangements.

3. Issues having defence implications dealt with under this Article shall not be subject to the procedures set out in Article J.3.

4. The policy of the Union in accordance with this Article shall not prejudice the specific character of the security and defence policy of certain Member States and shall respect the obligations of certain Member States under the North Atlantic Treaty and be compatible with the common security and defence policy established within that framework.

5. The provisions of this Article shall not prevent the development of closer co-operation between two or more Member States on a bilateral level, in the framework of the WEU and the Atlantic Alliance, provided such co-operation does not run counter to or impede that provided for in this Title.

6. With a view to furthering the objective of this Treaty, and having in view the date of 1998 in the context of Article XII of the Brussels Treaty, the provisions of this Article may be revised as provided for in Article N(2) on the basis of a report to be presented in 1996 by the Council to the European Council, which shall include an evaluation of the progress made and the experience gained until then.

Article J.5

1. The Presidency shall represent the Union in matters coming within the common foreign and security policy.

2. The Presidency shall be responsible for the implementation of common measures; in that capacity it shall in principle express the position of the Union in international organizations and international conferences.

3. In the tasks referred to in paragraphs 1 and 2, the presidency shall be assisted if needs be by the previous and next Member States to hold the Presidency. The Commission shall be fully associated in these tasks.

4. Without prejudice to Article J.2(3) and Article J.3(4), Member States represented in international organizations or international conferences where not all the Member States participate shall keep the latter informed of any matter of common interest.

Member States which are also members of the United Nations Security Council will concert and keep the other Member States fully informed. Member States which are permanent members of the Security Council will, in the execution of their functions, ensure the defence of the positions and the interests of the Union, without prejudice to their responsibilities under the provisions of the United Nations Charter.

Article J.6

The diplomatic and consular missions of the Member States and the Commission Delegations in third countries and international conferences, and their representations to international organizations, shall co-operate in ensuring that the common positions and common measures adopted by the Council are complied with and implemented.

They shall step up co-operation by exchanging information, carrying out joint assessments and contributing to the implementation of the provisions referred to in Article 8c of the Treaty establishing the European Community.

Article J.7

The Presidency shall consult the European Parliament on the main aspects and the basic choices of the common foreign and security policy and shall ensure that the views of the European Parliament are duly taken into consideration. The European Parliament shall be kept regularly informed by the Presidency and the Commission of the development of the Union's foreign and security policy.

The European Parliament may ask questions of the Council or make recommendations to it. It shall hold an annual debate on progress in implementing the common foreign and security policy.

Article J.8

1. The European Council shall define the principles of and general guidelines for the common foreign and security policy.

2. The Council shall take the decisions necessary for defining

and implementing the common foreign and security policy on the basis of the general guidelines adopted by the European Council. It shall ensure the unity, consistency and effectiveness of action by the Union.

The Council shall act unanimously, except for procedural questions and in the case referred to in Article J.3(2).

3. Any Member State or the Commission may refer to the Council any question relating to the common foreign policy and may submit proposals to the Council.

4. In cases requiring a rapid decision, the Presidency, of its own motion, or at the request of the Commission or a Member State, shall convene an extraordinary Council meeting within forty-eight hours or, in an emergency, within a shorter period.

5. Without prejudice to Article 151 of the Treaty establishing the European Community, a Political Committee consisting of Political Directors shall monitor the international situation in the areas covered by common foreign and security policy and contribute to the definition of policies by delivering opinions to the Council at the request of the Council or on its own initiative. It shall also monitor the implementation of agreed policies, without prejudice to the responsibility of the Presidency and the Commission.

Article J.9

The Commission shall be fully associated with the work carried out in the common foreign and security policy field.

Article J.10

On the occasion of any review of the security provisions under Article J.4, the Conference which is convened to that effect shall also examine whether any other amendments need to be made to provisions relating to the common foreign and security policy.

Article J.11

1. The provisions referred to in Articles 137, 138, 139 to 142, 146, 147, 150 to 153, 157 to 163 and 217 of the Treaty establishing the European Community shall apply to the provisions relating to the areas referred to in this Title.

2. Administrative expenditure which the provisions relating to the areas referred to in this Title entail for the institutions shall be charged to the budget of the European Communities.

The Council may also:

—either decide unanimously that operational expenditure to which the implementation of those provisions gives rise is to be charged to the budget of the European Communities; in that event, the budgetary procedure laid down in the Treaty establishing the European Community shall be applicable;

—or determine that such expenditure shall be charged to the Member States, where appropriate in accordance with a scale to be decided.

TITLE VI. PROVISIONS ON CO-OPERATION IN THE FIELD OF JUSTICE AND HOME AFFAIRS

Article K

Co-operation in the fields of justice and home affairs shall be governed by the following provisions.

Article K.1

For the purposes of achieving the objectives of the Union, in particular the free movement of persons, and without prejudice to the powers of the European Community, Member States shall regard the following areas as matters of common interest:

1. asylum policy;
2. rules governing the crossing by persons of the external borders of the Member States and the exercise of controls thereon;
3. immigration policy and policy regarding nationals of third countries;
   (a) conditions of entry and movement by nationals of third countries on the territory of Member States;
   (b) conditions of residence by nationals of third countries on the territory of Member States,

including family reunion and access to employment;

(c) combating unauthorized immigration, residence and work by nationals of third countries on the territory of Member States;

4. combating drug addiction in so far as this is not covered by 7 to 9;

5. combating fraud on an international scale in so far as this is not covered by 7 to 9;

6. judicial co-operation in civil matters;

7. judicial co-operation in criminal matters;

8. customs co-operation;

9. police co-operation for the purposes of preventing and combating terrorism, unlawful drug trafficking and other serious forms of international crime, including if necessary certain aspects of customs co-operation, in connection with the organization of a Union-wide system for exchanging information within a European Police Office (Europol).

Article K.2

1. The matters referred to in Article K.1 shall be dealt with in compliance with the European Convention for the Protection of Human Rights and Fundamental Freedoms of 4 November 1950 and the Convention relating to the Status of Refugees of 28 July 1951 and having regard to the protection afforded by Member States to persons persecuted on political grounds.

2. This Title shall not affect the exercise of the responsibilities incumbent upon Member States with regard to the maintenance of law and order and the safeguarding of internal security.

Article K.3

1. In the areas referred to in Article K.1, Member States shall inform and consult one another within the Council with a view to co-ordinating their action. To that end, they shall establish collaboration between the relevant departments of their administrations.

2. The Council may:

—on the initiative of any Member State or of the Commission, in the areas referred to in Article K.1(1) to (6);

—on the initiative of any Member State, in the areas referred to in Article K1(7) to (9):

(a) adopt joint positions and promote, using the appropriate form and procedures, any co-operation contributing to the pursuit of the objectives of the Union;

(b) adopt joint action in so far as the objectives of the Union can be attained better by joint action than by the Member States acting individually on account of the scale or effects of the action envisaged; it may decide that measures implementing joint action are to be adopted by a qualified majority;

(c) without prejudice to Article 220 of the Treaty establishing the European Community, draw up conventions which it shall recommend to the Member States for adoption in accordance with their respective constitutional requirements.

Unless otherwise provided by such conventions, measures implementing them shall be adopted within the Council by a majority of two-thirds of the High Contracting Parties.

Such conventions may stipulate that the Court of Justice shall have jurisdiction to interpret their provisions and to rule on any disputes regarding their application, in accordance with such arrangements as they may lay down.

Article K.4

1. A Co-ordinating Committee shall be set up consisting of senior officials. In addition to its co-ordinating role, it shall be the task of the Committee to;

- give opinions for the attention of the Council, either at the Council's request or on its own initiative
- contribute, without prejudice to Article 151 of the Treaty establishing the European Community, to the preparation of the Council's discussions in the areas referred to in Article K.1 and, in accordance with the conditions laid

down in Article 100d of the Treaty establishing the European Community, in the areas referred to in Article 100c of that Treaty.

2. The Commission shall be fully associated with the work in the areas referred to in this Title.

3. The Council shall act unanimously, except on matters of procedure and in cases where Article K.3 expressly provides for other voting rules.

Where the Council is required to act by a qualified majority, the votes of its members shall be weighted as laid down in Article 148(2) of the Treaty establishing the European Community, and for their adoption, acts of the Council shall require at least fifty-four [sixty-four] votes in favour, cast by at least eight [eleven] members.

Article K.5

Within international organizations and at international conferences in which they take part, Member States shall defend the common positions adopted under the provisions of this Title.

Article K.6

The Presidency and the Commission shall regularly inform the European Parliament of discussions in the areas covered by this Title.

The Presidency shall consult the European Parliament on the principal aspects of activities in the areas referred to in this Title and shall ensure that the views of the European Parliament are duly taken into consideration.

The European Parliament may ask questions of the Council or make recommendations to it. Each year, it shall hold a debate on the progress made in implementation of the areas referred to in this Title.

Article K.7

The provisions of this Title shall not prevent the establishment or development of closer co-operation between two or more Member States in so far as such co-operation does not conflict with, or impede, that provided for in this Title.

Article K.8

1. The provisions referred to in Articles 137, 138, 139 to 142, 146, 147, 150 to 153, 147 to 163 and 217 of the Treaty establishing the European Community shall apply to the provisions relating to the areas referred to in this Title.

2. Administrative expenditure which the provisions relating to the areas referred to in this Title entail for the institutions shall be charged to the budget of the European Communities.

The Council may also:

— either decide unanimously that operational expenditure to which the implementation of those provisions gives rise is to be charged to the budget of the European Communities; in that event, the budgetary procedure laid down in the Treaty establishing the European Community shall be applicable;

— or determine that such expenditure shall be charged to the Member States, where appropriate in accordance with a scale to be decided.

Article K.9

The Council, acting unanimously on the initiative of the Commission or a Member State, may decide to apply Article 100c of the Treaty establishing the European Community to action in areas referred to in Article K.1(1) to (6), and at the same time determine the relevant voting conditions relating to it. It shall recommend the Member States to adopt that decision in accordance with their respective constitutional requirements.

TITLE VII. FINAL PROVISIONS

Article L

The provisions of the Treaty establishing the European Community, the Treaty establishing the European Coal and Steel Community and the Treaty establishing the European Atomic Energy Community concerning the powers of the Court of Justice of the European Communities and the exercise of those powers shall apply only to the following provisions of this Treaty:

   (a) provisions amending the Treaty establishing the European Economic Community, the Treaty establishing the European Coal and Steel Community and the Treaty establishing the European Atomic Energy Community;

   (b) the third subparagraph of Article K.3(2)(c);

   (c) articles L to S.

Article M

Subject to the provisions amending the Treaty establishing the European Economic Community with a view to establishing the European Community, the Treaty establishing the European Coal and Steel Community and the Treaty establishing the European Atomic Energy Community, and to these final provisions, nothing in this Treaty shall effect the Treaties establishing the European Communities or the subsequent Treaties and Acts modifying or supplementing them.

Article N

1. The government of any Member State or the Commission may submit to the Council proposals for the amendment of the Treaties on which the Union is founded.

If the Council, after consulting the European Parliament and, where appropriate, the Commission, delivers an opinion in favour of calling a conference of representatives of the governments of the Member States, the conference shall be convened by the President of the Council for the purpose of determining by common accord the amendments to be made to those Treaties. The European Central Bank shall also be consulted in the case of institutional changes in the monetary area.

The amendments shall enter into force after being ratified by all the Member States in accordance with their respective constitutional requirements.

2. A conference of representatives of the governments of the Member States shall be convened in 1996 to examine those provisions of this Treaty for which revision is provided, in accordance with the objectives set out in Articles A and B.

Article O

Any European State may apply to become a Member of the Union. It shall address its application to the Council, which shall act unanimously after consulting the Commission and after receiving the assent of the European Parliament, which shall act by an absolute majority of its component members.

The conditions of admission and the adjustments to the Treaties on which the Union is founded which such admission entails shall be the subject of an agreement between the Member States and the applicant State. This agreement shall be submitted for ratification by all the contracting States in accordance with their respective constitutional requirements.

Article P

1. Articles 2 to 7 and 10 to 19 of the Treaty establishing a single Council and a single Commission of the European Communities, signed in Brussels on 8 April 1965, are hereby repealed.

2. Article 2, Article 3(2) and Title III of the Single European Act signed in Luxembourg on 17 February 1986 and in the Hague on February 1986 are hereby repealed.

Article Q

This Treaty is concluded for an unlimited period.

Article R

1. This Treaty shall be ratified by the High Contracting Parties in accordance with their respective constitutional requirements. The instruments of ratification shall be deposited with the government of the Italian Republic.

2. This Treaty shall enter into force on 1 January 1993, provided that all the instruments of ratification have been deposited, or, failing that, on the first day of the month following the deposit of the instrument of ratification by the last signatory State to take this step.

Article S

This Treaty, drawn up in a single original in the Danish, Dutch, English, French, German, Greek, Irish, Italian, Portuguese and Spanish languages, the texts in each of these languages being equally authentic, shall be deposited in the archives of the government of the Italian Republic, which will transmit a certified copy to each of the governments of the other signatory States.

IN WITNESS WHEREOF, the undersigned Plenipotentiaries have signed this Treaty.

Done at Maastricht, on 7 February 1992.
[Here follow the signatures]

Note on the Presentation of the Indexes

Our main problem has been to devise a citation method which gives readers all they need in order to find a particular provision swiftly and unerringly, but gives no more than that. The difficulty stems from the fact that in their national versions the texts printed above are laid out in different ways. The US text is divided into seven major parts called Articles, which are subdivided into Sections, and these are often subdivided into clauses. The German Constitution is divided into main parts or chapters, then into articles, which are further subdivided into clauses. The French text is divided into titles, then into articles, which are often subdivided into *alinéas* or paragraphs. After its Preamble, the Russian text is divided into two sections, of which the first is by far the longer, since the second contains only the transitional provisions. The first section sets out the constitution proper in a number of chapters, subdivided into articles, and further subdivided into clauses. The EC Treaty is divided into Parts, then Titles, then articles, then paragraphs.

In all of these there is an element forming the building-block, and in all save one these blocks are called 'articles', and are numbered consecutively through the whole text. Thus to find a particular building block one needs only its number, and not that of the chapter, part, or title to which it belongs. We therefore omit this latter information in our citation, so that, for instance, references to the right to petition for redress of grievances are given in the form: FRG 17, RF 33, EC 8d. The exception to this method is the US constitution where the building-blocks ('sections') are not numbered consecutively but start afresh within each part (called Article). Here therefore, we give the Article number followed by that of its section. Only four of the Amendments to the US Constitution were given their own numbers on adoption (13–16). The others have since been added and are found in Congress documents. They are used in these indexes, so that for instance the reference to the right to petition is Amdt. I.

A further complication arises from the way in which the texts treat the elements smaller than the building-block of the 'article'. In an ideal world these provisions would themselves be numbered consecutively within each article, so that one could just cite RF 14(1) for the proposition that Russia is a secular state. In fact this usually works for Russia and Germany. In the French constitution the *alinéas* are unnumbered and indicated only by paragraph indentations: thus to cite the corresponding provision one has to refer to France 3 para. 1. The original text of the US constitution likewise left the sections' separate clauses unnumbered, but numbers have since been added and appear in Congress documents. They are used here in brackets, so that US I 8(3), for instance, refers the reader to the provision conferring on the US Congress the power to regulate inter-state commerce.

In addition we have adopted a number of abbreviations (listed in the Table of Abbreviations) and conventions: 1789 refers to the French Declaration of that year; 1946 to the preamble to the French constitution of that year. Both are incorporated by its preamble into the operation of the 1958 constitution. The German Constitution (art. 140) incorporates parts of the Weimar constitution of 1919 relating to religion; they are printed as an appendix to the German text and our indexes cite them as W. The UK references are to the paragraph numbers of the chapter describing the UK constitution. Finally, it should be remembered that the ECHR, EC, and TEU extracts printed here and cited in the indexes are but a small part of the full international texts.

Analytical Index

		USA	FRG	France
Constitutions				
I	Constituent power	Preamble, VII	Preamble	
II	Sovereignty	Preamble, Amdts IX, X	20(2)	3
III	Amendment			
	(1) Method	V	79(1)–(2) 85, 89	7 last para.,
	(2) Unamendable provisions		79(3), 81(4), 115e(2)	89 last para.
IV	Territorial application		Preamble para. 3	1
V	Scope and duration	Preamble	129, 133–4, 146	90–2
VI	State and religion	VI(3), Amdt I	140, W136–9, 141	2 para. 1
VII	Language			2 para. 2
VIII	Flags, symbols, etc.		22	2 paras 3–5
IX	Constitutional review of legislation etc.			
	(1) Competent organ	III 2(1)	93(1)	61
	(2) Effects of ruling	VI(2)	94(2)	62
X	Relation to international law			
	(1) Compatibility with treaties			54
	(2) Ratification of treaties	II 2(2)	32, 59	52
	(3) Internal effect of international law	VI(2)	25, 100(2)	55
	(4) Transfer of competences to international entity		23, 24 15, 1958 88–2	1946 para.
Federations				
I	Constituent units			
	(1) Designation, membership	IV 3(1), VII	Preamble	
	(2) Boundaries		29, 79(3), 118	
II	Division of powers			
	(1) General residuary power	Amdt X	30, 70(1)	
	(2) Supremacy clause	VI(2)	31	
	(3) Conflicts			
	(a) Competent organ	III 2(1)	93(3)–(4)	
	(b) Effects of ruling		94(2)	

RF	UK	ECHR	EC	EU
Preamble	5–6	Preamble	Preamble, 247	Preamble, R
3(1)–(3)	10–19, 46		1	A
16(1), 92(3), 134–6	8			N
4(1)	28–39		227	
Sec. 2(1)–(6)			240	Q
14	20–4			
26(2), 68 70(1)			217, 248	S
125(2)(a)–(b), (4) 125(6)			173, 177(b) 174, 176	
125(2)(d), (6) 86(c), 106(d)	25, 27		228.2	
15(4), 69	26, 144			
79			238	
5(1)–(2), 65, 137(2)				O
67, 71(m), 72(b), 102(1)(a), 106(e)				
76(4), (6)			3b	
15(1), (2), 76(5), (6)				
125(2)(b), (3)(b)(c)				
125(b)				

	USA	FRG	France
(4) Exclusive federal powers			
(a) Common market/customs union provisions			
(i) Taxing/borrowing	I 8(1)–(2), Amdt XVI	105, 108(1), 115	
(ii) Foreign and internal commerce	I 8(3), 9(5), (6), 10(2)	73(5)	
(iii) Bankruptcy	I 8(4)		
(iv) Currency, credit	I 8(5), (6), 10(1)	73(4), 88	
(v) Postal service	I 8(7)	73(7)	
(vi) Intellectual property	I 8(8)	73(7)	
(vii) Loans	VI(1)		
(viii) Transport/communications		73(6)	
(b) External affairs, defence, security			
(i) Treaties and ambassadors	I 10(1), II 2(2), 3	24, 32, 59, 73(1)	
(ii) Armed forces	I 8(12)–(16), II2(1)	65a, 73(1), 87a–b, 115b	
(iii) War and peace	I 8(10)–(11)	26(1)–(2), 115a, 115l(3)	
(iv) Invasions and security	I 8(15), IV4	73(10, 50a, 57a, 91, 115a	
(v) Asylum		16a	
(c) Citizenship	I 8(4), IV2(1), Amdt XIV	16, 73(2), 116 1	
(d) Capital city, new states, boundaries	I 8(17), IV3		
(e) Miscellaneous social	I 9(8)	72, 75	
(f) Juridical	III 1–2, VI(2)	92–100	
(g) Other		73(3)	
(5) Powers exclusive to the constituent units	Amdt X	70(1)	
(6) Concurrent/alternative powers		72, 74, 74a, 105(2), 125	
(7) Subsidiarity		72(2)	
(8) Collaboration between federation and units		73(10), 91a–b	
(9) Federal deconcentration to constituent units			
(a) General administration		83–5, 87c–d, 89(2), (3), 90(2)	
(b) Finance and fiscal administration		108(2), (3)	

RF	UK	ECHR	EC	EU
71(g), 74, 106(c)				
71(k)			3(a)–(c)	
71(g), 75(1)(2), 106(c)				
75(4)				
71(c)				
71(j), 106(d)			228–31	
71(l), 102(1)(d)				
71(j), 106(f)				
71(l)				
71(c), 89(a)			8, 8a–e	K1.1 B para. 3
70(2)			216	
71(l) 71(d)(n)(o) 71(p)(r)				
73				
72			3a	
78(1), (3)			3b 198a–c	B last para. K
78(2)				

RF	UK	ECHR	EC	EU
				F.1
77			5	J.1
			169, 171, 192	
77				F.1
130–3	40–5			
10, 94, 99, 104–8	46, 50–2		137, 138b, 145	
95, 105(5)	10–11		137, 138b	E
97				
97(2)	59			
98	56, 62 60			
100(2)			143	
99(2), 100	57		139	
	74		141	
104	71–6		189a–c	
102(3), 103(3), 105(2)	74		141, 148.1	
105(5), 107(3), 108(2)			148.2, 189a–c. 203	
105(4)			189b(3)–(6)	

		USA	FRG	France
II	Upper chambers			
	(1) Composition	I 3(1)–(2), II 2(3)	51	24 para. 3
	(2) Officers	I 3(4)–(5)	52(1)(2)	32
	(3) Membership qualifications	I 3(3)	51(1)	25
	(4) Term of office	I 3(1)–(2), Amdt XVII	51(1)	25
	(5) Procedure	I 5(1)–(4)	52	43–4, 61 para. 1
III	Lower chambers			
	(1) Composition	I 2(1), (3)–(4)	38(1) 25	24 para. 2,
	(2) Officers	I 2(5)	40(1)	32
	(3) Membership qualifications	I 2(2)	38(2)(3)	25
	(4) Term of office	I 2(1)	39(1),	25 115h(1)
	(5) Procedure	I 5(2)	40(1), 42(2), 121	31, 43–4, 45, 61 para. 1
	(6) Dissolution		12	
IV	Respective powers of upper and lower chambers	I 2(5), 3(6), 7(1), II 2(2), Amdt XII	76–9	45, 46
V	Relationship to executive see Executive branch			
VI	Relationship to judiciary see Judicial branch			
Executive branch				
I	Head of state			
	(1) Election	II 1(1)–(2), Amdt XII	54	6–7
	(2) Qualifications	II 1(4)	55	
	(3) Deputization	II 1(5), Amdts XX(3), XXV	57	7 para. 4
	(4) Payment	II 1(6)		
	(5) Oath of office	II 1(7)	56	
	(6) Term of office	II 1(1)	54(2)	6 para. 1
	(7) Re-eligibilityAmdt	XXII	54(2)	
	(8) Removal	II(4)	61	68
	(9) Powers	I 7(3), II 1(1), 2–3	39(3), 58–60, 63–5, 67–9, 81(2), 82(1), 115a(3), (5), 115h	5, 9–19, 30, 52, 54, 56, 61, 64–5, 80–2

RF	UK	ECHR	EC	EU
95(2)	53–5			
101(1)	55 53–5 53			
101(4), 102(3)	55, 71–6			
95(2)	58			
101(1)	61 59			
96(1)	57, 60			
101(4), 103(3), 104(2)(3)	62, 71–6			
109, 111(4), 117(3), (4)	60			
101, 102, 106	62, 66–9			
10	87–90			
80				
81(1)(4), 92(2), 102(1)(e)				
81(2)				
92(3)				
82				
81(1)				
81(3)				
93, 102(1)(f), 103(1)(g)				

83–92, 107,
  108, 109,
  111, 115(3),
  117
	91			

		USA	FRG	France
II	Head of government	*see* Head of State		
	(1) Election/appointment		63, 115h(2)	8 para. 1
	(2) Qualifications		66	23 para. 1
	(3) Deputization		69(1)	
	(4) Term of office		69(2),(3)	8 para. 1
	(5) Removal		67	8 para. 1
	(6) Powers		39(3), 58, 62, 64–5, 81, 87a(4), 91(2), 93(1)2, 94(1), 111, 113–14, 115b	12 para. 1, 16 para. 1, 19, 21–2, 39, 49–50, 54, 61 para. 2, 82 para. 1, 89, para. 1
III	Governments and cabinets	II 2(1)–(2)	62, 64, 67–8, 76, 80, 81, 84–6	11, 13 para. 1, 20, 22–3, 36, 38–9, 41–5, 48–50
IV	Individual ministers			
	(1) Appointment/removal	II 2(2)–(3), 4	64(1), 69(2)	8 para. 2
	(2) Qualifications	I 6(2)	66	23
	(3) Powers and duties	II 2(1)	58, 64(2), 65, 80, 95(2)	21 para. 2, 22
V	Civil servants	II 2(2)–(3)		1789 6, 15; 1958 20 para. 2, 21 para. 1, 23 para. 1

Judicial branch

		USA	FRG	France
I	Courts/judiciary			
	(1) General	I 8(9), III 1–2	92, 95–6, 101	64, 66 para. 2
	(2) Access	III 2(3), Amdts V, VI, VII	19(4), 101	
II	Constitutional tribunal	III 2(2)	93–4, 99–100, 115g	56–63
III	Extraordinary courts		101	
IV	Judges			
	(1) Appointment	II 2(2)	60(1), 94–5	65
	(2) Independence	III 1	97–8, 132	64 para. 4
	(3) Accountability	II 4	96(4), 98	65
V	The Procuracy			83(f), 102(1)(h), 129

RF	UK	ECHR	EC	EU
83(a), 103(1)(a), 111	92–3			
83(c), 117 112, 113	94 98–100			
83(b), 110, 114–17	101–13			
112(2)	114			
	115			
71(r)	116–19			
10, 118	120–34	19	154, 164, 168	L
46(1)(2), 123		6	173	
125				
118(3)				
83(f), 102(1)(g), 119, 128	133		167	
120(1), 121–2	131–4		167	

	USA	FRG	France
III Rights and duties			
(1) General	Amdts I–X	1–20	1789; 1946
(2) Substantive rights			
(a) Property	Amdts V, XIV 1	14–15, 74(14)–(15); W138	1789 2, 7, 14, 17
(b) Privacy, beliefs, etc.	VI 3, Amdt I	4, 10	1789 10, 11
(c) Social rights			1946 5, 6, 7, 8, 10, 11
(d) Other	Amdts I–IV, XIV1	137(1)	1789 14
(3) Procedural rights			
(a) Access to justice	I 9(2)–(3), 10(1), Amdts V–VIII, XIV 1	19(4), 101	1789 7
(b) Fair trial	Amdts V, XIV1	101	1789 8
(c) Other		1789 9	
(4) Liberties and equalities	IV 2; Amdts XIV 1, XIII, XV, XVII, XIX, XXIV, XXVI	2, 3, 5, 33 13; 1946	1789 1, 4, paras 3, 12
(5) Duties		12a	1789 7, 13; 1946 para. 5
Constitutional offences	I 2(5), I 3(6)–(7), II 4, III3	18, 26(1)	68

RF	UK	ECHR	EC	EU
17–64, 103(1)(e)	156–63	1–18		F.2
34–6			222	
23–33 37–44		8–10		
52				
46–8, 120(2), 125(4)		2(1); 13		
49–51		6		
22 19		14	6	
57–9				
3(4), 13(5), 93, 103(1)(g), 125(7)				

Alphabetical Index